From the Tanjore Court to the Madras Music Academy

From the Tanjore Court to the Madras Music Academy

A Social History of Music in South India

By
Lakshmi Subramanian

OXFORD
UNIVERSITY PRESS

OXFORD

UNIVERSITY PRESS

YMCA Library Building, Jai Singh Road, New Delhi 110001

Oxford University Press is a department of the University of Oxford.
It furthers the University's objective of excellence in research, scholarship,
and education by publishing worldwide in

Oxford New York

Auckland Cape Town Dar es Salaam Hong Kong Karachi
Kuala Lumpur Madrid Melbourne Mexico City Nairobi
New Delhi Shanghai Taipei Toronto

With offices in

Argentina Austria Brazil Chile Czech Republic France Greece
Guatemala Hungary Italy Japan Poland Portugal Singapore
South Korea Switzerland Thailand Turkey Ukraine Vietnam

Oxford is a registered trade mark of Oxford University Press
in the UK and in certain other countries

Published in India
by Oxford University Press, New Delhi

© Oxford University Press 2006

ISBN-13: 978-0-19-567835-2
ISBN-10: 0-19-567835-4

Typeset in 10/12 Times
by Star Compugraphics, Delhi 110 096
Printed in India at Ram Printograph, New Delhi 110 051
Published by Oxford University Press
YMCA Library Building, Jai Singh Road, New Delhi 110 001

For Mannargudi Naganatha Iyer
(A Cherished Memory)

Preface and Acknowledgements

This book grew out of an impulse to capture a childhood memory and to make sense of it as a student of history. Growing up in Calcutta, as part of the Tamil community in the city in the late 1960s, it was de rigueur to learn Karnatic music as it was to attend annual concerts or *kacheris* organized by fledgling music associations like the Rasika Ranjana Sabha. The experience even if it seemed tedious at times, proved invaluable for it brought me in very close proximity to a traditional teacher, who in terms of his lineage, musical approach and temperament, and of his life experiences in modern urban India embodied the complex, cultural transformation that an entire generation of practitioners had undergone. It is to him and his memory that this book is dedicated.

The memory was stoked nearly three decades later when I spent one summer term in 1996 in Oxford and chanced upon a nearly continuous series of the *Journal of the Music Academy Madras* from 1929 to 1970. Reading through the journals along with the proceedings of the All India Music Conferences that were held regularly every year from 1916 onwards, had me thinking about the ways in which a nationalist discourse was framed for the reconstitution of the performing arts in India, about what music meant for nation building and for the individual enthusiast, and conversely what the changing material context meant for the performer and the art form. That in itself, I thought was enough material to begin with in telling a story about music, its makers and managers in modern India. My enthusiasm was encouraged by a small group of friends and music lovers in Calcutta, who in their own individual ways were trying to document a history of modern classical music in India. Their support and encouragement persuaded me to present a preliminary paper on the subject in a conference organized under the aegis of the Centre for Studies in Social Sciences, Calcutta in 1998. The conference in many ways was a defining moment in the making of this monograph as it forced me to think deeper about the subject and investigate the possibility of expanding my methodology for the research. Trained as a historian with a particular fetish for archival research, it was initially difficult to combine anecdotal material and fieldwork with the printed source but the exercise in the end proved rewarding for it facilitated a more critical reading of received wisdom.

The debts that I have incurred in writing this book are many. My deepest thanks go first and foremost to Jon Barlow, who, as my severest critic and unfailing friend, has been with the book since its inception. To Adrian McNeil, Sugato Marjid, and Amlan Dasgupta, for giving me numerous opportunities to share my research findings and urging me on from the wings, I owe a special word of acknowledgement. My colleagues at the Centre, especially Tapati Guha Thakurta and Janaki Nair who spared their time to read and comment on the manuscript at various stages, have been a source of constant sustenance and cheer. Indira Peterson gave me a wonderful opportunity to present my work, when she invited me in February 2004 to address the Barbara Stoler Miller Conference on the Performing Arts in Columbia University. Indira has always been a source of inspiration for me, and her interest and confidence in my work has egged me on even as early as 1996, when we met for the first time in the School of Oriental and African Studies. The Conference introduced me to a number of colleagues and fellow travellers—Mathew Allen, Devesh Soneji, Saskia Kersenboom Story, and Hari Krishnan—whose work in so many ways reinforced my own endeavour. It also enabled me to set up a dialogue with Janaki Bakhale, whose work on V.N. Bhatkhande promises to be a major intervention in the history of Indian music in the nineteenth and twentieth centuries.

In these six years I have had the privilege of working in some of the finest libraries in India and abroad. I am especially grateful for the help of librarians, archivists, and others at the National Library in Kolkata, the Adyar Library and Research Society in Chennai, the Roja Muthiah Research Library in Chennai, the National Centre for Performing Arts in Mumbai, the Nehru Memorial Museum and Library in Delhi, the India Office Library in London, and the Indian Institute in Oxford. A special acknowledgement goes to the authorities of the Madras Music Academy and the Thanjavur Maharaja Serfoji's Sarasvati Mahal Library for permitting me to reproduce illustrations from their publications.

Finally, a very special thanks to my mother and daughter who, above all, helped me to lighten up when the process of writing and rewriting threatened to overwhelm all sense of humour.

Contents

Illustrations

Introduction

It is logical that India should be the one country in the world, where music in its connection with and expression of life should be so aware of the spiritual service of music. In India, life is religion and religion is life. Until the advent of the Muhammedans into India, there was no secular type of music. In South India, all the themes are still religious only and a music party is more like a prayer meeting than an entertaining concert.

Margaret Cousins, 1935

Cousins' observations, more in the nature of prescriptions, are telling. She eloquently summed up the social and aesthetic aspirations, and the politics of cultural representation of an entire generation of publicists and patrons. By the time Cousins had published her celebrated work on *Music of the Occident and Orient*,[1] the performing arts in south India, and particularly music, had undergone fundamental changes in terms of patronage, content, presentation, and reception. This in turn engendered radically new modes of representing the tradition in discursive practice and locating it in a new institutional space. The dynamics of cultural consumption and its representation were rooted as much in the imperatives of modernity and nation building as in the development of a new auditory culture in south India from the second half of the nineteenth century. The emergence of new orders of patrons and listeners transformed modes of consuming and reflecting upon music—its performance, interpretation, and preservation—which set in motion a complex process of what one may call the 'reinvention of tradition'.[2]

Ironically perhaps, the making of a classical tradition, which was a response to the predicament of modernity, and entailed the identification of the authentic classical tradition focused on a repertoire barely a hundred years old. The making of the modern classical music tradition in south India was thus both an act of staging as well as an accretion of cultural production in the eighteenth and nineteenth centuries. It lent itself to and depended upon new forms and networks of patronage, which rested nevertheless in deeply pervasive and culturally patterned conceptions of power and authority. The process was not uncontested for it inevitably undermined the position and status of those traditional communities of performers who did not have the wherewithal to stake a claim in the transformed public culture of modern India. Subsequently, the very notion of a national classical tradition and its exclusive custodianship came under attack.

The making of the modern classical tradition forms the principal focus of the present study. In plotting this process, I have, as the title suggests, chosen two coordinates: the Tanjore court of the late eighteenth and early nineteenth centuries and the Madras Music Academy that was formed in the first decades of the twentieth century. Implicit in the choice is the assumption that the Tanjore court particularly under Serfoji II (1798–1832) displayed a markedly new temperament in relation to cultural practices and consumption. Equally important is the historical fact that the same court even if indirectly, spawned the individuated artist composer whose engagement with the art form expanded the scope of musical creativity. Was the Tanjore experience—the musical revolution the court oversaw—then the defining moment for an appreciable shift in the development and organization of the musical tradition? Or was it merely a chance and ad hoc coming together of eccentric artists whose moral and material economy was far removed from the modern world of art and performance, constituted by new agents—the urban listener, the critic, the nation builder, and the student? On the other hand, the Madras Music Academy, founded in 1928, 'in pursuance of the recommendations of the All India Music Conference held in Madras in 1927 during the Congress week',[3] presided over what was quintessentially the world of modern classical music, a form it reinvented as a self-conscious cultural practice and wove into the larger and compelling narrative of nation building.

In the context of this cultural project, its historical antecedents, ideological compulsions, and institutional location, the book raises larger questions of identity and imagination, and how the influence of nationalism and the nation form worked into the creation of an auditory habit, and of the signification attached to it. In other words, its concern is not restricted to the production of knowledge about music in the nineteenth and twentieth centuries or to the institution building process for its practice. Rather, the book ventures to tease out the ambivalence and ambiguities that informed these practices, anticipating the dilemma of the modern Indian middle class in negotiating a retrieved past for the present. How musicians and their patrons constructed a canon for classical music, the enthusiasm with which amateurs and professionals straddled the worlds of myth, practice, and the modern disciplines of history and musicology to provide a stable basis for their cultural claims and self-description, constitute the principal themes of the study.

And yet unlike the case of the visual arts, the indivisibility between the spheres of professional and public knowledge were not clear-cut in the case of the performing arts especially in south India. This derived from an underlying solidarity that characterized the community of performers and publicists who not merely shared ties of caste and kin but who entertained common aesthetic concerns generated by the experience of colonial modernity. What distinguished the activities of the Madras Academy was the ability to enlist the cooperation of influential segments in the traditional performing community and work out through them, a comprehensive programme of constructing a classical canon. The process of construction involved a selective appropriation of elements and genres from the earlier and more inclusive tradition associated with the Tanjore court.

Given this focus, what the book does not set out to do is to come up with a historical account of musical development in south India in the nineteenth and twentieth centuries. On the other hand, it departs from conventional scholarship on the subject, which has tended to be largely the work of music scholars and musicologists whose focus has been on aesthetic conceptions and attributes of Indian music and their underlying philosophical basis over time. In terms of method, these studies have relied upon anecdotal material, contemporary experience and analysis of normative texts in Sanskrit that have generally been seen as important indexes of the art form.[4] The method has not been entirely unproblematic; a recent intervention by R. Sathyanarayana,[5] mentions that the inherent tendencies in the older historiography of music to conflate myth with historical time and geographical space resulted from an uncritical use of oral material and normative texts. It is only recently that there has been a shift in focus and an attempt to locate the practice of music in a concrete social milieu, within a larger political and cultural economy. The works of Raymond Reiss, Daniel Neuman, Bonnie C. Wade, Allyn Miner, Adrian McNeil, Jon Higgins, and Mathew Allen for instance, belong to this category.[6] While working within the framework of musicology, these works nonetheless focus more closely on the social organization of music in modern India and raise larger questions about the social relationship of musicians and their selection, recruitment, and training, none of which were random processes. In this context, I would be remiss if I failed to mention a forthcoming work by Amanda Weidman on the violin as a vehicle for conveying *Karnataka Sangeetam* or Karnatik music[7] to modernity as well as for preserving its authenticity, and how developments in instrumental music in the nineteenth and twentieth centuries became critical in the articulation of a classical canon.[8] Weidman makes a powerful case for the violin and its emergence as a central accompanying instrument, and in the process, questions the so-called liminality of colonial influence in the dynamics of modern classical music. The jettisoning of the fiddle image, the key role accorded to violin as the perfect accompanist to the voice and its explicit association with modernity is seen and demonstrated as an integral and important moment in the making of the modern classical music tradition in south India.

The present work attempts to push these questions of tradition and its reinvention further. It focuses largely on the late nineteenth and twentieth century social milieu in which questions of modernity and tradition became implicated in the self-fashioning of the consuming communities, on the one hand, and the changing imperatives of the performers, on the other. It examines in greater detail the context in which patronage and politics shaped performance, its reception and transmission, and how in the process, the performing arts became central to the cultural project of nation building.

In 1803, Maharaja Serfoji II, the Maratha king of Tanjore known for his love of music and patronage of the arts, composed a number of marching tunes, in slow and quick movement for the Tanjore military band.[9] These novel though perhaps trivial compositions were remarkable for being notated in the European manner, a practice that was not traditionally associated with musical activity in India, where notation of any sort was rare and elementary. Equally intriguing was the king's interest in developing a new etiquette for musical performance—story has it that he once placed sentinels with drawn swords all around his music room with orders that whosoever shook his head during the performance should be decapitated![10] In 1820, the same court issued a number of orders regulating the sartorial equipment and social status of court dancers, who were forbidden certain colours and restricted to use only prescribed modes of conveyance.[11] At the same time, the king used the performing arts as a vehicle for expressing his own individual engagement with new ideas—in his celebrated composition *Devendra*

Kuravanji (Fortune-teller Play of the King of Gods), one of the central motifs was the heliocentric system, the essentials of which were conveyed to Indrani, the wife of the king of gods when she posed the question, 'Tell me, does the earth revolve around the sun, or does the sun revolve around the earth? What is the moon's orbit, and what planets revolve around the sun? What is the diameter of the earth sphere?' The fortune-teller gave the queen a complete account of the heliocentric system, and then listed the known continents, countries, rivers, and capital cities of the known globe thereby expressing the king's preference for the new taxonomy and empirical knowledge of the natural sciences.[12]

Serfoji's improvisations may be seen as important indications of an individual ruler's response to cross-cultural intersection in nineteenth-century India prior to the entrenchment of British colonial hegemony. Less than a century later, we encounter a similar preoccupation with techniques of reproducing musical language, the streamlining of a new aesthetic, and the promotion of new compositions foregrounding the nation and its virtues as the central motive in the new discourse that developed around music and the performing arts in southern India. A discourse that has been understood as modern and reflecting transformed notions of cultural consumption and social identity. A.M. Chinnaswami Mudaliar, one of the early pioneers of mapping the musical terrain of south India and rendering it intelligible to a wider audience (by presenting Indian compositions in European notation), complained in 1893 that systematic efforts had not yet been made to bring on record, in a complete and authentic form, the real music of the country. Equally lamentable were 'the convulsions, grimaces and ungraceful gesticulations, which inseparably accompany the performance of almost every musician of the east'.[13] A couple of decades later, the Madras Music Academy, in an attempt to boost new compositions selected a composition entitled 'In Praise of Bharat Mata' as its winning entry in the *kriti* competition of 1931.[14]

Do we detect in Mudaliars' enterprise and in the Madras Academy's initiative a continuation of an earlier project flagged off by the Tanjore court? Were the Maratha rulers harbingers of a new orientation in musical culture, where a break from an earlier framework was being registered? The question is of larger interest for there is a growing consensus in historical scholarship that economic processes and social formations in the eighteenth century generated critical shifts in modes of thought and analysis, of which historiography was one notable example. A new conceptual mode formed the basis of a history-writing project that assigned greater value to facticity, sequence, and to individual author-ship.[15] Can the same be said of developments in the field of performing arts? Did the Tanjore court's production and advocacy of music, capture a new stage in the development of the art form?

While it was under the reign of the Mughal emperor Muhammed Shah, that Delhi perfected the *Khyal* genre[16] of Hindustani classical music, it was under the dynamic rule of the eclectic Maratha rulers of Tanjore, that the musical tradition of southern India reached the high point of its evolution. The organization of the Tanjore principality in its early days reflected the dynamism of the seventeenth-century Maratha warlords, but the consolidation of the state and the development of its cultural profile expressed in vernacular cosmopolitanism located Tanjore within a larger context. The development of music, in eighteenth-century Tanjore, testified to the vital role of the Maratha state and its rulers whose patronage became a critical determinant in the evolution of the performing arts tradition in south India.[17] By virtue of its location at the crossroads of cultural and religious influences, the Tanjore court was able to respond to a more inclusive and diverse musical conception that accommodated diverse genres, styles, and compositions in several languages. At the same time, the court to establish and safeguard its status as the premier cultural arbiter, encouraged its musicians to adopt standardizing techniques in the form of song exercises, to facilitate transmission and thereby create a standard for music and performance. It was in this musical atmosphere that Tanjore's celebrated trinity emerged whose creative output further refined the musical tradition, taking it to new heights. Later commentators saw the intervention of the trinity, especially of Tyagaraja as an important shift that was instrumental in providing a foundational basis for articulating a clearer definition of traditional music. Thus Tanjore, through its court and the individual musicians who lived and worked in the cultural milieu of the city, saw the working and reworking of a resilient musical tradition that carried with it the potential of 'classicism', 'modernity', and 'difference'—all of which inevitably surfaced in the cultural politics of the following decades.

In the intervening years, between the decline of Tanjore and the rise of Madras, the trend to assemble and establish a classical music idiom, gathered momentum. This, while commanding the accessories of an older or earlier repertoire, registered a new emphasis in terms of presentation and musical values making it especially attractive and accessible for later communities of patrons and performers. However, the shift from Tanjore to Madras was by no means uninterrupted. There was a rupture at multiple levels, in terms of patronage, locus, and modes of consumption and signification leading to what scholars have called a 'reinvention of the tradition'. Behind the process of redefining the tradition, was the formation of a new social identity around the educated middle class of colonial south India. As an integral part of its self-imaging, this class attempted to straddle the world of tradition it had lost and hoped to retrieve, and the world of modernity that colonial education and administration promised.

Implicit in the recasting of tradition from the late nineteenth century was a complex and even paradoxical engagement with the notion of modernity. What was colonial modernity all about? What was different in conceptual terms between the Tanjore initiative and that of the later nineteenth-century project spearheaded by Indian publicists and early nationalists? Did the latter merely sharpen the contours of an ongoing debate and self-reflection about defining and engineering *the tradition*, relegating in the process other traditions and practices, thereby making conflict and contestation inevitable? These are some of the questions this work will address. It was during the closing decades of the century that nationalism became a powerful reference point and the emergence of a new sense of the public provided an alternative conceptual framework for the production and consumption of cultural artefacts and practice.

To locate and define modernity, in the context of non-European societies that did not follow the same progression to development, or had their historical destinies thwarted by the advent of colonialism is not an easy task. There has been, in recent years some debate around the category of the early modern in Indian history, whether it represents a period or a conceptual framework to explain the nature of social and political developments in the eighteenth century, or was it a period of transition to colonialism and colonial modernity. Research on the eighteenth century regimes in India, their antecedents and social anatomy has definitively established the dynamism of new social alignments that sustained regional political structures and generated novel discursive practices that spoke of a shift in political conceptions of governance and statecraft. Simultaneously, there were new modes of engagement with science and art mediated by the growing interaction with Europeans, Serfoji's cabinet being an instance in point. In southern India, where the process of state formation involved competing claims for honour and status,[18] ritual and performative practices became especially significant leading to a sharper appreciation of performing arts. What began as a ritual prerequisite became in time an aesthetic pursuit with unexpected consequences, especially in Tanjore,[19] where a line of eclectic Maratha kings emerged as patrons and performers and attempted to set in motion a process of canon formation.

What drove the Maratha kings remains ambiguous. That the early Maratha rulers of Tanjore were creative and personally disposed to the performing arts, that they assigned a definite value to patronage and performance as a ritual as well as an artistic endeavour, is well known. One may legitimately suggest that this was in consonance with the political tradition and culture of post Nayaka regimes in south India. However, it is also important to record the individual sensibility of a king like Serfoji II (1798–1832), who straddling different worlds simultaneously, wrote and patronized traditional music and read and appreciated Shakespeare with the same facility. Bishop Heber was smitten with the Raja's erudition, and as he wrote in a letter to R.Wilmot Horton:

I have been passing the last four days in the society of a Hindoo prince; the Raja of Tanjore who quotes Fourcroy, Lavoisier, Linnaeus and Buffon fluently, has formed a more accurate judgment of the political merits of Shakespeare than that so felicitously expressed by Lord Byron; at the same time, he is much respected by the English officers in his neighbourhood as a real good judge of the horse, and a cool, bold and deadly shot at the tyger. The truth is that he is an extraordinary man who having in early youth received such an education as old Schwartz, the celebrated missionary could give him, has ever since continued, in the midst of many disadvantages preserve his taste for and extend his knowledge of European literature while he has never neglected the active exercises and frank soldierly bearing which become the descendant of the old Maratha conqueror and by which only in the present state of things, he has it in his power to gratify the prejudices of his people and prolong his popularity among them.[20]

The catholicity and curiosity of Serfoji's temperament, stoked no doubt by Schwartz, was in full display in virtually everything that he embarked upon, whether it was his disposition to record and preserve systems of knowledge or extend education facilities to his subjects. A new spirit of enquiry and regeneration matched the deference to tradition and the existing order. Reverend Robinson who took the opportunity to visit a Christian congregation, fifteen miles from Tanjore, spoke eloquently of the Raja's generosity in sustaining the establishment. 'This chatram,' he remarked, 'had saved many hundreds from perishing, when a severe famine and cholera prevailed in Ramnad, Shivaganga, and Madura districts. There is a charity school attached to it—in which children are instructed in Tamil, Gentoo, Mahratta, Sanskrit, Persian, and English language.'[21] The emphasis on a multilingual curriculum was in a sense integral to the cultural profile of the Maratha state of Tanjore where the simultaneous circulation of Tamil, Telugu, and Marathi reflected the diversity of the state's cultural and political inheritance. As an erstwhile Nayaka centre that had supported and sustained the Telugu, speaking court and literati, the city had developed a rich poly-lingual and multi-layered culture that extended from the Brahmanical temple establishment to the Telugu-speaking court and finally to the popular world of the mystic saints poets who spoke and sang in Telugu, Tamil, and Kannada and even occasionally used the Manipravala, a Marathi prototype. The advent of the Marathas reinforced this latent tendency for cultural assimilation and became a powerful catalyst in the full maturing of the performing arts tradition in southern India. Just as new literary genres in eighteenth-century south India developed in response to the political, economic, and social dynamics of the period, the full-fledged evolution of music and dance forms was a reflection of the extraordinary diversity and richness of cultural and religious interaction. Two processes contributing to the emergence of a definitive musical idiom came to operate in tandem—one directly initiated by the court and the other by developments outside the existing hierarchies of court and canon.

While it is impossible to plot the making of the musical tradition in south India with any great precision, it is evident that by the fifteenth century, the interweaving of ritual singing, dramatic practices, and devotional music had produced a complex musical conception with myriad expressions and distinct communities of practitioners. An extensive system of melodic entities (ragas) and a repertoire of musical compositions (kriti, *varnam, javali*, and *padam* among others) in a number of languages that fitted the needs of temple ritual as well as court performance and devotional expression were in circulation.[22] The multiple dimensions of the tradition found expression in its structural organization: there were ritual temple specialists (devadasis and *Oduvars*) who danced and sang as part of their ritual duties, and specialized in certain musical genres; there were professional singers attached to courts who had a grounding in musical grammar and belonged to the upper castes, mostly Brahmins, who combined knowledge of the scriptures, Sanskrit with a reading of conventional musical texts, and there were the peripatetic singer-composers who were engrossed in the poetics of devotion.[23] These groups participated in a shared musical culture that was inextricably linked to the social and moral landscape of the region.

The court took an added interest in the arts and its protection, partly out of concern with the status that made up south Indian politics and partly out of a genuine taste for art. The Nayakas, like their predecessors in Vijayanagar were especially active as patrons, poets, and cultural engineers. They sponsored a major project of classification of melodic structures and a systematic theoretical compilation of musical texts and knowledge. The defining of the 72-reference scale (1660) by Venkata-makhin, son of Govinda Diksitar and minister for three generations of Nayaka rulers in Tanjore, became a landmark in the canonical fixing of the emerging tradition. It gave practicing musicians and composers a detailed template to work out melodic combinations with a degree of precision, and a standard of reference for performance.[24] The essentials of an accepted classical music of the southern region, in terms of song texts, its theoretical conventions as laid down in traditional texts with their supporting commentaries, the compositions that were sung by court performers, and even standardized song exercises that were part of 'correct' training, had all coalesced by the late seventeenth century to enable an articulation of a distinct regional musical art form. Tanjore had become the seat of music and staked its claim early on as the premier cultural arbiter, at least as far as the performing arts was concerned.[25]

What particularly marked the efflorescence of performing arts in Maratha Tanjore in the eighteenth century was the emergence of individual composers whose output added a rare artistic quality and lucidity to the existing musical framework. The creativity of Tanjore's trinity,[26] and in particular of Tyagaraja (1767–1847), refined and expanded the tradition in a manner that enabled later observers to identify their contribution as *the classical* tradition. In two somewhat distinct but not unrelated ways, the court and the individual musician came together in an artistic engagement that experimented with traditional music in new ways while taking care to provide it with stable guidelines. For the court, the emphasis seemed to be on the questions of training and prioritizing certain genres in the performance repertoire, which upheld the idea of authenticity and hierarchy of styles and genres. The Maratha rulers, notably Serfoji II, were interested in establishing cultural standards for performance.[27] This priority can be seen both as a traditional status resource and as a new and keen sensibility oriented towards classification and preservation of knowledge for some sort of subsequent scanning and scrutiny. It is in this connection that the idea of notation, however basic, became relevant. The idea of notation was not just a personal fetish with Serfoji. It appears in a simple way to have had an impact on contemporary singers and composers like Tyagaraja, who, it is suggested, also came up with a rudimentary notation. In this, he was not necessarily seeking the mechanical reproduction of music but was instead, attempting to stress authorship and establish a clear basis for his individual style, an idea that became even more important to his disciples. In terms of style, Tyagaraja's music represented a rejection of the excessively ornate court music. His focus was on an improved song text that in terms of language was simple but provided ample scope for musical interpretation. The result was a refined three-part kriti with *sangatis* or melodic variations built into its structure and designed to bring out the fullest potential of the melodic design. His approach was intensely personal and in jettisoning the existing formulaic conventions of court music and patronage, the composer defined for himself a new space of creativity.[28] In the succeeding decades, his compositions and the ideals that it embodied became identified as the authentic art form—developing out of the creative tension between the individual vision of the artist and a range of social, formal, and historical constraints.

The dissemination of Tanjore's musical culture in the late nineteenth century especially into the colonial city of Madras and to the smaller courts of Mysore, Ramnad, Ettayapuram, and Travancore went hand in hand with the formation of a new consuming elite. As beneficiaries and participants of colonial education and administration, the new elite entertained a markedly modified approach to culture and its consumption. In contrast to their predecessors, who earlier in the century had patronized music and performing arts as part of an older regimen of status and ritual practice involving the sharing and contesting of honour, the new elite's relationship with music and culture was more intimate and consciously individualistic. This was the product both of a sensibility shaped by the complexity of colonial experience at the psychological level and altered circumstances in which the tradition was relocated and transformed. It was not merely the spatial relocation but a fundamental change in auditory conception: a break in terms of listening and meanings assigned to the experience. The dissemination of Tyagaraja's style by his disciples and students, was an important element in this experience as it fed the imagination of the new middle class in all sorts of subtle and complex ways. Even as they settled down in the enclaves of the colonial metropolis partaking of its western learning, acquiring new aspirations of social status and economic success, they began to project their cultural inheritance into the foreground in an altogether new manner. This involved both a subjective aesthetic experience and a discursive process that attempted to inscribe a set of meanings on India's traditions.

An interesting and distinguishing feature of the emerging discourse on musical reform and revival was its deployment of the English language. This was partly informed by the brahmin elite's appreciation of the language as a vehicle of modernity and professional mobility and partly by the derivative nature of their discourse that carried the familiar overtones of Orientalist appraisal and evaluation. It is not therefore, a matter of coincidence that the primary sources for a study of music in twentieth century south India should be largely if not entirely in English language sources. There was admittedly from the 1920s a reflection of elite concerns in Tamil weeklies like the *Ananda Vikatan*, that carried a section on arts but these were mostly written in the form of music criticism and occasionally satires. Predictably, the challenge to the classical music project from the advocates of the Tamil movement was framed in the Tamil language but this did not in any sense reflect a conceptual shift in the framing of the alternative tradition.

The emerging discourse on performing arts reflected an all India phenomenon but the case of the southern version was more intimately tied with the question of an elite's selfhood and self-representation. The elite in Madras city was predominantly brahmin, with the result that a brahmin reading of the musical heritage followed. The consumption of music became tied up with questions of identity that appeared to have immediate roots in Tanjore's classical past, which had accommodated ideals of artistic creativity, spiritual expression, and canon formation. This held a powerful appeal to the new middle class in south India emerging as consumers and custodians of culture with a near existentialist urgency. The middle-class intervention became a defining moment in setting out the performance.

This is not to posit an exclusively Brahmanical political and cultural hegemony or to suggest that other influential caste or status groups were excluded from the politics and process of cultural consumption. We know from David Washbrook's work that, notwithstanding the advances made by brahmins in colonial education and administration, they were incapable of mobilizing and sustaining large-scale movements without the support of the city patrons who had extensive rural and landed connections.[29] Where there was a perceptible shift, it was in relation to the dynamics of the transformed public space that accompanied the displacement of old elite groups. This was accompanied by foregrounding the patronage of art for its own sake rather than connecting it with an ostensible ritual context. Within and alongside this, there was the influence of British Orientalism and its evaluation of India's performing arts—where the tradition was described in a particular manner that produced a new frame of reference for understanding, consuming, and in the end, reinventing the tradition.

Orientalist appraisal of southern India's musical traditions tended to emphasize its distinctiveness in relation to both the European system as well as to the system that prevailed in north India. The difference, in case of the former, derived from the relative absence of harmony and the stress on melody, and in the case of the latter, the adherence to an older tradition of music that was ostensibly less influenced by the Islamic interlude, whose influence in the peninsula was perceived to have remained peripheral. The most influential voice in the nineteenth-century European discourse on music in the peninsula was that of C.R. Day who while eloquent in his appreciation of Indian music was responsible for projecting the relative 'purity' of the southern musical tradition. Taking the cue from his predecessors, Day argued quite forcefully that the isolation of the peninsula from the 'excesses' of Muslim rule was responsible for the preservation of its musical culture against alien influences and for the higher status of its practitioners. The dominant Islamic presence in northern India and the formation of a court culture resulted in the increasing association of music with Muslim performers and in a growing prejudice among high-caste Hindus against the profession.[30]

That Orientalist depictions obscured the reality of old and celebrated Sufi musical lineages fostering a mystical devotion which transcended sectarian boundaries, or the complex interaction between Hindu and Islamic culture embodied in the shared cultural taste of Vijayanagar and Bijapur in the sixteenth and seventeenth centuries, was not something that the new patrons of the arts cared to consider.[31] The Orientalist discourse was taken as implicitly true and the cumulative effect of their pronouncements was the emergence of a self-conscious agenda for redefining the tradition of music and laboriously situating it within the parameters of textual authenticity and a new moral sensibility that was deemed properly Hindu and adequately spiritual. The agenda was contingent, both on abstract conceptions of spiritual essence as well as concrete social values and expectations of the new middle class.

The new concerns of the middle class were located within the changing urban context of south India—in the wake of musical entertainment that developed in Madras in the second half of the nineteenth century. The influx of musicians from older centres to the new city, the popularity of *harikathas*[32] (a kind of musical theatre that deployed song, scripture, and dramatic narration) helped in the formation of a genuine listening habit. For sons of brahmins who had been sent to Madras to study and eke out a living in the lower rungs of colonial bureaucracy, these theatrical and musical performances were not only a form of recreation and entertainment, but were also an important vehicle of accessing a past that had disappeared in the wake of an altered political and social reality. The need to invoke that past became increasingly sharper as the new elite faced the moral crisis implicit in the fact of colonial subjugation in the public/political domain, and the disturbing questions it raised about the quality and potential of India's heritage. An upshot of this complex pursuit of self-discovery was the production of a derived discourse on music and performing arts—a discourse that ultimately conjoined with nationalism to articulate a national cultural project. This hinged on discovering the tradition and subsequently investing it with attributes of classicism and antiquity, even while striving to locate it within a modern context.

As the beneficiaries of new learning and print revolution, the imagination of the colonial middle class was captured by the possibilities of assembling a collective identity based on standardization and fixity of language. Their case was made easy by the nature of musical revolution that had taken place in Tanjore during the early nineteenth century and resulted in the refinement of the song text integrated with that of melodic movement associated with specific lineages of Tyagaraja. At the same time, given the nature of the organization of musical tradition in terms of community composition, the brahmin disciples who were the immediate bearers of the tradition were also part of the modernizing process associated with printing and education. They were in a vantage position of disseminating the Tanjore style that was subsequently marked off as the classical paradigm through the new technologies of printing and institutional spaces of modern education, and became in effect purveyors of tradition as well as agents of modernization. This left its imprint on the histories they wrote and circulated of music and musicians.

The circulation of biographies and of song texts in the public domain facilitated a particular appreciation of the composer's personality and his artistic genius, both of which assumed a new significance. The production of biographies and circulation of harikathas retold the story of the brahmin composer's life emphasizing the composer's sterling moral character, his single-minded musical devotion, his rejection of any and all sorts of material gain, and fleshed out his rather low-profile life with more nourishing images of dramatic action and self-reliance.[33] Whatever the intent of the actual biographers and performers, the result was the invention of a legend that in William Jackson's opinion could serve as a holding pattern for religious sentiment and grassroots values, and for the social order in a quickly changing world.[34] This coinciding with a prodigious dispersal of music in the nineteenth century—thanks to the efforts of musicians like Veena Kuppier, Patnam Subramania Iyer, Poochi Srinivasa Iyengar, and Muthiah Bhagavatar—resulted in the development of a genuine musical culture in Madras city and the principal courts. It produced a heightened awareness of the tradition, the need to suitably catalogue and classify it, and make it an integral part of the larger cultural project that accompanied early nationalist activity.[35] In particular, the circulation of song texts in manuscript form generated discussion about the potentialities of standardization and a definitive reading of musical texts and melodic form.

The articulation of a self-conscious cultural project may be dated to the 1870s, when the Madras branch of the Gayan Samaj was established ostensibly to promote music among the middle class, to take appropriate steps to preserve the tradition in some sort of suitable format and to link it with the new institutions of learning, that happened to be the natural constituency for the middle class.[36] The issue of locating music among the middle class was especially important in northern India, where the actual practice of music was in the hands of Islamic lineage musicians, and had fed deep-seated prejudices among middle-class Hindus. In south India, given the dominant presence of high-caste *Bhagavatar*s (musician-teachers) in the profession, middle-class publicists found it easier to take up the art form both as practitioners and custodians. However, the question of disseminating it raised the two imperatives of melodic and textual authenticity and of establishing a particular artistic hierarchy around Tyagaraja. These features were clearly evident in the pioneering efforts of Chinnaswami Mudaliar who published in 1893 his *Oriental Music in European Notation*. In its introduction, he made a strong case for notation as the only viable means to standardize and preserve Indian music, as well as for a more critical evaluation of Tyagaraja, whose work, he described as 'by far the most scientific, charming, voluminous and variegated in all Dravidian music'. Mudaliar described Tyagaraja as being scrupulous in his choice of disciples in order to retain the purity of his compositions and conceptions.[37] Such a reading was reinforced by other writings that followed in this vein and exercised a powerful appeal to the middle class, especially in the context of an emerging project of national reconstruction through education and culture.

To the sheer interest and pleasure derived from listening to music was now added an increasing enthusiasm for learning the art form and inscribing on it exceptional sacral features, that made it exceptionally Indian and that set it off against the materialist and extroverted dimensions of western culture. The modern, as expressed through a proper pedagogical method of transmission, was constantly held in balance by the traditional and the classical which invoked the spiritual essence of the art form, and the sublime character of the composers who cared for neither power nor gain but chose personal devotion as the only moral choice for salvation. In Madras, the middle-class project was further revitalized by inputs from the Theosophists who exulted the Hindu past, celebrated the vigour and merits of the Brahmin caste and viewed music and performance as an extension of collective religious expression. Under the circumstances, the serial invocation of tradition and modernity became very central to the self-definition of the brahmin elite and produced a distinct approach to the understanding and representation of music and its artistic ideals. The two categories were not seen as mutually contradictory or exclusive. As far as actual lifestyle practices went, consumption and appreciation of classical music were part of the inner religious life of the elite that adhered to several ritual practices in a public manner. The celebration of sixtieth and seventieth birthdays—the *Shastirabdapoorti* or *Bhimarathashanti*—which often included musical performances as part of the celebrations, became coeval with a distinct culture even as the new patrons achieved and aspired for material advancement in the public sphere with their access to colonial education. It became imperative therefore, to reconstruct the artistic heritage around the modernizing project of education and social reform—a tendency that was virtually ubiquitous throughout India. In Madras city, the leading lawyers and publicists like V. Bhashyam Iyengar,[38] who were ardent patrons of music, conferred with Theosophists to undertake a systematic programme of music education. Margaret Cousins, as a committed Theosophist and a member of the Madras University Senate became a key figure in the project as she pressed for the inclusion of music in the university curriculum. For Cousins and her band, music was invaluable as a means of regenerating the spiritual life of the nation. As she wrote,

The Culture of Nationalism ... has developed the demand for national culture. Any analysis of the national value of music will bring as its corollary an understanding of the value of national music and for its inclusion in the curricula of schools and colleges so that young India may grow up in the image of the young Krishna with his beloved flute and that of Saraswati radiant with the Veena.

For realization of this ideal, Cousins identified notation as 'the instrument for a more widely spread knowledge of scientific music and the handmaid of the new type of music teacher'. Equally, she was fully aware of the changes in the physical space of performance and wrote rather approvingly of the socializing habits of the Mylapore music lovers.

Recounting her experiences during a concert in Mylapore Sangam, she wrote:

The hall is a large cadjan roofing attached to the wide verandah of a house shut right away from the road by one of the street houses. This ensures complete silence unlike conditions in the city halls. Clean matting formed the seating accommodation for about 200 people and around it were 2 rows of benches and chairs. The verandah formed the platform on which the performers sat on a dais covered with a handsome cloth. A section of the hall near the musicians was reserved for ladies without the stupidity of an intervening and blinding purdah such as I had endured elsewhere...dignity and devotion pervaded the environment of the performance.[39]

The familiar tropes of dignity, devotion, and educational potential of music, were fully in keeping with the temper of the times, particularly of the educated publicists and self-appointed custodians of Indian culture. Like religion, music was sacred and therefore had to be divested of all accretions of sensuality and corrupt usage. Even more than religion, it had to prove its classical credentials by taking recourse to textual locations, even though the very notion of classical music as the twentieth century consumers saw it, was of recent origin and hardly a hundred years old. What mattered was the need to establish an identifiable standard for the art form that would not only pass western scrutiny but one that would reinforce the essence of Indian culture. It was here that the idea of the classical as a validating category became so important. The idea of the classical had multiple connotations of antiquity, lineage, textual rigour, and above all, resonated with the essential spirituality of India's tradition. The pursuit of the classical as an idea was thus not solely an aesthetic one. It was generated by the inner logic of nationalist thought that, Partha Chatterjee claims, demarcated a distinct domain of sovereignty. According to Chatterjee, nationalism had an inner and outer domain,[40] and the former was sovereign and not open to any negotiation and compromise. In south India, classical music lay at the very core of that inner domain.

The search for classicism and spirituality in music, whereby every musical performance became a kind of congregational prayer was in effect, a collective urge to nurture and celebrate the sovereign domain of culture. In the process, the classical had to be represented, reinvented to make it more acceptable to an altered and modern sensibility. One feature of the project was the notion of standardization, and in music the chosen instrument was notation which was seen as a marker of western classical music and implicit in its power. In the overall context of Indian classical music, southern and northern, it would be too simplistic to equate the use of notation with modernity. For Indian music, the use of notations was peculiarly double-edged. It standardized a rich tradition of music making and facilitated appreciation but the very process of standardization had the potential of reducing it and thwarting individual creativity. The project of being modern could be both liberating and subjugating.

The project had its share of detractors and casualties. For implicit in the project of defining and delimiting the modern classical tradition was the compulsion to ensure the accessibility of the art form to the middle class. This required not merely a spatial relocation of the art form in a new setting or even a new pedagogical framework of transmission, but a re-evaluation of ritual performers and performing communities whose social position, functions, repertoire did not conform to the imperatives of the new patron and consumer. The redefining of the classical and its other became a convenient vehicle for marginalizing part of the repertoire that ritual performers specialized in. The dyad between the classical and the non-classical was orchestrated through arbitrary notions of pure music as opposed to applied music, in which music was not necessarily of a simpler variety but one which applied music to a specific purpose like that of dance, drama, or ritual performance. This construction reflected the social imperatives of the cultural project relating to the position of ritual performers, like devadasis and became a convenient rationale for assigning them and their repertoire a distinctly lower position within the artistic hierarchy. It also enabled an organization like the Academy to fend off the claims of language politics in Tamil Nadu articulated by the Tamil Isai movement. What the Academy did to neutralize the counter claims of Tamil music as well as to accommodate the musical genres associated with the devadasi repertoire was to integrate them into the concert repertoire of classical music and present them as light classical. It was not clear, as Mathew Allen has argued,[41] where classicism lay— whether it was inherent in the compositions themselves or whether it lay outside in the web of meanings and signification imposed on them by successive cultural engineers. The consequences of their intervention were the streamlining of the concert format, the redefining of a classical tradition that was firmly located within the institutional space of modern performance and education in India. In bringing music into the domain of the modern educational system designed for the middle class and into commercial recording and state sponsored broadcasting, the Madras Music Academy played a singularly important role.

To conclude, the framing and development of the classicist discourse was closely connected with the sociology of performance in the twentieth century. It responded to the immediate needs of cultural nationalism that had to compulsively retrieve a heritage that was appropriately antique, authentic, and classical, to the compulsions of modernity that demanded a wider dissemination of the tradition among the middle classes through newly emerging conduits of education, and finally to the imperatives of actual artistic performance in a contemporary setting. While with the Maratha ruler Serfoji II or with the Raja of Travancore Swati Tirunal, the engagement with new modes of listening or evaluating musical performance was one of the many choices and mediated only partly by the early European encounter, in the case of the Madras Music Academy and the constituency, what it represented was fundamentally different. The middle-class elite as reconstructed colonial subjects operating in a transformed public space not only listened to music differently, but chose to describe and value the auditory experience from a new perspective altogether. The imperatives for the new consumers were partly informed by the changing social context of performance, by the emergence of a market for musical entertainment, but more significantly by a need to ascribe a moral function to music. The articulation of a new ethically driven aesthetic of modulating the appreciation and representation of the tradition was clear in the Academy's discourse and in the interventions that followed.

NOTES

1. Margaret Cousins, *The Music of Orient and Occident: Essays Towards Mutual Understanding*, B.G. Paul & Co., Madras, 1935, p. 17ff.
2. Mathew Harp Allen, 'Rewriting the Script for South Indian Dance', *The Drama Review*, 41(3), 1997, pp. 63–100. Also see Mathew Harp Allen, 'Tales Tunes Tell: Deepening the Dialogue between "Classical" and "Non-Classical" in the Music of India', *Yearbook for Traditional Music*, vol. XXX, 1998, pp. 22–52; Lakshmi Subramanian, 'The Reinvention of a Tradition: Nationalism, Carnatic Music and the

Madras Music Academy', *Indian Economic and Social History Review*, XXXVI(2), 1999, pp. 131–63.

3. 'The Madras Music Academy: A Brief Resume of its Origins, Aims and Achievements with an Appeal for Generous Support by the Hon'ble Dr. U. Rama Rao', *Journal of the Music Academy Madras*, (hereafter *JMAM*) vol. I, Madras, 1930. pp. 79–81.

4. Swami Prajnanananda, *Historical Development of Indian Music*, Firma K.L. Mukhopadhyay, Calcutta, 1973. Also see his *Sangitasara Samagraha*, Ramakrishna Vedanta Math, Calcutta, 1956; Raghava Menon, *Indian Music*, Bombay, 1974; Ram Avatar Veer, *History of Indian Music and Musicians*, Pankaj, Imprint, New Delhi, 1987. For the southern musical tradition, see R. Ranga Ramanuja Ayyangar, *History of South Indian (Carnatic) Music From Vedic Times to the Present*, published by the author, Madras, Bombay, 1972. Also see P. Sambamoorthy, *A Dictionary of South Indian Music and Musicians* (3 volumes), The Indian Music Publishing House, Madras, 1971.

5. R. Sathyanarayana, *Karnataka Music as Aesthetic Form*, PHISPC, Centre for Studies in Civilization, New Delhi, 2004, pp. 144–6.

6. Raymond E. Reiss, 'The Cultural Setting of South Indian Music', *Asian Music*, nos 1–2, 1969 pp. 22–31; Jon B. Higgins, 'From Prince to Populace: Patronage as a Determinant of Change in South Indian (Karnatik) Music, *Asian Music*, no. 7, 1976 pp. 20–6; Daniel Neuman, 'The Social Ecology of Indian Music' in O.P. Joshi (ed.), *Sociology of Oriental Music*, ABD Publishers, Jaipur, 2004; and also Neuman's, *The Life of Music in North India: The Organization of an Artistic Tradition*, Manohar, New Delhi, 1980. Gerry Farrell, *Indian Music and the West*, Clarendon Press, Oxford, 1997. Allyn Miner, *Sitar and Sarod in the Eighteenth and Nineteenth Century*, reprint Motilal Banarasidass, Delhi, 1997; Adrian Mcneil, *Inventing the Sarod: A Cultural History*, Seagull Books, Calcutta, 2004.

7. I am using the term Karnatik music as a synonym for Karnataka Sangeetam. Authors have tended to use this term interchangeably with Carnatic (the English derivation of the Mughal Suba of Karnataka that included well-defined areas of the peninsula including coastal Andhra and Tamil Nadu).

8. Amanda Weidman, *In the Kingdom of the Voice: Music and its Subjects in Modern South India*, Duke University Press, (forthcoming). See chapter I on the violin.

9. Sarasvati Mahal Library, Tanjore, Catalogue no. 2551. Raja Serfoji's *Compositions of Military March with Notation for Band Music*, 1803, 1685(a).

10. A.M.C. Mudaliar in his *Oriental Music in European Notation* mentions this story. See *Oriental Music in European Notation*, edited by Gowri Kuppuswami and M. Hariharan. Reprint, Delhi, 1982 (first published 1893), pp. 9–12.

11. R.S. Shelwankar, *Report on the Modi MSS in the Sarasvati Mahal Library, Tanjore*, pp. 15–16ff. Observations on Bundle no. 3.

12. Quoted in Indira Viswanathan Peterson, 'The Cabinet of King Serfoji of Tanjore. A European Collection in Nineteenth Century India', *Journal of the History of Collections*, 11(1), 1999, pp. 71–9.

13. A.M.C. Mudaliar, *Oriental Music in European Notation*, Cosmo, Delhi, 1982, pp. 10–11.

14. *JMAM*, vol. II, no. 4, 1931, p. 240ff. 'Sangeeta Vidwan' T.R. Vishwanatha Sastri's composition was adjudged the best entry for 1931.

15. V.N. Rao, David Shulman, and Sanjay Subrahmanyam, *Textures of Time: Writing History in South India*, Permanent Black, Delhi, 2001.

16. Bonnie C. Wade, *Khyal: Creativity within North India's Classical Music Tradition*, Cambridge University Press, Cambridge, 1984.

17. S. Seetha, *Tanjore as a Seat of Music*, University of Madras, Madras, 1981, pp. 22–3ff., pp. 71–88.

18. C.A. Bayly's work on northern India during the period of British expansion was influential in setting out new terms of reference for understanding the development of regional polities in India during the eighteenth century. The various regimes and regional power structures in eighteenth-century India reflected the dynamism of the political elites in creating and consolidating new social alignments and adopting new cultural practices to stabilize their power. The experience in south India was not markedly different. The case of Ramnad, mentioned here is elaborated by Pamela Price, *Kingship and Political Practice in Colonial India*. Cambridge University Press, Cambridge, 1996.

19. Ibid., p. 27. Price mentions Tanjore as the ultimate destination for artistic demonstrations. The Setupati of Ramnad made it a point to visit Tanjore in the late 1720s where he had the opportunity to show off his prowess. 'There were competitions of wrestling, boxing, sword-fighting, and bull fighting in connection with festivals and function of the States (*sic*) in which the King (of Tanjore) was present.' The Navaratri celebrations in Ramnad and the Dusera festivities in Mysore were well known as sites for performance when the state sponsored on a large-scale artistic performances.

20. Bishop Reginald Heber, *Narrative of a Journey through the Upper provinces of India from Calcutta to Bombay 1824–25 with Notes upon Ceylon. An Account of a Journey to Madras and the Southern provinces*, 1826, 2nd edn, vol. III MDCCCXXVIII, pp. 456–9.

21. Ibid., p. 458.

22. Ludwig Pesch, *The Illustrated Companion to South Indian Classical Music*, Oxford University Press, New Delhi, 1999.

23. Mathew Allen, 'Tales Tunes Tell', pp. 22–52.

24. An old-fashioned but comprehensive treatment of the development of south Indian music is available in R. Ranga Ramanuja Ayyangar, *History of South Indian (Carnatic) Music*. Also see E.M. Ramakrishnan, *Fundamentals of South Indian or Karnatic Music in a Nutshell*, Sakaraa, Madras, 1967. The contribution of medieval saints in Karnataka is well documented by R. Sathyanarayana in his *Music of Madhava Monks of Karnataka*, Gnana Jyothi Kala Mandir Bangalore, 1988.

25. Ibid. Also see S. Seetha, *Tanjore as a Seat of Music*.

26. The trinity refers to three celebrated composers in eighteenth-century Tanjore, namely Syama Sastri (1762–1867), Tyagaraja (1767–1847) and Muthuswamy Diksitar (1776–1835).

27. S. Seetha, *Tanjore as a Seat of Music*, pp. 118–19ff.

28. William Jackson, *Tyagaraja, Life and Lyrics*, Oxford University Press, Madras, 1991. Also see William Jackson, *Tyagaraja and the Renewal of Tradition Translations and Reflections,* Motilal Banarasidass, Delhi, 1994. Also see Ludwig Pesch, *The Illustrated Companion to South Indian Classical Music* and P. Sambamoorthy, *A Dictionary of South Indian Music and Musicians,* and *Great Composers*, The Indian Music Publishing House, Madras, 1970.

29. David Washbrook, *The Emergence of Provincial Politics*, Cambridge, 1976; Indian edition, Vikas Publications, New Delhi, 1977, pp. 84–5, 107–24, 218–29. A

contemporary depiction of the city's elites and their consumption of the performing arts is available in the Sanskrit text *Sarvadevavilasa*. Edited with introduction and notes by V. Raghavan, The Adyar Library and Research Centre, Madras, 1958.

30. C.R. Day, *The Music and Musical Instruments of Southern India and the Deccan*, 1891, Reprint, Low Price Publications, New Delhi, 1990, 1996, pp. 1–2.

31. Phillip Wagoner, 'Sultan Among Hindu Kings: Dress, Titles and the Islamization of Hindu Culture', *The Journal of Asian Studies* 55(4), 1996, pp. 851–80.

32. R. Ranga Ramanuja Ayyangar, *History of South Indian (Carnatic) Music*, pp. 258–69.

33. William Jackson, *Tyagaraja and the Renewal of Tradition*.

34. Ibid. Also see Jackson, *Tyagaraja Life and Lyrics*, pp. 22, 60–1.

35. R. Ranga Ramanuja Ayyangar, *History of South Indian Music*, pp. 316–17. Also see *JMAM*, vol. XXXIX, 1968, p. 29 for paper read by Chennakesaviah on the spread of Tyagaraja's compositions in Mysore. Also see *JMAM*, vol. XXIII 1947, pp. 20–1ff. On 26 December 1946, there was a demonstration by Tyagam, a grandson of Umayalpuram Krishna Bhagavatar, a direct disciple of Tyagaraja, of the composer's work. This was prefaced by a lecture on the composer's life and work. Also see the biographical notices of post Tyagaraja generation of singers that the Academy's journal came up with every year. For details on Muthiah Bhagavatar, K.Varadachariar, T.S. Sabesa Ayyar and Umayalpuram Swaminatha Iyer, see *JMAM*, vol. XIV, 1943. pp. 31–6.

36. *Hindu Music and the Gayan Samaj Published in Aid of the Funds of the Madras Jubilee Gayan Samaj*, Bombay, 1887.

37. Chinnaswami Mudaliar, *Oriental Music in European Notation*, pp. 29–30.

38. Bhashyam Iyengar was one of the early members of the Gayan Samaj besides remaining one of the most important patrons of music.

39. Margaret Cousins, *The Music of Orient and Occident*, pp. 132–4.

40. Partha Chatterjee, *The Nation and its Fragments: Colonial and Postcolonial Histories*, Oxford University Press, New Delhi, 1993, pp. 121–2ff.

41. Mathew Harp Allen, 'Tales Tunes Tell'.

Music Comes to the City

'*Dharma Migu Chennai*'[1] (Madras is replete with piety)—so sang Ramalingaswamy,[2] a nineteenth-century saint poet as he expressed his approval of the city's sacral landscape dotted with temples, tanks, and rest houses. A curious testimonial for a city, which had capitulated to the power of the English East India Company 'intent on destroying the good' and as far removed from dharma as anything could be. If the aerial protagonists of the *Visvagunadarsa Campu*, written in the latter decades of the seventeenth century[3] had protested against the polluting presence of the white faced Hunas in the 'town', their successors preferred to play down the visibility of the foreigner and chose instead, to extol the virtues of the city's indigenous notables who had emerged as *sampradayika*s, the custodians of dharma and tradition. The eighteenth and early nineteenth century Campu poets seem not to have been too far off the mark—as recent historical research has shown, Madras in contrast to her counterparts, Bombay and Calcutta projected a distinctive indigenous urbanism that drew from the larger cultural hinterland of Tondaimandalam.[4] Originating in a humble fishing hamlet, Madras developed through the seventeenth century into a key-trading centre for Europeans and their Indian partners and emerged as the southern locus of British commercial and political power. The dynamics of the city's transformation in terms of its trading profile and urban fabric were unique. It produced at one level a very distinct hybridity of demographic composition and, at another, fostered a particular urban culture with strong if not overriding traditional overtones. The urban space that early colonial Madras represented was, according to Susan Neild Basu, an amalgam of three separate overlapping societies: the suburban village cluster which formed part of the pre-colonial agrarian society of Tondaimandalam, the predominantly Indian commercial cum artisan agglomerates, responding to the needs of the European trade settlement in Madras, and the distinct colonial urban/suburban society that emerged during the nineteenth century reflecting British colonial interests and policies.[5] In the interstices of these three layers a distinct Tamil cultural identity emerged, one that drew from an older, shared and living repertoire of religion, arts, performance, and ritual practice even while attempting to make a crossover to modernity. It compelled an abiding engagement with inventing and reinventing cultural traditions that had to be appropriately classical, adequately nationalist, and uniquely authentic. The central vehicle for this synthesis of identity was found in Sangeetam, music and dance, which became the most striking and significant forms of expression in the city's cultural life.

Madras and her Notables in the Eighteenth Century

Until the late eighteenth century, Madrasapatnam, Fort St George, and its satellite town, the 'petta' constituted a kind of frontier society in the sense that a loose and informal structure of personal relationships, often described as friendships characterized the urban fabric. It was a society where European traders worked in close collaboration with the Indian dubashes who facilitated their commercial transactions and the supply of produce from the artisan communities settled in parts of the town. Madison Mines, in his work on caste identities in early colonial Madras, describes the society as being plastic and personalized.[6] There was no clear and consistent social divide between British and Indian, and relationships between the two groups were in constant flux. Although technically, the Company constituted a suzerain power under the rights of its lease of Madras and its charter, in practice, the city was weakly administered and lacked strong institutions. Personal status and relationships were critical, and as Mines has demonstrated, it was the will of the big man that prevailed for the greater part of the century.

The dubashes held the pride of place among Madras's notables. Through their capital assets, linguistic skills, and personal influence they became vital collaborators of the Company servants and emerged as the principal movers of indigenous society in Madras. Proximity to the English Company, especially the governor, was an important determinant of local influence. We have references to the misdoings of Ankanna, the dubash to Governor Macrae. In the words of Sunka Rama and Tambu Chetty (both dubashes), he exercized 'unlimited authority over the town and had extracted from them (the aforesaid) 3700 pagodas several times'.[7] The Madras dubashes came from a miscellany of castes; Brahmins, Pillais, and Vellalas, all of whom combined land holding with their commercial pursuits and continued to pursue their traditional social activities in the new social space.[8] Large numbers of Vellalas, the traditional rural elite of the Tamil country who owned substantial land holdings and participated in the revenue administration of the local rulers, took up business as interpreters and collaborators of the English Company but without severing their links with the rural hinterland. The linkages were mediated through control of ancestral properties in the larger hinterland through the cultural, social, and traditional connections with agrarian society. The interplay between ritual position, wealth, and colonial urban status was an important and distinguishing feature in the growing prestige of the Madras dubashes. While they made regular visits to ancestral villages and participated in customary festivities as patrons and donors, they simultaneously attempted to replicate the traditional order in the new city of residence. Well-established practices such as temple building, management of religious institutions and charity endowments and the consumption and patronage of the performing arts were deployed to this end. These were critical strategies in perpetuating the status of the big man (*talaivar*) and went a long way in creating by 1800 the illusion of Chennai as a dharmic city. Thus in spite of the dominating presence of the Yavana whose 'national vice' were 'beyond words', who did not 'have the habit of washing themselves after answering calls of nature', the city of Madras became the site for the sport of the notables.

The Sanskrit literary text *Sarvadevavilasa* (Sport of all the Gods) written around 1800 by an anonymous brahmin in the mixed prose poetic Sanskrit genre known as the Campu, offers a rare and graphic description of the public life of Madras and the centrality that performance and patronage assumed in the mapping of the city's social order.[9] For local elites, the deployment of insignia, that is the public performance of ritual, was an important marker of status and a means of defining and delimiting urban space.

For the eighteenth-century author of the *Sarvadevavilasa*, who may well have anchored the work for the gratification of his merchant patrons, Chennai with its dense cluster of temples and tanks, was a hallowed city, which drew to its precincts pundits, musicians, and artists from all over.

Significantly many of the principal suburbs mentioned in the *Sarvadevavilasa* as sites of principal temples, were by 1800, part of the English East India Company's territory though they continued to be administered under the traditional system of *mirasi* tenure. There were two notable exceptions—Triplicane and Pudupakkam, where superior rights over village land had been granted to local temples and their managers—the *dharmakarta*s under the shotrium form of tenure. At the end of the eighteenth century, even after the presence of the English Company and increasing European investment in urban property had altered the existing power structure in the Madras region, the cultural profile and orientation of the city remained traditional. The temple set the tone of the city and its activities were mediated through its patron donor whose piety earned him prominence in the city's social life while his capital ensured him a secure place within the Company set up. In such a city, musicians and artists could expect the support and generosity of patrons like Vedacala, Kalingaraja, and Sriranganayaka.[10] Here, leisure and arts could flourish. The comments of the *Sarvadevavilasa* were echoed in Company discourse as well. The Madras officials of the English East India Company were struck by the temple-centred proclivities of their client merchants. As the Governor of Madras, Pigot wrote to the Court of Directors in 1756, 'in this country, men who are fond of showing their wealth and grandeur have as yet found no better means of displaying them than by the building of temples'.[11] In fact, the Company authorities in their early enthusiasm to fit into traditional modes of political behaviour and social influence, even bought the privilege of country music 'at very great charge' and mentioned that it was looked upon as one of the 'greatest grandeurs that can be'.[12]

The new temples brought with them a fair share of disputes among their worshippers. The 1750s saw wrangles between the two subcastes of the Vaishnavite Iyengar community—the Vadakalais and Tenkalais over invocation practices and prayers in the Triplicane temple and one that dragged on till the 1780s.[13] This related to the thorny problem of language in ritual and use. The Vadakalais appear to have introduced a new liturgy in Tamil in the temple that was under their charge, an addition that was not acceptable to the rival sect. The issue of vernacular liturgy was, in fact, of fairly old standing—as early as the twelfth century, Ramanujam, the principal Vaishnavite leader had instituted reforms that included formal recitation of devotional songs (Alwar compositions) in temple liturgies and opening the temple to fuller participation by sudras whom he called Sattada Vaishnavas. Their involvement lasted till the fourteenth century, when there was a resurgence of brahmin dominance in temple affairs and a return to more orthodox forms of prayer.[14]

With temples and their patrons came music and performance as an integral constituent of ritual practice and aristocratic etiquette or *mariyadai*.[15] White umbrellas, flags, drums and torches, dancing girls were all common *viruttu* that embodied an individual or group's *manam mariyadai*.[16] At the same time, the development of the classical music in south India, or at least one stream of it had been very closely linked with the temple, which since Chola times had operated in tandem with royal courts to emerge as the principal locus of culture, in both its normative as well as performative aspects. Ritual specialists and traditional communities of performers undertook the practice of celebratory music as part of daily temple worship, wherein the presiding deity enjoyed full honours with music and dance. The association of women ritual specialists with the worship of a deity was of long standing and was possibly related to the idea of female sexual energy and harnessing it for the benefit of the community. The female entity carried with it not only unbridled power and energy but also an implicit potential for inauspiciousness and degradation that came in the wake of widowhood. Both these ideas worked together to produce in early Tamil society, the figure of the bard or the *virali*, who had magical powers and supported the life essence of the king.[17] Their presence was in the nature of a protective amulet safeguarding him against malign influences and exhorting him with song and gesture to lead his people to victory. An equally powerful compulsion was to contain female energy by deploying it in the service of the deity, and at the same time isolating it from the inner domain of mundane marriage, which always carried with it the dangers and slur of widowhood. The result was as Saskia Kersenboom Story has argued,[18] the development of the devadasi tradition, which predated its formal location in the temple.

Ritual music thus constituted a vital component of temple worship. All festivities were accompanied by singing and, as C.R. Day had occasion to comment, 'There is hardly any festivity in India in which some part is not assigned to music—and for religious ceremonies it is universal.' Temples had their bands or what was known as *melam*s. There was the *peria melam*, the big band of wind instruments with the *nadaswaram* as the lead instrument. The drone and drums—the *othu*, *thavil*, *talam*, and *sankhu*, accompanied the nadaswaram player. In contrast to the peria melam was the *chinna melam* (literally small band) consisting of dancing girls accompanied by male musicians and other accompanists. Both the melams were constituted by composite non-brahmin castes, referred to sometimes as the Mangalavandulu caste and at others as Isai Vellalas.[19] The melams had a repertoire that suited the requirements of the temple—propitiatory as well as entertainment—but it was by no means an exhaustive representation of the complex musical tradition prevalent in south India. For, temple related ritual music constituted only one element in the making of a musical tradition, and the temple based community comprised only one set of practitioners in what was essentially a polyvalent and multilayered practice in terms of language, content, and structure. Furthermore, the tradition was not singular or fixed, but continued to organically evolve absorbing new musical ideas and modes of expression. In fact, it was during the eighteenth century under the active patronage of the Tanjore court, that certain core segments of the musical tradition were systematically identified and promoted as 'pure music', a tendency that was pushed with greater vigour by the consuming elite of the new city nearly a century later.

A Genealogy for Karnatik Music

Understanding the emergence of what we now call the Karnatik musical tradition requires a close examination of the gradual development of a regional cultural expression that responded to what Kapila Vatsyayana calls certain critical mobile principles.[20] Among these principles, she distinguishes the levels of time representing conservation as well as flux, of locus comprising the factors of indigenous creation and mobility, of cultural state, social realities, and genres reflecting the functions of art form vis-à-vis its audience. Going by what the fourteenth century theorist Kallinatha (1446–65), the principal commentator of the *Sangeeta Ratnakara* had to say of the music of Karnataka Desa as a distinct variant of the larger Indian musical tradition, modern musicologists and scholars have argued that this variant was specific to the area lying between the Krishna and the Kaveri.[21] However, a recent intervention by R. Sathyanarayana suggests that this is a fallacious assumption derived from an erroneous conflation of modern and medieval texts and that the term Karnatik music came into circulation only in the nineteenth and twentieth centuries.[22] Even so, what is borne out by the evidence of musical practice points to the slow coalescence of regional tendencies and musical culture in the area corresponding to modern south India.

How did this regional tradition crystallize? What were the principal catalysts and how inclusive was it of local musical and religious experience on the one hand, and of the larger musical culture on the other? For, it is clear that the courts of the Deccan and the peninsula from about as early as the post-Sangam period (fifth century AD) tended to reflect an interface between the assertion of local culture and of an expanding Sanskrit culture, evident in the language of inscriptions[23] as well as in the juxtaposition of Vedic Brahmanical religion with local devotional practice. With musical expression and improvisation, the process of adaptation and borrowings was even more perceptible. What emerged as the music of Karnataka Desa was, in effect, a mélange of linguistic and musical expressions derived from a variety of melodic sources and theatre practice, local, regional, and Indian.

The area between the Krishna and the Kaveri rivers represented in a sense, a microcosm of the political and cultural experience of the Deccan plateau and the peninsula further south. Politics here, was marked by long and endemic conflict between the two geographical zones, the western Deccan and the Tamilaham that corresponded to the vast plateau areas enclosed by mountains along the coast on the one side, and the fertile plain south of Madras on the other. The division of the peninsula into the plateau kingdoms on the west and the coastal kingdoms on the east increased the desire of each to control the entire waterway, particularly the Krishna and the Godavari. An even more lucrative zone was around the fertile Kaveri basin that supported and sustained impressive polities, the subjugation of which informed the politics of the Hoysalas and Kakatiyas.[24] The period of prolonged political conflict saw the rise and fall of several dynasts—some more successful than others but almost all contributing to a rich and inclusive culture that found manifold reflection in art, architecture, and performance. Even more significant than political connections that could either disrupt or integrate, was the rise and spread of bhakti or devotional religion and the sensibility that it fostered through the pilgrimage circuit and the circulation of poetry and song. Early medieval devotional poetry was poly-lingual; composers, commentators, and singers often crossed over from Sanskrit to Tamil, from Kannada to Marathi, and even improvised the *grantham* script to write Sanskrit with greater ease.[25]

The ascendancy of the Tamilaham towards the end of the first millennium BC is associated with the rise of three chieftaincies—the Cholas, Cheras, and Pandyas—located around the lower Kaveri and the west coast of southern India. While the earliest Tamil writings date from the second century BC, it is from the first century AD that we come across the emergence of a poetic corpus of very high quality, known as Sangam literature (100 BC–AD 300). Sangam poetry accorded a very special and exalted place to bards and referred specifically to *panns* and *pannars* or singers of panns. Panns are now understood to represent ancient Tamil melodic entities that were suitable for bardic lore, whether these were the precursors of modern ragas is difficult to ascertain. What is clear is that panns reflected the workings of a rich musical culture in southern India but over time became part of a recitative tradition, used more extensively in singing devotional songs like the *Tevaram* hymns of the Saivite saints, thereby preserving its unique Tamil resonance.[26]

The extension of what historians call the classical pattern into south India accompanied the emergence of regional kingdoms like the Pallavas and the Chalukyas in the Tamil country and the western Deccan in the fifth, sixth, and seventh centuries AD. These kingdoms drew their inspiration from the classical phase of north Indian kingship and demonstrated their adherence to Vedic Brahmanism, the new social alliance with the brahmins, and the patronage of Sanskrit literature and theatre all of which, set in motion a complex, cultural interchange of ideas and styles. This found reflection in language and literary development, architecture, and the performing arts, wherein, it was expressed in terms of the *Desi–Margi* paradigm. A seventh century inscription of a Chalukya king at Badami mentioned Kannada as the local Prakrit or natural language and Sanskrit as the language of culture— a distinction that underscored the difference in the social context of languages and literatures.[27] In the case of music, the Margi–Desi distinction in all probability derived from regional interpretations of Sanskrit drama.[28] While *Marga* referred to the classical phase of Sanskrit drama, resting on texts and strict application of compositions and melody, the Desi came to represent regional traditions, employing regional song texts and incidental music resting more on improvisation than on fixed composition. Negotiating the two traditions were *Vaggeyakaras* or interpretive practitioners, who, it is suggested, undertook the act of translation in the period between the third and the seventh centuries AD.[29]

The process would appear to have continued through the following centuries, even though our understanding of the forms of theatre music and dance in the period of Chola ascendancy in the peninsula (nineth–twelfth centuries) is only impressionistic.[30] While epigraphic information is replete with references to the hierarchy of performers in temples and the grants they enjoyed for their maintenance, we do not have too many leads about the kind and variations of dramatic performances, theatre, music, and dance that were current. Devotional poetry, at least in the Tamil-speaking area, was sung in traditional *panns*—the *Kuttanul* text of this period talks both of extinct melodies as well as those in limited circulation.[31] It was in the aftermath of Chola decline and in the tentative articulation of power by the first line of Vijayanagar kings in the fourteenth century, that a distinct musical tradition, prevalent over an identifiable region, emerged. The two critical constituents in the making of this culture were provided by devotional poetry and song and a broader and more expansive cross-cultural inheritance produced by the politics of Vijayanagar and the Deccan Sultanates, whereby new languages, new forms of compositions, and new melodic improvisations moved into the core region of Tamilaham, which became the cradle of a distinct regional musical practice.

The integration of diverse eco-cultural zones in the plateau by the Vijayanagar dynasty (1340–1565)[32] had important consequences especially in the domain of literature and the performing arts. Conventional wisdom has tended to characterize Vijayanagar as the 'Hindu bulwark against Mohammedan conquest'[33] and to see the court as the standard bearers of Hindu culture and Sanskritik traditions. It is only recently, that historical scholarship has contested these assumptions, suggesting instead, that the Hindu culture of Vijayanagar was, in fact, deeply transformed by its interaction with Islamic culture.[34] Simultaneously, there was a close engagement with regional linguistic practices as the court actively promoted the use of languages like Telugu. The dictates of politics and governance necessitated the appointment of Telugu deputies to different and distant parts of the realm, which in turn, drew the Tamilaham into the larger cultural universe that the refigured southern India accommodated. The adoption of Telugu as the court language and the language of poetry and music and the preference for Sanskrit and Brahmanical traditions, had a particularly favourable reception in Tanjore, the core region of Cholamandalam, which emerged and remained for more than five centuries the seat of classical music in south India.

Modern historical reconstruction of the south Indian musical tradition takes, as its starting point, the emergence of Vijayanagar (1340).[35] Tradition credits the saint composer Vidyaranya with the founding of the empire as well as with laying the theoretical foundations of Karnatik music. The subsequent centuries saw the maturing of a musical culture produced by the interface of Hindu devotionalism, Islamic mysticism, and of a court sponsored initiative in promoting literacy and musical production in vernacular. Among the principal literary genres promoted and patronized by the Vijayanagar court, the *prabandham* was the most significant. According to Saskia Kersenboom Story, this was an important determinant in the consolidation of the performing repertoire of the devadasis in temples and courts.[36] Musicologists recognize the prabandham as the precursor of later forms such as the *Dhrupad* in the north and the kriti or *kirtanam* in the south. Changes in poetic composition, whereby the relation between the inherent rhythmic quality of the literary text and its melodic vocal rendering, became somewhat closer and more organically dynamic than in the older configurations of text and melody. This facilitated the emergence of the prabandham as a musical genre, which was accompanied by the crystallization of a system of ragas and *mela*s or melodic entities and scales. A raga may be defined as the particular quality of intonation and order of relations between notes in a scale (mela) that is derived from the seven *svara*s of the Indian gamut, namely *sa re ga ma pa dha ni* in either their whole or half-tone forms. A raga yielded and facilitated a distinct and recognizable melodic flavour or character that was persistent throughout all the permitted variations, known and improvised, from the smallest to the most extended, and at all tempos.

The adoption of the raga mela system in musical practice did not find a correspondence in musical scholarship, which remained locked in antiquated definitions of *grama* (the earliest name given to a collection of notes definitely related to one another by certain measurable intervals not of a haphazard nature) *murchana* (a subsequent development with seven notes strung together, but not necessarily on one octave as know them today) and jati[37] (the final stage when murchanas became disciplined into a harmonious relationship which projected consonance of certain fixed entities, that is, one note fixed as sa or tonic r drone note, one as final note, a predominant note which had a great deal of emphasis, and one relating to it in tonality). The decay of musical scholarship, reasons for which are obscure, meant that by the fifteenth century, there was virtually no one who understood either old classical theory or who could square it with contemporary practice, which by this time had been considerably influenced by Persian music mediated largely through Sufi practices. The legends of Amir Khusro (1235–1325) suggest that by his time, Islamicate life in northern India had at least reached a level of integration in local culture that a widespread hybridization of melodies and styles was inevitable. For southern India too, going by the observations of Kallinatha, the geography of music had changed and among the elements that marked the change were a complete disappearance of the grama-jati-murchana and its replacement by a repertoire of ragas all based on the universal tonic sa, and representing, however, approximately a catalogue of the melodic possibilities of the music of the subcontinent and given order by a system of scalar rules.[38] Supporting the growing dominance of the sa, was the emergence of the tanpura that evolved as a hybrid of the Central Asian tambur and the bin.

The adoption of the *raga mela* system, which Acharya Brihaspati suggests, was an adaptation of the Persian style of mukams, came at a time, when devotional practice associated with bhakti fostered the production of song texts in vernacular and whose composers experimented with new melodic influences. The songs of the Talapakkam composer Annamacharya (1408–1503) are a case in point; a prolific composer in Telugu he belonged to a group that propagated a society free of caste divisions and was known to have composed in ragas such as *Thejjuji*, which most probably drew from a Persian *mukam*.[39] In a similar vein, we have the compositions of Madhava monks—Sripadaraya, Vysaraya, Vijayendra, and Raghavendra, who improvised with rhythm and prabandha structures and produced a variety of song texts like the kriti, vrittam, padam, and javali.[40] What distinguished these compositions was their spontaneity while manifesting the amalgamation of the four elements of raga (melody), tala (rhythm), *prameya* (theory), and prabandha (song) that had gradually emerged as the key attributes of improvisational music. Their activities worked in tandem with the court's sponsorship of musical theory leading to the production of the *Swarakalanidhi* (1550) of Ram Amatya, the minister of Krishna Deva Raya followed by *Raga Vibodha* (1609) by Somnatha Kavi and the *Sangeetha Sudhanidhi* (1614) by Govinda Diksitar. These tests did not necessarily reflect accurately or entirely the changes that the practice of music had registered and, their tendency to adhere to convention by using the *Sangeeta Ratnakara* of Sarangdeva (AD 1230) as their normative model only served to widen the gap between what was largely a stagnant theory with a living practice and also to perpetuate later myths of a relatively pure and unalloyed southern musical tradition. Some modern scholars like Walter Kaufman see Ram-Amatya as among the first theorist to try and establish a link between an old theory filled with countless obscure quotations from various sources and the actual performance practices of his time. It was Ram-Amatya who suggested the use of twenty melas, a plain seven-tone scale that represented the tone material of a group of subordinate melodies or *janya* ragas.[41] On the other hand, scholars like Brihaspati do not see the work in the same light and argue that the work referred endlessly to the *Ratnakara* and even went to the extent of referring to *Hejjuji* as a grama raga.[42] However, to suggest or even assume that projects such as the *Swaramelakalanidhi* or the ones that followed were guided by the imperatives of modern identity politics that would have to discount the Islamic influence or claim an exaggerated continuity with the *Sangeeta Ratnakara*, would be an act of prolepsis.

What may be said with some certainty, is that the court was interested in encouraging musical scholarship and reconciling, however, ineffectively, the gaps in old understanding and new practice and that the collaboration, between court and composer or singer, often only tacit, and also over time a community of listeners. A key figure in this proves was undoubtedly Purandaradasa, (1484–1564) who was not only a prolific composer of padams and devotional songs but was also among the first to develop a teaching methodology for the tradition. He fixed the basic scale for a number of musical exercises and a graduated course of vocal compositions that came to be regarded as basic training for musicians. Best known for his *gitam*s and *abhyasaganam*s (literally song exercises), Purandaradasa had an abiding influence on later practitioners both in his setting out definite guidelines for melody and rhythm and in his deriving rudimentary pedagogic techniques to facilitate transmission.[43] His contribution epitomizes an enduring tendency in improvisational music in India, in which, as Lewis Rowell has suggested, there was a continuous movement towards spontaneity and free expression held in balance by certain controls derived from a complex adaptation of textual tradition.[44]

Recent studies[45] on the Islamicization of Hindu culture at Vijayanagar permit us to raise questions about the nature of Indo-Islamic interaction in the domain of music. The sharing and appreciation of a composite musical culture at various levels, in the Bahmani and Vijayanagar empires and subsequently in the successor states that emerged thereafter, would point to being part of what Herman Goetz called a '"national civilization", which was neither Hindu, nor western, nor Central Asian but to which both Hindus and Muslims contributed'.[46] Ibrahim Adil Shah II (1580–1627) and his fascination for the music of Telugu and Marathi brahmins, the Nawab of Golconda's patronage of Ksetragna, the sixteenth century advocate of erotic padams are suggestive of the complex Indo–Islamic interaction in music mediated principally through Sufi and Vaishnav devotional practice. What added to the dimensions of this experience in southern India was the sustained attention that Vijayanagar and its successor courts paid to the formalization of musical theory with all its inconsistencies and the continued association of high-caste practitioners with both theory and the practice of music. Both these had important consequences for the future, when the question of retrieving the tradition and representing it as traditional, textual, and authentic assumed a new meaning altogether.

The battle of Talikota (1565) signalled the end of the Vijayanagar empire and its subsequent division into a series of what has come to be known as Nayaka regimes of Tanjore, Madurai, Ikkeri, and Jinjee. Of these, the Tanjore polity was especially important in establishing and retaining its role as cultural arbiter, a functional role that was a result of 'chance and necessity'. Saskia Kersenboom Story argues that the relative smallness in the material base of the kingdom forced its rulers to 'stay in a kind of relic position which left no scope for expansion and initiative, but only the amalgamation of different streams of culture and their consolidation and preservation'.[47] The Tanjore Nayaka rulers, besides being consumers were themselves composers and as such were keenly interested in promoting musical scholarship and literary productions. As poet princes, both Raghunatha Nayaka (1600–34) and Vijayaraghava Nayaka (1633–73) were important patrons of arts, composed prabandhas and plays, elevated the status of Telugu as a court language, and sustained musical scholarship. It was under their initiative and patronage that two important treatises were written, the *Sangita Sudha* by Govinda Diksitar and the *Caturdandiprakasika* (1660) by Venkatamakhin, who outlined a scheme of 72 reference scales or *melakartas*. This was a landmark for despite the modifications that followed in the succeeding centuries, it gave a basis for musicians to work out melodic combinations systematically and actually use the work as a reference point in their own practice.

These developments along with the imperatives of Nayaka kingship that negotiated with the arena of the temple and ritual performance appears to have produced a complex assemblage of musical practice and conception, and a corresponding hierarchy based on patronage, training, and functions in the field of the performing arts. There were court-based scholars who compiled and commented on and authored musical treatises, there were high-caste court musicians who had access to formal training, who performed in court and who became spokesmen for the more canonical version of the tradition. Below them were ritual singers and dancers, the devadasis, who worked within the precincts of the temple but who could negotiate between the court and the temple. Together, they constituted the cultural economy of Nayaka rule, which recent commentators have suggested, worked out a new model of hedonistic kingship.[48] The new kings were great exemplars of wealth, they projected an image of uncalculating, profligate generosity to poets, hungry brahmins, courtesans, deities, and above all, their own insatiate bodies.[49]

The emerging hierarchy in the profession of music and performance was reinforced by developments in the eighteenth century. It was during this period (1676–1856), that Maratha rule was consolidated in Tanjore and the city experienced a spectacular burst of artistic creativity. Of particular significance in this cultural efflorescence was the articulation of a definite canonical standard for *sampradaya* or traditional music. It covered the critical areas of composition and melody and rhythm

Figure 1: Serfoji II and Shivaji II.
Courtesy: Painted Manuscripts of the Sarasvati Mahal Library

structures while projecting a new normative model for the devout performer-musician, immersed in his practice. The collaboration between the court and the musician, musician and devotee produced far reaching, even if in fact, unforeseeable results in terms of content, musical grammar, normative ideals, and pedagogic models for future transmission. The court's role was seminal in the process of standardization. It did not content itself with patronizing veterans and established musicians like Virabhadraiyya, Kasinathaayya, and Margadarsi Seshayya but through them attempted to formulate conventions and guidelines for training, practice, and presentation.[50] It was in this context that a crop of celebrated composers made their mark among whom, the trinity—Tyagaraja, Diksitar, and Syama Sastri—attained exemplary eminence by virtue of an artistic conception that transcended the more conventional and ornate forms of court music.

It was thus, not entirely fortuitous that eighteenth-century Tanjore saw the coming together of brilliant composers who in their own distinct and individual ways, extended and enriched the contours of the existing tradition and in the process created what one may legitimately describe as a new if not proto-modern form for classical music, one that expanded the scope and inflection of romantic-devotional expression, in which the artist's labour followed or was seen to follow his existential self-realization. New, because it definitely marked a departure from the existing conventions of love poetry and devotional music or even art music that had been patronized by the court; new also because it improvised with existing material to create a form that represented a more individual approach to melodic delineation and rhythm structures. Thus even while responding to their received inheritance of theoretical training, artistic context, social experience of ritual and worship, and of a rich and elaborate musical education, the trinity were fully alive to the expanding possibilities of refining the structure of song text, of delineating and improvising on melodic modes, and of marrying music and song more effectively. The ability of Tyagaraja in particular to discover a free and unfettered artistic space to improvise and function freely derived perhaps in part from the difficult material situation that Tanjore was undergoing in the wake of the Mysorean invasions of Haider Ali, and in part from a deep existential angst that drove the poet to contemplate on music and devotion as a reaction to secular hierarchies of power and status. The result was, according to William Jackson, the reconstituted kriti as a simple and integrative cultural form that synthesized refinement and codification with simple devotion making it a vehicle of liberation for difficult times to come.[51]

The Tanjore trinity, each in their own way represented a distinct, subjective, and individual artistic ideal that came together to produce a remarkably composite, yet richly diverse template of musical ideas and expression. For instance, Tyagaraja, belonged to a musical family well versed in the pedantic aspects of the tradition and with access to a range of linguistic skills and benefited from a rather traditional musical education—his teacher being Sonti Venkatrammiah, a leading court musician, well known for his erudition and performance capabilities. This, combined with an intensely personal, spiritual commitment produced a rare musical and artistic energy. Tyagaraja's engagement with music was coeval with his devotional and inner life and he, perforce, shunned the politics of performance. His individual genius and imagination were oriented to simpler expressions of devotion and poetry that were part of the peripatetic bhakti saints' circuit. His blend of a simple devotional idiom, almost folk-like in expression and a rigorous art music with its complex structures of rhythm and melody resulted in a rare combination of simple devotional music and art music which revolutionized the musical sensibilities of his society. He perfected his expressive vehicle in the kriti[52] (a three-part song text) and the accompanying sangatis or variations that played around the idea of refrain but more expansively and imaginatively giving full scope for elaborate development of the melodic mode. Parallel to this ran the idea of the ideal musician who was not lured by lucre and whose single-minded steadfast devotion to god transcended all worldly pursuits. Thus Tyagarja's kritis were as much vehicles for melody as they were for personal salvation. His versatility created a wide spectrum of moods in a variety of song types. His grounding in musical grammar led him to compose in many different and rare melodic modes. Later commentators observed his 'struggle against the secularizing trend which was fought out in the context of the Tanjore Courts relation to music'. Twentieth century recensions of the Tyagaraja legend emphasized the composer's distaste for court patronage and art music sponsored by the court as well as the music associated with the devadasis.[53] While the former underplayed the element of simple poetry and musical clarity, the devadasi repertoire was seen to play up the idea of erotic entertainment. For Tyagaraja, the pursuit of music as the supreme vehicle of devotion was best achieved in combining lucid poetry with musical freedom and a perfectly balanced sense of rhythm. To quote from an observation that appeared in the souvenir volume of the Tyagaraja Mahotsavam in 1945,

The principles of *Sangatis* that Tyagaraja introduced in *kirtanas* transformed the recitative hymn into a piece of art music of high aesthetic merit. But for this compositions would not form the bulk of concert programmes today. Songs of other composers will not pass muster unless they are adapted to the requirements of sangati. In this great change, the two elements of discipline and freedom are dexterously reconciled by engrafting the *alap padhati* on the *gita marga*. This simple achievement is enough to confer on him undisputed sovereignty in the domain of Indian music.[54]

If Tyagaraja embodied one stream of artistic improvisation, then Muthuswamy Diksitar represented an equally powerful voice in the changing auditory landscape of south India. More than Tyagaraja, his life and career were informed by the richness and variety of southern India's cosmopolitanism—his family's connections with regional courts like Tanjore and Ettayapuram as well as with the Company's establishment in Madras fostered an exploration of new ideas. Diksitar himself participated in the traditional circuit of pilgrimage and made frequent visits to Kashi, where he encountered north Indian musical traditions, especially dhrupad singing, which left a permanent impression on his artistic persona. Like his senior contemporary, he worked on the kriti as the chief vehicle of poetic and musical expression although for the most part he employed a two-part form. His compositions were in Sanskrit, and dense in poetic description and philosophical import and named as a kind of melodic signature the specific melody in which they were set. Modern musicologists maintain that Diksitar scrupulously adhered to the Venkatamakhin system of melodic classification and nomenclature jettisoning the subsequent scheme introduced by Govindacari in the eighteenth century, and one that Tyagaraja preferred.[55] This did not necessarily suggest an ultra conservative disposition for we find significant instances of what one may call a 'modern' temperament in terms of response to new inputs. His exposure, through his family, to European military music in Madras inspired him to compose Sanskrit lyrics for tunes such as 'God save the King'—quasi European airs that came to be known as *Nottusahitya*. Again, his brother Baluswamy Diksitar was among the first to take to the violin, an alien instrument that over time gained complete acceptance.[56] The difference in approach and musical conception lay in the slower and more solemn melodic delineation that suited Diksitar's creativity and reflected the diversity of the musical climate of Tanjore. Both composers were clearly products of their environment, and both wished to define a new space for musical expression that was not bound to the conventions and requirements of court music but could draw on the existing pool of musical expression to develop an altogether new musical idiom.[57]

The third figure in the trinity was Syama Sastri, a Tamil-speaking brahmin who like his contemporaries came from a musical family. He learnt the rudiments of music from his father and uncle, was initiated into musical mysticism by Sangeeta Swami (his identity is not clear) and finally trained under a prominent Tanjore court musician, namely Gopala Iyer. The latter was the court musician of Serfoji II and was credited with a number of important compositions especially varnams that were considered essential exercises for vocal music. Syama Sastri was considerably influenced by his teacher and evolved a unique style in his compositions that speak both of his training and of his immediate personal inheritance, for he belonged to a family of officiating priests who combined ritual service with musical expertise. Although his output was not prodigious, his three hundred odd songs stand out as exquisite finished pieces and reputedly earned Tyagaraja's appreciation. Modern critics see in the compositions a refined conception of song grounded in perfectly integrated rhythm and note combinations.[58]

This efflorescence of artistic creativity and the cultural agenda of the Maratha court coincided to produce a definitive aesthetic canon for art music. The court's encouragement of the performing arts had not only provided patronage for performing musicians, it also promoted guidelines for presentation and stimulated improvisations and compositions. The plethora of compositions expanded the repertoire for performers and set important aesthetic parameters that they had to adhere to. The location of the trinity, albeit, outside the formal domain of the court deepened the musical culture as both court and performers acknowledged the richness of their intervention. The widespread dissemination of their work, however, was not mediated through the Maratha court; in fact, it was largely a mid-nineteenth century phenomenon.[59] The immense influence of the trinity, especially Tyagaraja derived from the disciple tradition that he developed and which, in less than half a century enjoyed primacy as the standard bearer of classicism. It is interesting and important to note that art music continued to thrive in Tanjore well into the nineteenth century and that it was not before the 1870s that the great influx of musicians into Madras city became a marked feature of the changing cultural scene in south India. This in turn coincided with the coalescence of a high-caste predominantly brahmin elite in Madras city and that articulated its own cultural sensibility, and produced a new mode of cultural consumption and patronage.

Musicians on the Move

The movement of music and musicians into the colonial city of Madras occurred in two phases and encapsulated two very different stages in the evolution and presentation of classical Karnatic music. The *Sarvadevavilasa*, the eighteenth century work on Madras, spoke quite expansively on the presence of musicians and the patronage they enjoyed from the city's notables. These musicians appear to have been the court variety, excelling in the technicalities of melody and rhythm and adhering to the pre-Tyagaraja tradition of court music. Their forte remained the *pallavi*[60] (elaboration of a sole theme melodically deploying a brief text consisting of one or two lines); the refined and embellished kriti had not arrived. The early arrivals constituting largely of merchant magnates, whose artistic sensibilities were informed by existing conventions of ritual music, temple honours, and proto-court performance were impressive. Thus we have extensive references to temple dancers, to temple processions and attendant ritual music, and to well-known court musicians who visited Madras even as they maintained links with the Tanjore court. The dancers and courtesans who enjoyed the patronage of the magnates also maintained connections with Tanjore and represented very definitely the performative aspect of a court centred tradition. This is evident in the description of courtesans like Manga, who was reputedly well versed in music and drama, of Minakshi and Narayani all of whom enjoyed extensive patronage in the city.

The migration of musicians into the new city continued through the century and was part of the general process of artistic relocation following the decline of the Tanjore court. This did not, however, mean that connections with Tanjore were entirely disrupted or that the cultural influence exerted by the city disappeared. In fact, the circulation of musicians, and musical ideas continued to move along the traditional axis of Tanjore-Madurai-Ramnad, Ettayapuram, and later Mysore and Madras and thereby giving currency to the idea of a unitary cultural model, to which performers always had occasion to refer. Here, the initiative undertaken by the lineage of Tyagaraja's disciples was, especially significant. The saint-composer, if later biographies are to be believed, carefully selected disciples, upon whom he could rely to retain the authenticity of his compositions.[61] Some of them made tentative efforts in preserving the old compositions with a rudimentary form of notation. Particularly among his chief disciples in disseminating the tradition and bringing it to the new city by way of public performance and through the newly emerging medium of print, were Venkatramana Bhagavatar and his son Krishnaswami Bhagavatar, and Veena Kuppier (1798–1860) who made a Telugu manuscript of Tyagaraja's kritis in 1826. Other distinguished pupils were Manambucavadi Venkatasubbu who taught an entire generation of musicians like Mahavaidyanatha Iyer (1844–93), Sarabha Sastri (1872–1904), Fiddle Venkoba Rao, and Patnam Subramania Iyer (1845–1902). Virtually all of them, belonged to musical families, had well-established linkages with the Tanjore court, acknowledged the influence of Tyagaraja and the tradition that he represented, learnt his compositions and thereafter pursued careers in the new city of Madras as well as in court centres like Mysore, Travancore, Ettayapuram, and Ramnad.[62] Poochi Srinivasa Iyengar who became court musician of Ramnad and trained a number of disciples among whom mention may be made of Salem Doraiswami Iyengar, Kutralam Srinivasa Iyer, and Mannargudi Krishnamurti Iyer. Similarly, Patnam Subramania Iyer trained Ramanathapuram Srinivasa Iyengar, C.S. Krishnamurthi Iyer, Guruswami Iyer and the Enadi sisters. In establishing the Tyagaraja lineage in Travancore, Muthiah Bhagavatar played an important role with performance in Tirunelveli and Tirichirapalli.[63]

In Madras city itself, the space for performance both as a public activity as well as a private occasion around a wedding or birthday celebration continued to increase quite rapidly, thereby encouraging the post-Tyagaraja generation of musicians to take up permanent residence in the city. This had to do with the lifestyles of the city's successful professionals, for whom consumption of music was not only a matter of aesthetic pleasure or a marker of status and culture but an articulation of what Emile Durkheim would call, a collaborative need to formalize togetherness by adhering to common symbols and practices.[64] Admittedly, this was not an entirely unprecedented practice; a close look at the social world of Tanjore in the nineteenth century reveals the importance of such practices among notables—Brahmins, Vellala, and Chetty patrons as well as heads of religious organizations.[65] However, what distinguished the engagement of the brahmin elite in Madras was the enhanced symbolic significance they attached to the practice of listening and appreciating music, thereby participating in the construction of a sense of community, with exclusivist overtones. At the same time, their engagement with issues of social reform and education lent a new inflection to their appreciation of music and culture and opened the possibility of integrating music into a new system of education. The interplay between the imperatives of devotion (shared experience within the community) and of professional skill and training (musical education in modern secular spaces) found expression in the changing modes of patronage for music by the leading notables of Madras. Leading lawyers and notables like Bhashyam Iyengar, Dewan Bahadur Raghunath Rao, and their associates participated in the deliberations of music associations like the Gayan Samaj and the Tanjore Sangeetha Vidya Mahajana Sangam, and became major patrons and spokesmen for reform.[66] Musicians were encouraged to perform in public as well as in family events; occasionally, permission was even sought from the courts to lend their musicians.[67] The appreciation of the city notables became synonymous with taste and refinement. In 1904, when the agent of Kudipi Kolam zamindar approached the Mysore palace for the loan of the court musician Veena Subanna, he mentioned in his letter that 'the leading and distinguished gentlemen of Madras such as the Hon'ble Justice Subramania Iyer and Shri Bhashyam Iyengar and others desire to have Veena Subanna's kacheri[68] or musical concert and as his name is well spoken of in Madras, he is requested to state terms and railway expenses from and to reach Madras before the day fixed (i.e. for the marriage).'[69]

The ramifications of the expanding network of musicians through courts, private contacts in Madras city, and their own kin connections produced interesting results. For one, the Tyagaraja tradition or *parampara* as conveyed through a small but closely integrated caste group located primarily in Tanjore and to a lesser extent in Tirunelveli, was firmly entrenched. The lineage and musical style associated with it, was foregrounded as being classical and traditional with all the hallmarks of rigorous training and musicological excellence. Both exponents and patrons of the Tyagaraja lineage became zealous guardians of their inheritance. Modern technologies of printing and transmission through schools and institutes were deployed to that effect. C.S. Ayyar who wrote *Sri Tyagaraja kritis for Beginners* in 1898 mentioned in his preface that his object was to convey a sense of the teaching methods before his time, when his father was a violinist and learnt from an Umayalpuram musician (Tyagaraja's lineage) and was taught a specific number of compositions. He compared them with the list of compositions that were taught to his elder daughters in 1919–21 by Sabesa Iyer, also of the same lineage and concluded by saying that these were the proper basis for any musical training and urged his readers to make them the backbone of 'musical education'.[70]

An important factor in the growing popularity of music and the development of musical taste in Madras was the spread of musical theatre performances called harikatha or *kathakalaksepam* from about the latter decades of the nineteenth century. This was essentially a narration play, with song, extempore discourse, and dramatic interpretation, and was organized around an epic story or religious theme. As an art form, it drew its inspiration from Marathi harikatha and local story-telling practices, but unlike either of these, the new form demanded a deep knowledge of Sanskrit scriptures, a song repertoire, and histrionic talent. Periaswamy Sastri was among the early improvisers of the harikatha and is, in fact, credited with the invention of the kathakalaksepam. A retired musician, he came up with a new form of performing a religious discourse and showed a rare talent for training gifted men. One of his protégés was Krishna Bhagavatar, who he took under his wing in 1865 in Tanjore. Six years later, the twenty-one year old having undergone training in music, dance, Sanskrit and physical culture, took to the stage and mesmerized his audience in Madras.[71] The songs used in performance were predominantly Tyagaraja's compositions[72] that were especially appropriate as expressions of pure devotion. Others followed suit—Pandit Laksmanachari (1857–1921), and Pancapakesa Sastri whose rendering of the Ramayana in Madras was immensely popular. These performances had the desired effect of creating a genuine appreciation of music so much so that to society's amazement, an individual like Mangudi Chidambara Bhagavatar gave up a promising career in the Bar to take up kathakalaksepam.[73] The performances accelerated the circulation of many compositions and created an awareness of the richness and potential of the repertoire. At the same time, they fostered a sense of selfhood, especially of the brahmin community giving them not just a form of entertainment to consume and patronize, but also a sharpened sense of cultural identity. As Ranga Ramanuja Ayyangar reminisced in his later days, the kathakalaksepam promoted devotion to god, reverence for the Vedas and Puranas, and respect for the national ideals of culture and aesthetics. The portrayal of sentiment through poetic song and its ability to compel the attention of a large audience to an exemplary presentation had a powerful impact on individual psychology, and served as a suitable agent for solidarity.

The consolidation of the eighteenth century inheritance and its dissemination in the post-Tyagaraja generation in the second half of the nineteenth century was a critical stage in the making of the modern classical music idiom in southern India. This, in a sense, predated the articulation of a self-conscious cultural project by the western educated middle-class elite of Madras city. In this, both the cultural politics of the Tanjore court and the organic development of an urban musical culture fostering a shared space of affective identity were important factors. The court through its patronage and engagement had refined and extended taxonomy of musical knowledge and practice that fixed the tradition around a specific range of coordinates. The improvisations of the trinity enriched the repertoire, besides investing it with a distinct character. It now emphasized the importance of the individuated composer who spurned court and patronage to evolve an autonomous relationship with the art form and, in the process gave a completely different dimension and direction to musical conception and practice. This quite inevitably captured the imagination of the middle class in the latter decades of the nineteenth century.

The New Gentry of Madras City

A major watershed in the changing social and demographic profile of Madras city occurred in the second half of the nineteenth century, when there was a clear shift in the location of elites in the city, the supercession of old elite groups, notably commercial, by the new professional elites. The shift, according to R. Suntharalingam,[74] occurred around the 1860s, when the first batch of graduates emerged from Madras University and took up positions in the professions. David Washbrook dates the shift two decades earlier, sometime in the 1840s, when the anglicizing impulse became the key rallying point of administrative policy.[75] Stuart Blackburn, in his work argues that one of the most significant consequences of Anglicization was the marginalization of vernacular journalism and the emergence of English as the principal language of public debate. This shift gave the brahmins a definite edge.[76] The emergence of the new brahmin elite was a direct outcome of the spread of colonial education and administration. The predisposition of brahmins to western education and professional service was evident from around the 1860s, when Tamil and Telugu brahmin lawyers began to attain prominence, wealth, and status as a professional group. Anil Seal's political arithmetic of the Madras Presidency revealed the absolute preponderance the brahmin sub-caste enjoyed in education and the services; in 1894, they represented 68.8 per cent of graduates in the city even while they barely accounted for 3.1 per cent of the total population.[77] Most of the brahmin entrants into the new city and the new world that western education and colonial administration embodied were from the districts of Trichinopoly, Tirunelveli, and Tanjore—the brahmin districts par excellence. Their adaptability and industry were identified as key attributes for their later success; as an official manual noted, 'there is hardly a pursuit, literary, industrial or professional to which they do not apply themselves with remarkable success'.[78] Why the community took so energetically to colonial education in the late nineteenth century is not clear—for we know from recent works that the groups to take advantage of the emerging print culture in Madras in the early nineteenth century were non-brahmins who, in fact, dominated the teaching scene in Fort St George College, and played a seminal role in copying and printing anthologies of Tamil grammar and poetics for general circulation. The early initiative did not give them a decided advantage, for with the formal establishment of western education and the opportunities that it encoded, it was the brahmin community which responded to the changes and rapidly established their presence as the premier group in Madras city. Professional success enhanced the ritual status of the community, which by the closing decades of the nineteenth century, was ready to negotiate with modernity and to recast their self-image in conformity with the new imperatives of colonial subject-hood. It was here that a major break occurred—while the older commercial elites of Madras city had neither the exposure to the modernizing influences of an urbanized society, nor engaged with the idea of modernity as a subjective experience, the new elite's rendezvous with western education and colonial governance produced an altogether different psychological response in relation to both their inherited culture as well as to the more immediate reality of modern politics and social ordering. A new mode of looking at the world emerged—a shifting of the episteme largely informed by the colonial discourse on progress, morals, and governance as well as by a need to articulate new forms of social identity. As a result, consumption practices, especially of culture changed. The case of the performing arts, especially music, assumed a special signification in the emerging process of cultural articulation in a colonial situation and constituted in the process, even if somewhat perversely, a defining moment in the re-definition of a classical tradition.

The deployment of music or, indeed the investment in temple building as part of mariyadai was for long constitutive of the traditional social order, where the landed and commercial elites held pride of place. The extension of this order into the growing city of Madras continued right through the late eighteenth and nineteenth centuries, leading to what David Washbrook calls elongation of linkages. Wealth to be translated into social status necessitated conventional modes of display and patronage that operated quite independently of the colonial presence and whose supporting apparatus of education did not fundamentally alter the parameters of consumption and reflection. This was not the case with the rapidly growing brahmin elite of Madras city, whose participation in culture in the late nineteenth century was informed by entirely new concerns and imperatives. Thus, even if it was the rich and influential magnate-patron whose competitive needs provided the necessary sponsorship for arts, temple management and other cultural markers, it were the western educated brahmin publicists who appropriated the tradition initially as a means of defining an exclusive social identity for themselves as a special group, and subsequently extending it to serve as part of the nation's unique cultural inheritance.

The crystallization of the professional elite, largely brahmin centred and the articulation of a specific cultural project coincided with the influx of musicians into the city and proliferation of music associations, and the popularity of musical-religious discourses (kathakalaksepam) in the city in the first quarter of the twentieth century. These developments had fostered a genuine listening habit among an urban audience that responded to music and dance not as a ritual experience, but as a kind of hybrid personal experience, that helped to negotiate the new professional life detached from the older moral economy. As migrants from Tanjore and Trichinopoly, they had an inside appreciation of the art form, which from their new social and spatial location in Madras, they could examine from a different perspective. Appreciation became both an aesthetic pursuit as well as an issue of taste and sensibility;[79] primers and teach yourself books came into the market, while middle-class families in Madras began to seriously entertain the idea of having their children learn music. Lawyers and barristers, recognized as city notables organized music performances as part of wedding celebrations,[80] and encouraged women and children to take up music. Musical culture was at the same time, seen as an integral part of personal religion—the hallmark of the brahmin's cultural identity, an inflection that was encouraged by the advocacy of Hinduism by the Theosophists. As Margaret Cousins observed, speaking of an occasion in Madras in 1926,

I remember my entire surprise when I met the musician in the private houses of Indian friends of cultured taste. I remember my entire surprise the first time I was asked to attend an evening party of a famous Madras barrister, I expected jollity and chatting and perhaps a little music; instead the entertainment had begun before I arrived and consisted of one singer giving a rendering in music of some religious song and all the legal luminaries kept silent all the evening profoundly engrossed in a religious theme.[81]

A heightened self-reflection mediated through music and religious performance combined with the Theosophist reading of the Hindu past and the special place accorded therein to the brahmin caste fuelled an enormous enthusiasm for Hindu culture, as a defining marker of an exclusive and closed identity in the inner domain, translated later into an Indianness that could exist quite robustly alongside the trappings of an emerging middle-class modernity.[82] Music enjoyed a special place in this invoked and imagined site of tradition, besides exercising a compelling and genuine appeal to its devotees, many of whom were, hardly, in all probability self-conscious cultural engineers. On the other hand, there was a definite pedagogic interest in the dissemination of music, an issue that began to engage the attention of princely states in south India, notably in Mysore and Travancore, thereby, heightening the tension between complementary and conflicting imperatives of devotion and virtuosity.

The intervention of the middle class and their engagement with classical music in an altered social context set the stage for recasting the tradition of performing arts. The shifting locus of patronage from court to individual salon to public domain, the emergence of the middle-class amateur musician who straddled even if uneasily the worlds of tradition and modernity, the growing concern to define and nurture the existing tradition as part of a nationalist cultural project and invest it with new overlays of meaning and signification, underscored the break with the past. The aesthetic experience was now caught up in complex discourses about tradition, selfhood, nation, identity, and culture. The result was that, the reception of music and its invocation as an emblem of an intimate identity and unique sensibility, produced new conceptions of classicism and aesthetics that had in the long run momentous consequences for the art form and its practitioners. It is to the discursive history of classical music in southern India, the constituents of the cultural project of the Indian elite and its southern variant that we shall now turn our attention.

NOTES

1. Quoted in V. Raghavan's introduction to the *Sarvadevavilasa*, The Adyar Library and Research Centre, Madras, 1958, pp. 2–4. Here, says Raghavan, 'we have a view of which saint Ramalingaswamy sang, "dharma migu Chennai"—Madras is full of virtue and piety'. Ramalingaswamy was a composer (1823–76) who came from Chidambaram.
2. For biographical details of Ramalingaswamy, see *The Life and Teachings of Saint Ramalingar* by S.P. Annamali, Bharatiya Vidya Bhavan. Bombay, 1973. Ramalingaswamy was born in 1823 and moved to Madras while still an infant. He had his education in Kanchipuram but it was in Madras that he gave long discourses and shared his poetry with his disciples such as Velayudha Mudaliar who later became Professor of Tamil in Presidency College.
3. 'Notices of Madras in Two Sanskrit Works' by V. Raghavan in *The Madras Tercentenary Commemoration Volume* (Humphrey Milford, Oxford University Press, London, Bombay, Calcutta, Madras, 1939), pp. 108–10.
4. Susan Neild Basu, 'The Dubashes of Madras', *Modern Asian Studies*, 18(1) 1984, pp. 1–31. Also see 'Madras in 1800: Perceiving the City' in Howard Spodek and Doris Srinivasan, (eds), *Urban Form and Meaning in South Asia*, Hanover and London, 1993, pp. 221–40.
5. Susan Neild Basu, 'Colonial Urbanism: The Development of Madras City in the Eighteenth and Nineteenth Centuries', *Modern Asian Studies*, 13(2) 1979, pp. 217–46.
6. Mattison Mines, 'Courts of Law and Styles of Self-Representation', *Modern Asian Studies,* 35(1) 2001, pp. 33–74.
7. J. Talboys Wheeler, *Madras in the Olden Times* Madras, 1861 in three volumes, vol. III, pp. 71–84. Petitions against Gooda Ankanna, Dubash of Governor Macrae.
8. Susan Neild Basu, 'The Dubashes of Madras', pp. 1–31.
9. *Sarvadevavilasa*, Madras, 1958, Introduction, pp. 5–6ff. Chapters 5 and 6 speak of the processions undertaken by the city's notables—Kalinga Raja, Venkatadri, and Vedacalam. Raghavan attempts to identify these names with actual historical figures; for example, he suggests that Venkatkrisna of Manali was the son of Muddukrishna of Manali who was dubash to Governor Pigot. Annaswami of Triplicane figures in the papers of the Madras collectorate from 31 January 1822, while Kalingaraja figures in Love's account.
10. Ibid., pp. 6–59.
11. Governor Pigot's letter to the Court of Directors is quoted in H.D. Love, *Vestiges of Old Madras 1641–1800*, vol. III, pp. 368–88.
12. H.D. Love, *Vestiges of Old Madras 1640–1800*, London, 1913, vol. II, p. 242.
13. Ibid., vol. III, pp. 388–90.
14. See Stephen Paul Hopkins, *Singing the Body of God: The Hymns of Vedantadesika in their South Indian Tradition*, Oxford University Press, New Delhi, 2002, pp. 34–5.
15. For Mines, the goal of merchants who controlled honours was not political rule. It was to use temples to establish their private reputation and influence to facilitate their enterprises. The division of the town into moieties and of these into caste

localities, each with its own set of temples, created limited constituency domains. This enabled a different set of prominent individuals to lay claims to temple honours on each domain. The English Company for the greater part of the eighteenth century adopted indigenous styles of social behaviour. Lionel Place, the collector of Chinglepet adopted the role of an indigenous king. He would call for all the dancing girls, musicians, and horses attached to the temple at Conjeevaram and distribute gifts and offerings. See Mattison Mines, 'Individuality and Achievement in South Indian Social History', *Modern Asian Studies*, 26(1) 1992, pp. 129–56.

16. H.D. Love, *Vestiges of Old Madras*, vol. III, pp. 385ff.

17. Saskia Kersenboom Story, *Nityasumangali, Devadasi Tradition in South India*. Motilal Banarsidass, Delhi, 1st edn, 1987. Reprint Delhi, 1998, 2002, pp. 11–7.

18. Ibid., pp. 23–8.

19. C.R. Day, *The Music and Musical Instruments of Southern India and the Deccan* (1891), Delhi Reprint, 1990, 1996, p. 97.

20. Kapila Vatsyayana, *Traditional Indian Theatre: Multiple Streams*, National Book Trust, New Delhi, 1979.

21. See Ludwig Pesch for instance. *The Illustrated Companion to South Indian Classical Music*, Oxford University Press, New Delhi, 1999, p. 320. Also Indira Menon, *The Madras Quartet*, Roli Books, Delhi, 1999.

22. R. Sathyanarayana, *Karnataka Music as Aesthetic Form*, PHISPC, 2004, pp. 149–50. Sathyanarayana argues that there were two treatises by the name *Sangitasudhakara*, one dated to the eleventh century by Haripala and the other composed by Kashinatha Apatulasi Paluskar in 1914, wherein the two categories, Karnatik and Hindustani music are clearly set out. Scholars have mistakenly attributed the first treatise to Haripala Deva, the ruler of Devagiri who did not compose any such musical work and who was actually named Harapala. According to Sathyanarayana, the name originated in Maharashtra in the early twentieth century and subsequently circulated in Tamil Nadu. While there would appear some truth in this assertion, namely that the process of categorization was part of the cultural politics of the twentieth century elites in the Madras Presidency, it is important to recall that we have clear references to Karnatik scholars and Karnatik musicians in Day's account (1891), to Hindustani musicians and Karnatik musicians coexisting in the Trivandrum court in the 1870s when the Gayan Samaj had occasion to speak with the ruler.

23. Romila Thapar, *Early India: From the Origins to AD 1300*, Allen Lane, The Penguin Press, London, 2002, pp. 326–7, 346–7.

24. Ibid. Also see Burton Stein, *Vijayanagara: The New Cambridge History of India*, Cambridge University Press, Cambridge, 1994, pp. 27–30.

25. Stephen Hopkins, *Singing the Body of God*, pp. 6–11, 30–1, 82.

26. Ludwig Pesch, *The Illustrated Companion to South Indian Classical Music*, pp. 12, 67.

27. Romila Thapar, *Early India*, pp. 326–7, 346–7.

28. Lewis Rowell, *Music and Musical Thought in Ancient India*, University of Chicago Press, Chicago, 1992, pp. 192ff.

29. 'Yattu Vaggeyakaren Rachitang Lakshanam, Deshiragadishu Prottang Tadganam Janaranjanam.' See *Sangitasara Samgraha of Sri Ghanasyamadasa*, edited with an introduction by Swami Prajnananda, Ramakrishna Vedanta Math, Calcutta, 1956,

p. 15. According to the editor, the Vaggeyakaras were experienced musicologists who 'formalized many of the aboriginal and folk tunes with the help of ten Sastric characteristics and incorporated them under the head of classical ragas'.

30. Saskia Kersenboom Story, *Nityasumangali*, pp. 29–31.

31. Ibid., pp. 29–31.

32. Burton Stein, *Vijayanagara*, pp. 27–30.

33. Robert Sewell, *A Forgotten Empire*, London, 1900.

34. Phillip B. Wagoner, 'Sultan Among Hindu Kings: Dress Titles and the Islamization of Hindu Culture at Vijayanagar', *The Journal of Asian Studies*, 55(4) 1996, pp. 851–80.

35. R. Sathyanarayana, *Music of Madhava Monks of Karnataka*. See Introduction and pp. 27–37.

36. Saskia Kersenboom Story, *Nityasumangali*, pp. 31–8.

37. Acharya Brihaspati, *Musalman aur Bharatiya Sangeet*, Raj Kamal, Delhi, 1934, pp. 31–2ff.

38. Ibid., pp. 37–8.

39. Ludwig Pesch, *The Illustrated Companion*, p. 190. Also see R. Ranga Ramanuja Ayyangar, *History of South Indian (Carnatic) Music*, pp. 143–4.

40. R. Sathyanarayana, *Music of Madhava Monks*. T.S. Parthasarathy on the other hand, suggested that the Kirtana in its earliest form appeared in the fourteenth century and that the earliest composer was Narayana Tirtha, the first of the band of devotional poets. See T.S. Parthasarathy, 'Composers of Indian Music' in Gowri Kuppuswamy and M. Hariharan, *Indian Music: A Perspective*, Sundeep Prakashan, Delhi, 1980, pp. 97–102.

41. Walter Kaufman, *The Ragas of South India*, Indian University Press, London, 1976. See Introduction.

42. A. Brihaspati, *Musalman aur Bharatiya Sangeet*, pp. 44–5.

43. R. Ranga Ramanuja Ayyangar, *History of South Indian (Carnatic) Music*, pp. 142–4.

44. Lewis Rowell, *Music and Musical Thought in Ancient India*.

45. Phillip B. Wagoner, 'Sultan Among Hindu Kings'. Herman Goetz, 'The Fall of Vijaynagar and the Nationalization of Muslim Art in the Dakhan', *Journal of Indian History*, 19, 1940, pp. 249–55.

46. Ibid.

47. Saskia Kersenboom Story, *Nityasumangali*, pp. 39–41.

48. V.N. Rao, David Shulman, and Sanjay Subrahmanyam, *Symbols of Substance Court and State in Nayaka Period Tamil Nadu*, Oxford University Press, New Delhi, 1992.

49. Ibid.

50. S. Seetha, *Tanjore as a Seat of Music*, pp. 71–88, 118–19, 250–2.

51. William Jackson, *Tyagaraja Life and Lyrics*, Oxford University Press, Madras, 1991, pp. 55–6, 88–90, 138–9.

52. In 1941, *The Indian Review* published an informative essay on Tyagaraja on the occasion of the saint composer's birthday celebrations. The article suggested that the composer had brought Karnatik music from its kirtana or recitative stage to kriti or lyrical stage. While earlier musician composers like Purandaradasa, Arunachala Kavi, and Vedanayakam Pillai had experimented with the kirtanas and which must have exercised a profound influence on the young Tyagaraja, it was

left to him to improvise with the form and, at the same time, to respond to the proliferation of other song forms like the *varnam*, *ragamaliga*, and *swarajati* and so on. See *The Indian Review*, Madras, February 1941, p. 140.

53. William Jackson, *Tyagaraja and the Renewal of Tradition: Translations and Reflections*, Motilal Banarsidass, Delhi, 1994, pp. 39–40.

54. *JMAM*, vol. XVI, parts I–IV, 1945, pp. 111–12ff. The Krishna Gana Sabha, an institution affiliated to the Academy published a souvenir volume on occasion of the Tyagaraja Mahotasavam in 1945. The extracts were published by the *Journal of the Music Academy Madras*.

55. R. Ranga Ramanuja Ayyangar, *A History of South Indian (Carnatic) Music*, pp. 233–6.

56. Amanda Weidman suggests that it is probable that Muthuswamy Diksitar heard many European melodies played on the violin along with his brother or with other court violinists during his travels. She also observes that what is remarkable about Diksitar's European airs is that none of them had the melisma or *gamaka* traditionally associated with Karnatik music and that the words seem only a mode of translating Western tunes into a recognizable and acceptable form. See chapter 1 in her forthcoming work earlier cited.

57. P. Sambamoorthy, 'Jatisvara Sahityas of Sri Muthuswamy Diksitar', *JMAM*, vol. XXI, 1950, pp. 130–31ff. Also see Ayyangar, *A History of South Indian (Carnatic) Music*, pp. 144ff.

58. P. Sambamoorthy, 'Syama Sastri: A Short Sketch', *JMAM*, vol. I, no. 2, 1930, pp. 99ff.

59. William Jackson, *Tyagaraja and the Renewal of Tradition*, pp. 56–119. Also see N.S. Ramachandran, 'Musical Image of Tyagaraja', *Sangeet Natak* (6) October–December 1967, pp. 19–35 and B. Dayananda Rao (ed.), *Carnatic Music Composers. A Collection of Biographical Essays*, Triveni Foundation, Hyderabad, 1994.

60. *Sarvadevavilasa*. See Introduction, pp. 46ff. and chapter 4 of the text where mention is made of Dorasami as a great musician. The editor identifies this figure with Pallavi Doraiswamy Iyer (1782–1816) who is supposed to have stayed in Madras with his maternal grandfather Nayan Venkatachala Iyer. Also see p. 55 verse 44.

61. P. Sambamoorthy, 'The Wallajapet Manuscripts', *JMAM*, vol. XIV, 1943, pp. 86–91. Also see discussions of the 1931 Music Conference, *JMAM*, vol. III (1–2) 1932, pp. 62ff. See views of Subramanya Shastriar.

62. William Jackson, *Tyagaraja and the Renewal of Tradition*. Also see Rao (ed.) *Carnatic Music Composers* (Relevant entries). Also see P. Sambamoorthy, 'Madras as a Seat of Musical Learning' in *The Madras Tercentenary Commemoration Volume*, Humphrey Milford, Oxford University Press, London, Bombay, Calcutta, and Madras, 1939, pp. 429–37. Here Sambamoorthy refers to the popularity of Veen Kuppier who organized spectacular concerts in his residence and that of Patnam Subramania Iyer in Madras.

63. *JMAM*, vol. XIV, 1943, p. 31. Biographical Notices of Harikesanallur Muthiah Bhagavatar. p. 33 of Sabesa Iyer and Sri Umayalpuram Swaminatha Iyer. Patnam Subramania Iyer and MahaVaidyanatha Iyer were acknowledged as the most important carriers of Tyagaraja's tradition. See lecture on Tyagaraja by Vidwan Bharatam Nallur Narayanaswamy Iyer in the 1946 Madras Music Conference. *JMAM*, vol. XVIII, nos 1–4, 1947, pp. 29–32.

64. Emile Durkheim, *Pragmatism and Sociology*, Cambridge University Press, Cambridge, 1983. Also see *The Rules of Sociological Method*, Collier Macmillan, London, 1964.

65. U.V. Swaminatha Iyer, 'En Charitram', *Ananda Vikatan*, 1940–2. This was subsequently published in a book form by his son in 1950. This has recently been translated by Kamil V. Zvelebil as *The Story of My Life: An Autobiography of Dr. U.V. Swaminatha Iyer* (English version), Institute of Asian Studies, Madras, 1994. Swaminatha Iyer's life and times is brilliantly analysed by Norman Cutler in 'Three Moments in the Geneology of Tamil Literary Culture', in Sheldon Pollock (ed.), *Literary Culture in History: Reconstructions from South Asia*, Oxford University Press, New Delhi, 2004, pp. 271–312.

66. *Hindu Music and the Gayan Samaj, Published in Aid of the Funds of the Madras Jubilee Gayan Samaj. Printed at the Bombay Gazatte Steam Press.* Bombay, 1887, p. 39, pp. 49–54. A. Pandithar, *Karunamirtha Sagaram; First Book —First Part. A Brief History of Indian Music*, pp. 220–38.

67. Rao (ed.), *Carnatic Music Composers*. Mention is made of MahaVaidyanatha Iyer (1844–93) performing on the occasion of a wedding in U.V. Srinivasa Iyengar's family. Iyengar was a well-known judge in the Madras High Court. Lavish marriages became common; E. Krishna Iyer mentions how Kalladaikuruchi, the 'Brahmin Chettinad' of Tirunelveli district was notorious for the lavish expenditure of its fortunes on spectacular marriages and choice musicians. See E. Krishna Iyer, *Personalities in Present Day Music*, Foreword by S. Doraiswamy Iyer, Madras, 1933. This was a collection of articles that Krishna Iyer contributed to the *Indian Express*.

68. The word 'kacheri' literally refers to a court of law. It may also be used to describe an assembly or public performance—and may be used interchangeably with the more common word *sadas*. Ariyakudi Ramanuja Ayanagar, regarded as the architect of the modern musical kacheri, suggested in one of his public addresses that a kacheri in its early phase was confined to a recital before a select gathering at the royal court or in the assembly on an auspicious occasion. See *Sri Ariyakudi Ramanuja Iyengar Commemoration Volume*. Published by Sri Ariyakudi Ramanuja Iyengar Centenary Commemoration Society, Madras, 1990, p. 13.

69. *Government of Karnataka Selections from the Records of Mysore Palace*, vol. I, *Musicians, Actors and the Artists,* Divisional Archive Office, Mysore, 1993, pp. 31–2. Letter dated 2 November 1904 from M.V. Subbanna addressed to His Highness Sri Krishnaraja Wodeyar Bahadur with enclosures.

70. C.S. Ayyar, 'Sri Tyagaraja Kritis for Beginners', *JMAM*, vol. XVIII, 1947, pp. 84–8.

71. R. Ranga Ramanuja Ayyangar, *History of South Indian (Carnatic) Music*, pp. 258–69.

72. Ibid.

73. Ibid.

74. R. Suntharalingam, *Politics and Nationalist Awakening in South India, 1852–1891*, University of Arizona Press, 1974.

75. David Washbrook, *The Emergence of Provincial Politics*, Vikas Publications, New Delhi, 1976.

76. Stuart Blackburn, *Print, Folklore and Nationalism in Colonial South India*, Permanent Black, New Delhi, 2003.

77. Anil Seal, *The Emergence of Indian Nationalism: Competition and Collaboration in the Later Nineteenth Century*, Cambridge University Press, Cambridge, 1968.
78. Quoted in Anil Seal, *The Emergence of Indian Nationalism*, pp. 96–7.
79. T.R. Venkatrama Sastri's address to the 25th Conference recalled his personal experience of listening to great musicians in Madras in the late nineteenth century. These made a profound impression on him urging him to take up singing and to think about music and musical reform seriously. See *JMAM*, vol. XXIII, no. 4, 1952.
80. 'Melam illada Kalyanama?' A marriage without music was inconceivable by the early twentieth century. This became often the butt of satire—the September 1936 edition of the *Ananda Vikatan* carried an imaginary conversation between Purushottam Iyer and his wife over organizing a music concert in connection with their daughter's Valakappu ceremony. This conversation, in effect, suggested a series of preoccupations on the part of the consuming elite in Madras—ranging from recordings to the new aesthetics of classical music. See *Ananda Vikatan*, 20 September 1936, Madras, pp. 28–9.
81. Margaret Cousins, *Music of Orient and Occident: Essays Towards Mutual Understanding*, B.G. Paul & Co. Publishers, Madras, 1935, pp. 131–2.
82. *An Artist's Miscellany on Society, Religion and Music* by Kumara Guru c. Subrahmanya Ayyar, Madras, R. Venkateshwar & Co., 1946, pp. 69–74. Here Ayyar describes his father's experience as he left his village to take up a job and how this relocation liberated him initially from webs of caste and kin, how western education introduced a certain rationality of approach, how he responded to music and the arts, and how eventually Anne Besant's speech inspired him to re-evaluate Hindu religion and philosophy. Ayyar himself learnt music with Sabesa Iyer and wrote a series of important pieces on music and violin.

Defining the Classical
THE NATIONALIST IMPERATIVE

In 1874, Balwant Rao Trimbak with his associates in Poona took the initiative to form the Gayan Samaj, an association of music lovers to revive what he described as 'taste for our musical science amongst the brethren of the upper class and to raise it up in their estimation' and to promote 'a sense of nationality in the sense of our possessing an indigenous art of singing'.[1] A year later, a member of one of Calcutta's leading bhadralok families, the Tagores of Pathuriaghata gave in to a compelling desire to present to the Europeans 'a collection of all that has been written on the subject of Hindu music by the Oriental scholars of Europe' appended with his 'humble comments'.[2] By 1885, the Gayan Samaj had established a branch in Madras where, the decision to cultivate the national music of India was endorsed.[3] Two decades later, a young Chitpavan lawyer, Vishnu Narayan Bhatkhande, gave up a flourishing legal practice in Bombay to devote all his energies to the collection of musical texts and compositions and pursue the art with a passion that found formal expression in 1916, when he addressed the first All India Music Conference convened under the auspices of the Maharaja of Baroda. 'I cannot but hope', he said on the occasion

that in a few years time, there will be an easy system of instruction of our music which will lend itself to mass education. Then will the ambition of India be fulfilled for the Indians will have music in their curricula of the universities, music instruction will be common and universal. And if it please Providence to so dispense that there is a fusion between the two systems of the North and South, then there will be a National Music for the whole country and last of our ambitions will be reached, for the great Nation will sing one song.[4]

The same occasion saw another Vishnu—Vishnu Digambar Paluskar—storm the rostrum, chide the organizers for indulging in verbiage and exhort them to allow music to speak for itself through song and not sermon.

The sudden effulgence of dramatic action, passionate oration, and purposeful deliberations that converged on music—indigenous/native/national—as the supreme aesthetic pursuit for all mankind, as a national treasure that had to be relocated within a new social context, raises an array of questions. Was this a random assemblage of individual desires or was it part of a complex, discursive exercise that had evolved over time? What shaped this exercise? Ideology or the changing networks of patronage and consumption? An Orientalist reading of the past and India's culture? Or nationalism and the nationalist imperative of celebrating the glory of the past in sharp contrast to the decline of the present? Why and how was the staging of the performing arts so important in the articulation of nation-hood? Admittedly, nationalism is an overburdened concept and its hegemonic stand open to contestation—yet as a symbol it was powerful in the reconstitution of culture in modern India, where the practice of representation was closely bound with the process of formation and reformation of social groups. This chapter proposes to focus on the practices and politics of representation—specifically on the staging of the musical tradition, which was continually reinvented, redefined, and invested with classical attributes. The exercise was contingent on the changing self-representation of consumers and patrons of music—in this case the brahmin elite of Madras, as well as on the unusual nexus between consumers and performers, both of whom were self-conscious participants in the experience of colonial modernity.

The Making of a Modernist Discourse: Orientalism, Print Culture, and the Madras Elite

The modern discourse on the performing arts, especially music, in nineteenth and twentieth century India was shaped largely in the convergence of Orientalist scholarship with print culture, and its dissemination among the urban Indian middle class. The former introduced new and inflected modes of understanding and appraising Indian culture, while the technology of print provided the convenient conduit to a new and eager public. Early European notices of India's music traditions were with rare exceptions, insignificant and desultory. Travellers, ambassadors, military men were as a rule partial to dance performances and the music that accompanied these shows. Their discrimination did not extend to the nuances or layers of music practice and production; in any case, the unfamiliarity of sounds and melodic arrangements precluded an easy sensory appreciation of the form. The French missionary, Abbe Dubois, for instance found Indian music unbearable:

Hindu Music, whether vocal or instrumental, may be pleasing to the natives, but I do not think that it can give the slightest pleasure to anyone else, however little sensitive be his ear. Their songs have always appeared to me uninspiring and monotonous, while from their instruments, I have never heard anything but harsh, high and ear splitting sounds.[5]

Captain Thomas Williamson was equally derisive in his responses when, in 1813, he wrote of unlucky listeners, 'who often are compelled, rather than give offence, to have their heads stunned, and their nerves disordered, by the monotonous and shrill notes which, for hours together, vibrate on their wearied ears. Such is the music of the East'.[6] Many of the early observers were army men or junior civilians not particularly interested in traditional performance barring the occasional *nautch* which had an element of the erotic and downright bizarre. It is therefore, not surprising that their observations were uninformed and missed the subtle aspects of what was a multi-layered art form. Many of them tended to see Indian music, as Hindu music, and even went as far as to identify Hindu songs from Persian airs. Lieutenant Fitzclarence, for instance, in describing a reception at a magnate's residence referred to a 'celebrated singer who sang tolerably well, not only Persian but Hindu songs accompanied by tom toms and two instruments, not unlike guitars. This man with the set of mimics and two sets of nautch women are always in the raja's pay and are part of his household and state'.[7] Here the Colonel was grounding his observations on a particular repertoire of performance, which accommodated dance and even ribald mimicry and lumped them together under the label of Hindu music. The mimics were an important part of the Mughal as well as regional courts and often acted as satirists much to the annoyance of the colonel. In his words:

The mimics are the worst kind of buffoons and accompany their acting by silly remarks and execrable attempts at wit. I recall seeing a set when I was in Hindustan in 1815, who in ridicule of our cutchery or court of justice went through a trial in which the judges were supposed to be European. The offender when about to enter on his defense is interrupted by a servant who announces that dinner is ready and the judges start up, pronounce the person guilty, condemn him to be hanged and run off to the table.[8]

The Colonel was not amused. Indeed, in an outburst of righteous indignation, he chose to look at the performance only as a rare reflection of the 'mildness and toleration of the British Government since even in public, actors feel that they can take such liberties with impunity'. John Hobart Caunter, a missionary who visited India in 1838, and had occasion to witness musical performances, identified what he thought was an Indian addiction to a bad habit:

The Hindus pretend to musical science and are therefore, disposed to reject that which nature teaches them. The consequence is that when they light unconsciously upon and sound a harmonious interval with its fundamental note, it breaks the monotony of their unisons and they consider it a blemish.[9]

There were some exceptions to this sort of amateurish reporting, and it was precisely those exceptions that provided a theoretical framework for the later representation of Indian music as a strongly text-based tradition. Sir William Jones, in his celebrated essay 'On the Musical modes of the Hindus' written in 1784, fore-grounded his passion for Sanskrit drama and classical Hindu texts in his analysis of music, which he described as being 'known and practiced not by mercenary performers only, but even by Muhammedans and Hindus of eminent rank and learning'.[10] Further, the Indian system was backed by an old and established textual lineage, and was 'minutely explained in a great number of Sanskrit books, by authors who leave arithmetic and geometry to their astronomers, and properly discourse on music as an art confined to the pleasures of imagination'.[11] Here, Jones was betraying his penchant for classical texts as a marker of cultural refinement and civilization. These texts had to be retrieved and translated—existing translations in Persian were far from adequate. In his words,

a man who knows the Hindoos only from Persian books, does not know the Hindoos; and that an European, who follows the muddy rivulets of Muhammadan writers on India instead of drinking from the pure fountain of Hindu learning will be in perpetual danger of misleading himself and others.[12]

It was therefore, critical to access old and authentic texts to gain a sound idea of the features of Indian music and to document its evolution and thereby to assess contemporary practice. Jones was convinced that had the older Hindu system of governance continued without interruption, religion would:

no doubt given permanence to systems of music invented as the Hindus believe by their Gods, and adapted to mystical poetry: but such have been the revolutions of their government since the time of Alexander, that although the Sanskrit books have preserved the theory of their musical compositions, the practice of it, seems almost wholly lost (as all the Pandits and Rajas confess) in Gaur and Magarha, or the provinces of Bengal and Bihar.[13]

Under these circumstances, it was not surprising, Jones informed his readers that 'modern performers on the Vina have little or no modulation, or change of mode, to which passionate music owes nearly all its enchantment'.[14] However, here Jones was not merely making a point about the divergence between textual convention and actual practice, but he was also introducing European terms of reference to explain the distinctive features and technicalities of Indian music. In his words,

The old musicians of India, having fixed on a leading mode to express the general character of the song, which they were translating into the musical language, varied that mode by certain rules, according to the variation of sentiment or passion in the poetical phrases, and always returned to it at the close of the air; many reasons induce me to believe; though I cannot but admit, that their modulations must have been greatly confined by the restrictions of certain modes to certain seasons and hours, unless these variations belonged merely to the principal mode. The scale of the vina, we find comprised both our European modes, and if some of the notes can be raised to a semi tone by a stronger pressure on the frets, a delicate and experienced singer might produce the effect of minute enharmonic intervals*; the construction of the instrument, therefore, seems to favour my conjecture.[15]

Sir William Jones' notices introduced three major modes of understanding the history of music and its development in the subcontinent, namely, an emphasis on a textual lineage that laid claims to antiquity and the Hindu past, the obfuscation of the textual tradition under Islamic rule, and the use of a European vocabulary to describe Indian musical expression. These were taken up and elaborated by enthusiasts such as William Ousely, Francis Fowke, Francis Gladwin, and Colonel P.T. French all of whom betrayed the same zeal for the authentic Sanskrit text and empathy with the mystical overlays of the tradition.[16] Additionally, Col. French in his essay titled 'Catalogue of Indian Musical Instruments' submitted to the Royal Irish Academy suggested that the more authentic versions of the tradition were to be found in the south of India, where it was cultivated 'as a science, long after it had ceased as such in the north'.[17] He mentioned that as early as the thirteenth century, the profession of music was found to be in an advanced condition in the south, that 'singers, male and female, musicians, and their Brahmin instructors, were taken with the royal armies and settled in the north'.[18] The cultivation of music as a science in ancient India did not however, according to the author, produce a move towards harmony, and as a consequence of which 'all Indian music is wanting in this most essential particular'. Col. French, however, was aware that most Europeans did not have access to the really fine expositions of classical music, and that what was ordinarily played out to them was sung by 'ill-instructed screaming and dancing women, at crowded native durbars, marriages and other ceremonies'.[19]

These early European observations set the tone and terms for the later Orientalist appraisal of Indian music that was to follow in the nineteenth century and one which exercised a marked influence on the nationalist reconstruction of India's musical tradition. On the one hand, there was the continual emphasis on the distinctiveness of the tradition that was in stark contrast to anything that the European ear was accustomed to, while on the other, there was a tacit acknowledgement of the antiquity and richness of the tradition, one that had lost its moorings because of political turmoil and the dislocation of an older social order. What is curious, and not entirely understandable, is that the emerging European discourse did not reflect in the slightest the critical changes taking place in musical practice in south India from the latter decades of the eighteenth century.

Later writings on India's music and musical traditions tended to emphasize the great divergence between theory and practice in Indian music, a gap that was attributed to the trauma of Islamic rule. C.R. Day's classic work titled *The Music and Musical Instruments of Southern India and the Deccan* (1891) exemplified this argument. Day was eloquent in his appreciation of Indian music as well as in his condemnation of prevailing European prejudice regarding Indian music. 'But it is hardly fair', he argued

that an art so little understood even among the natives themselves should be judged by such a criterion and then put aside as worthless because solitary individuals have been deceived by parties of outcaste charlatans whose object is mere gain. For that Indian music is an art, and a very difficult one, can hardly be denied. But to appreciate it, one must first put away all thought of European music and then judge of it by an Indian standard and impartially upon its own merits—of the ingenuity of the performer, the peculiar rhythm of the music and the extraordinary scale used. The recitatives, the amount of imitation, the wonderful execution and memory of the performer and his skill in employing small intervals as grace.[20]

Day here was not simply identifying the principal attributes of Indian music as he understood it, but was privileging one genre of performance over others—the skilled musician in contrast to the *natchni* or *chinna melam* chorus. At the same time, Day was responsible for pushing the argument of the relative purity of the southern musical tradition, arguing that the isolation of the peninsula from the excesses of Muslim rule was responsible for its preservation against alien influences and for the higher social status of its practitioners. The dominant Islamic presence in northern India and the formation of an Indo-Muslim court culture resulted in the increasing association of music and dance with Muslim performers and to the growing prejudice among high-caste Hindus to pursue the profession. The situation was different in the south, where the higher branches of musical learning were confined to brahmin families who combined ritual status and functions with knowledge of scriptures and Puranic texts, and who participated in musical activity. In Day's words, 'in later years, music became a distinct trade especially under Muslim rulers and passed into the hands of the lower orders and the unlearned, and to this cause operating through a long succession of years, the differences between Hindustani and Karnatik systems must in great measure be attributed'.[21] For Day, there was no doubt that the degenerate status of music in north India was caused by the long ordeal of Muslim rule. The detachment of the performing tradition from its textual basis in north India was accompanied by the appropriation of the art by Muslim practitioners, who had neither the skill nor the interest in setting out the tradition in writing.

Day was, however, critical of the existing texts on music, most of which in his view, adapted the principle they received to their ideas and encapsulated them in a string of quotations which were contradictory and inconsistent. As for texts in vernacular written by practicing musicians, these were no less unreliable and inadequate for they invariably tried to 'mix it with the absurdities of the pundits'. One of the reasons cited by Day for this was fear of criticism or ridicule and the need to gain acceptance among self-professed pundits. Day also detected a conspiratorial element in the production of flawed and confusing scholarship—'due to the great dislike all native musicians have to imparting instruction to any but a favoured few; indeed they rather prefer that the general public should continue in ignorance'.[22]

By the first decades of the twentieth century, there was an audible shift in European responses to Indian musical performance. The shift was partly informed by greater exposure to musical events of a higher standard, and partly by the early nationalist initiative in the reorganization of the performing arts. As Anne Wilson noted in her *Short Account of the Hindu System of Music* (1904), the British in India had, due to lack of exposure remained ignorant of the 'inherent and essential meaning' of India's cultural practices, notably music. One such occasion she wrote of was about a performance that featured a band of native musicians, who came and sat in a row on the ground with their drums, violins of pipes, and essayed a rendering that 'proved unfortunate and seemed to be synonymous with pandemonium. The discordant yells of men whose appearance suggested the extremities of toothache on their part tended to induce insanity in mine'.[23] However, her prejudices were overcome once she had the opportunity to attend a genuinely excellent performance and to listen to the expositions of Vishnu Digambar Paluskar[24] who was able to explain to her the principles of music. Likewise, Fox Strangways, who authored *The Music of Hindostan* in 1914 undertook a musical tour extending over six months in 1910–11 and discovered the pleasures of high quality performance. 'In a land not blessed with concert advertisements or concert notices, it is difficult for a stranger in the first place to find the best music, and in the second to know what the inhabitants think of it.'[25] He utilized local contacts to hear instrumental music of a high order in Mysore, Calcutta, and percussion in many arts of south India. His own experiences as a musical tourist led him to make general impressions about what he considered Hindu and Muslim singing, the differences between the two styles, were 'more easily felt than described'. The *ustad* was very much the vivacious performer with a penchant for more cheerful melodies, while the Hindu was the somber spiritualist opting for graver melodies and with his singing less broken up by rests and luxuriating in cross rhythm.

His song gives much more the impression of coming from the heart and of reaching out for sympathy rather than applause. You can more easily fancy him singing over his work or her over her household, and as has been mentioned, the Muhammadan has no cradlesongs.[26]

Strangways too, in his own way, was making a case for a particular kind of Hindu music that was part of a larger organic religious and social sensibility, and one that was not restricted to pleasure and the immediate sensation of entertainment.

To assess the cumulative impact of these pronouncements on the Indian elite and their efforts at cultural self-representation, it is necessary to examine the nature of social transformation in modern colonial India and the resultant emergence of a western-educated Indian middle class. In the case of south India, there was an additional determinant provided by the interface between the extension of the earlier Tanjore project into Madras city and the influence of the new learning and print-culture, the convergence of which generated a keener enquiry into India's culture and musical traditions. Printing in the Tamil country, as Stuart Blackburn points out, was already three centuries old, but it was in the first half of the nineteenth century, that it established a new literary culture and enabled a greater circulation of views and texts, and the production of Indian texts by Indians for an Indian audience. A distinguishing feature of the print led literary culture was the nexus between traditional pundits who had been prominent in courts and religious centres and British administrators who were on the look out for expertise in translation and the teaching of Tamil for running Fort St George College in Madras. Predictably, Tamil brahmins took the lead in translating Sanskrit texts while Mudaliars and Pillais were active in translating Tamil texts.[27] There was also a Tamil Christian network of pundits located in and around Pondicherry; an important scholarly link between Pondicherry and Madras had been established before Fort St George College, at the end of the eighteenth century. Muttuswami Pillai, who taught Ellis came from Pondicherry and wrote the first Tamil biography in 1820, in addition to his compilation of Catholic prayers, hymns and rituals, an edition of the *Tirukurral*, and an edition of the old Tamil grammar, *Cintamani Nikantu*.[28] The importance of these networks persisted; it is not entirely coincidental that Tamil Christians and Mudaliars with official British connections should have authored some of the pioneering works on music, its history, and future prospects.

The following years saw a stream of publications—collections of songs and notated compositions as well as a number of early biographies of Tyagaraja. In 1859, twenty songs of Tyagaraja with notation and eighty more without notation were published by Tirunagari Veena Ramanujayya.[29] In 1868, the text of *Prahlada Bhaktivijayam* appeared followed by that of *Naukacharitam*. The tendency to publish available and known musical compositions with notation by practicing musicians themselves was evident in the following years[30]—an enterprise that was fully supported by the consuming elites in southern India, including the princely states caught up with the agenda of modernization.

To what extent were these early publications and attempt at preservation of musical material a response to the Orientalist critique of India's musical traditions and performing culture? Only in part, for as suggested earlier, the idea of notation and preservation seems to have been a logical response to earlier developments in the eighteenth and nineteenth centuries. What Orientalist discourse did was to lend certain urgency and a distinct flavour to the process of self-reflection on the part of the south Indian elite. Their engagement was equally informed by the efforts of educated publicists in Bengal and Poona, for whom the articulation of a modernizing project for music was more immediately coloured by the Orientalist critique, which circulated the idea that in the north, Muslims had dominated the profession of music, while in the south, it had remained almost exclusively in the hands of the Hindus. This led Hindu reformists in northern India to valorize the southern experience— a phenomenon that, in turn, produced a sense of exceptionalism and pride in the south as the ultimate repository of tradition and traditional values. The response was confused and generated a discourse that professed its commitment to the idea of modernity and yet celebrated the notion of tradition, as a set of beliefs and practices thought to represent authentic culture. South India enjoyed a special if not exalted space in the pursuit of the authentic—self-appointed musicologists enthusiasts not only reinforced the older stereotype description of the peninsula as the cradle of uncorrupted Hindu culture, they also entered into a dialogue with their northern counterparts to devise a strategy for the reorganization of music as a scientific system with notation that would facilitate its transmission as an indigenous, authentic art form carrying with it the signs of an old and rich cultural past. Whether Indian music was an art or a science, why there was a sharp divergence between theory and practice were keenly debated. The categories in themselves had little signification except as tropes for setting out a discourse for claiming a tradition that could be presented and preserved in a context that was new and modern.

In 1875, Sourindro Mohan Tagore published *Hindu Music* and followed it up twenty years later by the *Universal History of Music Compiled from Divers Sources Together with Various Original Notes on Hindu Music*. In his preface to *Hindu Music*, Tagore implicitly accepted the European construction of the obscure Hindu theorist and the unlettered Muslim practitioner, and elaborated on the importance of reconciling theory and practice.

When from the theory of music, a defection took place of its practice, and men of learning confined themselves exclusively to the former, while the latter branch was abandoned entirely to the illiterate, all attempts to elucidate music from rules laid down in books, a science capable of explanation by mere words, became idle.[31]

And yet it was theory that caught Tagore's fancy when he laboured to write a history of Hindu music that continually reinforced stereotypes of the debauche practitioner and the somber Hindu theorist lost in his spiritual reverie. In his words:

Music has always been highly appreciated, especially, when its charms have not been prostituted to add to the allurement of licentious poetry. Hence it is that after, it had been methodized, the greatest men in this country admired it and patronized its professors, till in course of time, these becoming licentious, cast such a stigma on the science, that men of honour disdained to be numbered amongst its professors. At present most native performers of the noble science are the most immoral set of men on earth, and the term is another word for all that is abominable, synonymous with that of the most abandoned and profligate exercises under the sun.[32]

The need of the hour then was to bring back the patina of social respectability by reinvesting the practice with its sacral attributes and resurrecting the renouncer-musician, and by backing the practice with a strong theoretical base. The task at hand was daunting given the orality of the tradition and the absence of verifiable texts as referents, and the 'hatred of the natives to innovation'. And yet Tagore himself, ended up writing a history that was but a random collection of impressions, interspersed with raw ethnographic data and a reinforcement of the existing Orientalist paradigm. The work proved immensely influential and inspired his students like Loke Nath Ghosh to come up with what he called *Music's Appeal to India: An Original, Instructive and Interesting Story (Complete) Agreeable to the Taste of both Young and Old* and dedicated to S.M. Tagore. Ghosh too, was unequivocal in describing India's music as a noble science, whose decay originated from the Muslim conquest of India. Ghosh's work was in the nature of an autobiography, where the protagonist was the muse itself and who told the story of the unique land that Hindu India was, a nation famous for 'gentle disposition, good government and ingenuity in all sciences and arts'. The Islamic interlude proved traumatic for her and even the mighty Akbar was unable to help, for he made the blunder of:

Worshipping me not as goddess but as a common woman blessed with beauty. He could not appreciate my internal qualifications (theory) but gazed with admiration upon my external beauties (practice). The recultivation of music was commenced from the time of Akbar but the theoretical part was altogether rejected. From that time, the Hindus and Muslims only devoted themselves to practical music perfectly neglecting the scientific part of it. As a result, I fled from court and at last settled in England when Queen Elizabeth was on the throne. By and by, I became familiar with the Queen and I intended to subdue the power of the Muhammedan in India who have done so much injury to my countrymen and to induce her to grant a charter of incorporation to the English East India Company in 1599 for the purpose of opening a trade with the east. This opportunity at last enabled me to succeed in my aim by their becoming the conquerors of India and replacing the Muhammedan. As India has now become Her Majesty's Empire, I sincerely wish for the long reign and prosperity of Queen Victoria I came back to India, my place of birth and reached the metropolis on the evening of 3 August 1871. I began to live on the premises of the Calcutta Normal School, where I had access through the unwearied exertions of my most faithful devotees Professor Khetter Mohan Goswami and Raja S.M. Tagore. Here I have much gratification to observe that the theoretical part which had been shamefully overlooked from the time of Akbar has now gained a means to improve in its different branches by the assistance of several elaborate works composed by Professor Khetter Mohan Goswami and his student S.M. Tagore.[33]

The muse continued in this vein and exhorted the sons of India to pursue her with seriousness and with a scientific attitude. Ghosh made an impassioned plea for reorganizing the system of oral instruction that was neither scientific nor correct, a deficiency that had been aggravated by the lack of notation. He insisted on discovering traditional notation methods, which had been jettisoned by the Muslims.

The system of notation which was in use in this country at the time of Sumeshwar was abolished by the Mohammedans a few years after his death. The name of Sumeshwar must have gone forever from this world had not Professor Khetter Mohan Goswami and Raja Sourindro Mohan Tagore made researches upon the old Sanskrit texts. The system of notation which they have now adapted in their schools is an improvement upon that old one invented by Sumeshwar.[34]

Finally Ghosh's history also made an elaborate case for retrieving the spiritual and transcendental dimension of Indian music. In his view, only those who could wed musical practice with textual learning in Sanskrit had the moral authority, aesthetic expertise and the credentials to pursue music, at least of the classical and authentic variety. In his own words, if men are willing to worship me scientifically, let them learn Sanskrit and read Sanskrit. It is a shameful thing to be followers of the disciples of late Suremiah of the Northwest and Nidhu Babu of Bengal. These songs are voluptuous and have no connection to religion and morality. These songs are in a manner worthless, as they impress on the minds with vicious thoughts and immoral ideas. They are only loved by that class of men and women who have neither regard for their personal honour nor that of their country. The above class of men and women consist of dancing girls and Muhammedan Ustads. The Ustads and dancing girls together with several of the most vicious character are spreading evil and committing the most atrocious crimes in this country. Their influence is great. They can sing their songs in every place of worship without any compunction of feeling. Whenever their voices are heard I feel the greatest pain.[35]

Ghosh's history of music resonated with newly honed sensibilities of national honour, scientific application, and spiritual self-righteousness. Besides the personal debt that he owed to S.M. Tagore and his interest in the art, Ghosh was articulating the broad outlines of the incipient cultural project that educated Indians were engaged in by the latter decades of the nineteenth century. As beneficiaries of colonial education and patronage, the urban middle class developed a new mode of reflecting on culture and its consumption, partly as a self-reflexive exercise. Without for a moment discounting the deep personal engagement that many of them had as listeners and connoisseurs, there was a new compulsion to validate their cultural heritage. For this, it became necessary to highlight certain aspects of culture—those that were considered aesthetic, moral, and spiritual—as well as those elements that were scientific and modern. The earlier European critique provided the class with a convenient whipping boy—the illiterate Muslim practitioner of music who had corrupted what was inherently and intrinsically a pure, sacral, and scientific tradition while political loyalties to the new masters made it necessary to use European terms of reference in explaining the system of Indian music and to justify new and modern techniques of transmission and preservation. What followed was an increasing assertion of Hindu ideals in a westernized frame of reference and an attempt to project an authentic Hindu past through 'an interior historical focus to generate a rich image of classical Hindu culture'.[36] Alongside, the ideal had to be given concrete shape by making it compatible with modern life. Ghosh let his protagonist to urge sons of India not to 'delay', to 'come and worship' it immediately. 'I have come back to your country', it said, 'after centuries have passed' and am determined to remain here the rest of my days. Do not treat me as a common goddess. I am empowered by gods to make you all subordinate to my influences. However, I am sure that there are many honest minded gentlemen in this country who have long felt the necessity of worshipping me but they cannot carry out their wishes for want of scientific teachings. To one willing to worship me as an emblem of science, nothing is more desirable than to have certain fixed principles upon which to proceed and would serve as a standard but to the great misfortune of this country, the sacred task of worshipping me has been mostly confined to the notorious Ostauds who as a rule are generally illiterate without ever having received a scientific knowledge in their life. The oral teaching now prevalent in our country cannot be said to be a scientific and correct method.[37]

Ghosh's history found many takers; a number of music related journals made their appearance—some short-lived, others of longer duration but all of them taking up the cause of notation as the principle vehicle of modernization and reform, and of music education among the middle class.[38] In western India, especially Poona, there was a similar concern with the teaching of music and thereby relocating the art in a new space. The Gayan Samaj did not make explicit references to practicing musicians but instead chose to stress the necessity of imparting instruction in music by competent teachers. The members, however, did indicate their preference for educated students, thereby betraying the class character of the agenda, 'with the object of raising the status of the musical science and rendering it an accomplishment among the upper classes of our community as also of enhancing the refinement and culture of science itself'.[39] In its efforts to devise proper teaching methods and to disseminate music through new schools, the Samaj initiated a dialogue with practicing musicians and patrons in southern India, thereby giving wider currency to the idea of the relative purity and authenticity of south India's musical traditions. In 1882, the Raja of Travancore was approached by the Gayan Samaj and asked to report on the system of music and teaching techniques prevalent in his state, which in turn could serve as guidelines for the schools supported by the Samaj. The investigation produced interesting evidence. In Travancore, the raja stated that there were an impressive number of musicians although not all of them were of uniform quality, and that the most eminent among them belonged to the Tyagaraja lineage, which was implicitly recognized as the most influential in terms of musical style and quality. The raja also alerted the committee of enquiry about the problems of notation—he mentioned that Captain Day had anticipated many of these and also that music in Travancore was never taught by notation; instead it followed the system of scriptural learning by rote. The raja, by contesting the idea of the so called superior or scientific instruction in his country and of Indian music lending itself to notation, introduced yet another complexity in the emerging discourse on music instruction and reform.[40]

The establishment of a branch of the Gayan Samaj in Madras in August 1883 (also in Bombay on the same date) gave an institutional expression to the literary-musical culture that had by this time developed around the city's high-caste (predominantly brahmin but also with substantial Chetty and Mudaliar representation) elite. The Madras elite's initiatives were at this stage, different in tone and temper from their counterparts in Bengal. These arose from the differential nature of cultural participation, from a greater sense of continuity they enjoyed with their immediate social experience, and from the caste connections and linkages that tied the performer with the patron and located them in a commonly shared cultural and social space. This meant that the project was not as disabling for the performers whose collaboration with the new patrons was marked from the very beginning. The post-Tyagaraja generation of musicians, many of whom were his disciples, undertook the business of publishing biographical material on their teacher with his compositions. It was primarily from the performers that the production of anthologies and compilations came—an initiative in which they were fully supported by their patrons, in most cases, the courts of Mysore, Vijayanagaram, and Ettayapuram. Among these early publications, mention must be made of *Gayaka Parijatam* (1877), *Gayaka Siddhajanam* (1890 Part I and 1905 Part II), and *Gayaka Lochanam* (1902).[41] Many among the musicians had a toehold in the colonial administration and were thus part of the same social class that was articulating its self and identity through the narrative óf culture and practice. Kotiswara Iyer,[42] for instance, a musician of enormous influence was a translator in the Madras High Court, had his school education in Manamadurai, and graduated from Tiruchirapalli before embarking full time on his musical education. Even those who did not follow the trajectory of western education and colonial employment were not peripheral to this development—as a literate caste, their access to scriptural knowledge and Sanskrit learning and the local language was instrumental in reshaping their engagement. The Singarachalu brothers gave a new impetus to music publishing and were responsible for printing in notation some of the compositions of Tyagaraja and Syama Sastri. Their principal patron was the Raja of Vijayanagaram who financed their research tour in south India to gather material for preparing a series of graded books on south Indian music.[43]

Among the early works that dealt with music in south India, the most impressive one was authored by Chinnaswami Mudaliar, whose collaborative enterprise with Subbarama Diksitar, the court musician of Ettayapuram, embodied the new trend in cultural consumption. Chinnaswami Mudaliar, a Tamil Christian from Pondicherry with established linkages in the field of publishing, was a postgraduate from Madras University and employed as a superintendent at the Madras Secretariat. Combining his interests in publishing old anthologies of songs and musical compositions with a genuine appreciation of music, Mudaliar exhibited the characteristic enthusiasm for learning music and for collecting the authentic versions of traditional composers, and presenting them in a fashion that would facilitate future pedagogic ventures as well as render the art form more intelligible to his European superiors. He worked in close association with his immediate teacher Umayalpuram Krishna Bhagavatar from whom he learnt Tyagaraja's compositions and whose help he sought in annotating the composer's work.[44]

The interest of courts and aristocratic establishments (*samasthanam*) in the promotion of music, in terms of both supporting performances as well as sponsoring the publication of music texts and compositions, was in part a continuation of the cultural practices established and standardized by Tanjore. There was also simultaneously an engagement with new aesthetic conceptions as part of renegotiating new modes of political functioning. This was evident even in a small state such as Ramnad, where as Pamela Price points out, the dissatisfaction of its ruler, Bhaskar Setupati in maintaining the contractual obligations of lordship was revealing. The ruler had no illusions about the expertise of his court musicians; in 1893, his diary entries on two court musicians in 1893 went thus.

They are not by any means celebrated singers as they lack the first condition of good singing—a good voice. The father is outspoken...both are highly avaricious and a discontented lot altogether. They have a bad habit of speaking ill about others in their absence and praising whom they speak ill of in their presence. They are not to be trusted. But they dance attendance on me constantly and thus carry favour with me.[45]

Setupati's observations on the importance of voice in music or that of the musician's temperament and disposition, did not, however, reflect an artistic commitment, it merely expressed his own distancing from the older spaces of ritual, performance, and patronage. In fact, it was in

Mysore and Trivandrum that the initiative was more sustained and informed by the larger considerations of reform and pedagogy.

The growing interest in music among the educated elite in Madras and the princely courts, the circulation of biographies and anthologies, and the sponsoring of primers and musical instruction in print, had the important effect of framing a coherent agenda for reform and for streamlining an aesthetic. While the former was tied up with the larger issue of education, the latter was more intimately associated with the self-definition of the middle class. To this was added the imperatives of the new performance space that necessitated a more condensed repertoire, but which at the same time in the long run, opened the issue of standards—the need to establish an aesthetic standard that would mark off a classical performance from that of drama and of the harikatha, both of which used music extensively but did not take standards too seriously.

In fact, by the 1920s, with the expanding interest in dramatic activity, a critical element of which was the use of song,[46] serious reservations about artistic standards were voiced by sections of the city's elite. The *Daily Express* carried a series of articles on the subject in the 1920s focusing especially on declining musical standards in the harikathas. The articles drew attention to the unmusical din that accompanied these performances. It was equally critical of the subjects chosen by the harikatha performers, and exhorted the performers to jettison erotic and vulgar themes and instead adopt Puranic or nationalist themes. In the words of the critic, 'What with the gestures and gesticulations, dancings and prancings and jumping of the Bhagavatars, the harikatha performance as we know, is an enemy of morals and music.'[47] Continuing in the same vein, the article approved the efforts of individual performers to introduce harikathas on national leaders like Gokhale and Tilak, for these would enable the medium to become an instrument of propaganda for right social and political ideas.[48] These ideas gained ground steadily through the twenties and thirties of the century, when there was a clearer articulation of an all India nationalist project for music reform and education. In 1933, E. Krishna Iyer contributed a series of articles to the *Indian Express*, where he stated quite categorically that good music had to be sought for 'in a happy combination of natural music of sweet sound and human art of refined technique, practice and presentation'.[49] Additionally, there was in Madras city a proliferation of music concerts sponsored by associations or sabhas as they were known, and which in the opinion of self-professed critics and experts, was seriously jeopardizing the purity of classical music. Ranga Ramanuja Ayyangar in his reminiscences was never tired of pointing out how the market and the restructuring of the concert format, in response to the demands of the new clientele, seriously affected the quality of music.

The decline in standards began with the generation of musicians that appeared around 1920. The first blow fell on the pallavi. Mass oriented music scouted specialization and turned to the gallery for inspiration and encouragement. The mass mind is always impatient with what it cannot understand. Having paid the piper, it calls the tune that will tickle and titillate, rather than inspire and elevate.[50]

Here, Ayyangar, as a part of the reforming elite confronting the contradictions of reform and broadening the social basis of music, while adhering to notions of purity and classicism, was echoing a rhetoric that was slowly but surely put in place by the time of independence.

Education and Aesthetics:
Performing for the Nation

What began as a spontaneous, even if ad hoc expression of interest and identification with music, on the part of the middle-class elite, became a more concrete engagement by the first decade of the twentieth century. The community responded to the imperatives of nation building that demanded, on the one hand, the consolidation of secular spaces for a range of practices, including the arts and, on the other, the formalization of a classicist aesthetic that would legitimize the more precious and unique aspects of the nation's heritage. Consequently, the agenda for reform at one level was fairly simple and straightforward, namely to relocate the practice and learning of music within modern institutional spaces. At another level, the agenda was more complex. It sought to inscribe on the practice and performance of music a set of aesthetic attributes that were informed by both the sensibilities of the middle class and their social reform priorities. The determining of a common aesthetic denominator was linked to the construction of an acceptable heritage for the nation in the making that necessitated a process of artistic and social engineering. That the construction of such a standard was mediated through elite spokesmen who assumed the custodianship of India's musical culture, only underscored the importance of the art form in engendering a sense of solidarity and in imagining the larger community. Thus, as in art, as argued by Tapati Guha Thakurta, so in music, the categories of antiquity, classicism, artistic and national essence were arbitrary notions produced through a modern set of historical practices and institutions.[51] Nationalism was an important even if not exclusive determinant of these practices.

The importance of being national especially in the domain of culture, was understood primarily in terms of authenticity, as an essential precondition to the framing and freezing of an expressive legacy and its preservation by the deployment of modern technologies of reproduction and standardization. In privileging the idea of the authentic, there was an urgent need to showcase the textual elements in musical practice and to foreground the spiritual functions of the tradition. Here, especially in south India, the figure of Tyagaraja, as the foremost composer whose work embodied the quintessential elements of what classical music was or ought to be and whose life became a role model for aspirant musicians and listeners, became crucial. This had to do with the self-image of the brahmin community in Madras whose identity was articulated through the advocacy of a way of life. This was distinguished by a quotidian regime of discipline that extended not just to personal regimen and habits but to a larger collective sense of responsibility for upholding rituals and religious traditions. Furthermore, the emphasis on tradition was not just an atavistic reaction, but also a considered response to the processes of modernization that could hardly endorse either caste privilege or religious exclusivity. The community, by and large, considered themselves protagonists of modernity; even as they extolled the virtues of discipline and self-sacrifice, which they saw as the hallmarks of an older and traditional social inheritance, as well as essential preconditions to national regeneration. K.S. Ramaswami Sastri in his address *The Future of the Brahmin* (1935) defended the organization of the Brahmin Conference that he was presiding. The conference was not what it appeared—narrow, communal, and exclusive. It was an all India movement. 'The Brahmins', he said, 'have always tried to realize and enjoy the higher and more excellent things of life by the extensive cultivation of the spirit of renunciation in the spirit of the glorious teaching of the Upanishad. They have always tried to guide the secular life and spiritual life of the Hindu community without demoralizing or debasing it.' Sastri, therefore, exhorted the brahmins to safeguard *acharam* (ceremonial and social purity), bhakti (devotion) and *jnanam* (wisdom) and at the same time to adjust themselves to the new secular life and the modern spirit. For this, it was essential to lead a disciplined life (Sastri prescribed cold water baths to discipline the body and an education in

Sanskrit and the mother tongue), while remaining alert to the potential of science and technology, the most important aspects of modernity.[52]

The address epitomized not just the values impressed upon the community but the actual mechanisms of social practice that it opted for to mark out a distinct identity in a changing social context. As Sastri argued, the future for the brahmin lay in accepting and abiding by the lessons of modernity in the realms of science, industry, commerce, and administration. 'We have thus to preserve', the address reminded the community, 'our heritage and add to the gifts of modernity which have been brought to us by the west.'[53]

It is in this context that the reception of Tyagaraja's music by the Madras elite has to be understood. Here, William Jackson identifies the subgroup of Smarta brahmins as the principal catalysts in the remembering of tradition. He suggests, that historically, the group played a dynamic role in transmitting the Hindu tradition, in updating and redefining values that allowed for variety and diversity in religious expression.[54] As creative synthesizers, they bridged folk traditions with Sanskritic culture and were largely instrumental in popularizing Brahmanical traditions among lower castes. The ability to synthesize[55] remained a distinguishing feature of the group—Milton Singer had occasion to refer to the Smarta brahmin's initiative in organizing urban religious functions in Madras.[56] In the case of music, the centrality of the Smartas is striking. Not only were the principal composers part of this subgroup, the major patrons in twentieth-century Madras belonged to this category as well.[57] Without suggesting that the entire project was a Smarta driven brainwave, it does appear legitimate to argue that for the group, the projection of Tyagaraja as the ultimate synthesizer of simple bhakti traditions and high learning, as an exemplary composer who sought neither fame nor riches, and who sought salvation in the grace of devotion was integral to their self-definition.

Added to this was the compulsion to modernize and thereby establish firm foundations for a modern classical music culture. The virtues of standardization, spiritual regeneration, and authenticity became the guidelines for the emerging agenda of cultural reconstruction that developed explicitly nationalist overtones over time. The first concrete expression of the agenda came in 1912, four years before the celebrated first All India Music Conference was convened, when Abraham Panditar, the author of the *Karunamritasagaram*, organized the Tanjore Sangeeta Vidya Mahajana Sangam.

For Panditar, the conference was expected to provide a foundational basis for Indian music, especially Karnatik music, and thereby enable the system to retain its purity. 'So having our fears that the music of South India might get mixed with *Desikam*, in course of time and become corrupt like other music, we had to establish the *sangam*.'[58] The collaboration of the practicing musicians was seen as critical in the exercise and it was only through the combined efforts of musician and patrons, that the study of south Indian music could be promoted. The Sangam therefore professed its intentions of honouring the distinguished musicians, whose assistance would be solicited for the establishment of a modern academy. The Sangam, it was hoped by its founder member, would initiate a search for works on music and a publication programme of those compositions which had not been published. These were expected to serve as valuable teaching aids. The pedagogic imperative was never forgotten—in fact, it was for the teaching of proper music, that the Sangam hoped to intervene in the important business of purifying melodies by weeding out a few of the errors that had crept in.[59]

The Tanjore Conference, in its conception and plan of action was part of a larger all-India movement that gained momentum in the first decades of the twentieth century. Individual enthusiasts like V.N. Bhatkhande and V.D. Paluskar in Bombay, the Gaekwad in Gwalior, and the Wodeyars in Mysore combined their personal interest with a larger social programme of inducting music into the national life of the country by advocating an expanded system of education that would include music as curricula. By 1916, the year of the first All India Music Conference, the idea that music embodied the essence of the nation, and that its preservation and cultivation through a national system of education, was a matter of urgency had gained ground. Added to this was a history project, which Bhatkhande, the prime mover of the music conferences saw as critical in stabilizing the foundational basis of Indian classical music, especially Hindustani music.[60] This was important both for pedagogic purposes as well as to 'keep the system easily distinguishable' from the southern version. Subsequent conferences were even more explicit in their advocacy of the 'sacred and national cause of music' and of mass education in music. The second All India Music Conference saw the promotion of music as nation building, and alerted the nation builders to systematize music education. 'For all education has got to be systematic, and there is at the present day no common system of education for our Hindustani music.' It was in this conference that the authorities also pointed to the lack of a competent teaching faculty, a reference that underscored their negative appraisal of existing practitioners, who happened to be Muslims, and who were not part of the western-educated Indian middle class. The conference authorities expressed their disappointment in no uncertain terms when they argued that 'the teaching of music is in the hands of illiterate artists who cannot produce as good results either in point of quantity or quality as if there was a system of instruction and the instruction was in the hands of educated persons.'[61] This was a serious anomaly given the need to incorporate music as part of the general education system. On the other hand, the organizers were fully cognizant of the importance of enlisting practitioners to record their music and make an offering of it in the service of the nation. 'Our workers', the organizers announced, 'have to hasten to preserve in a permanent form by means of gramophone records the existing art of singing, the best specimens of which rest with aged artists.'[62] The latter had to be persuaded to realize the superiority of a national interest over a private interest. In other words, while the business of collection, the working out of theoretical outlines for music, the publication of primers, and a graded course of study remained with the educated middle class, the practitioners had to rest content with making a national offering of their expertise and performing skills. The framing of the project in such terms only widened the gap between theory and practice, a gap that the cultural engineers had wished to address and redress in the first place. In their words, theory was 'the backbone of practice, and when that perished, the practice was bound to degenerate'.[63] Thus the time had come, 'when the educated classes should take up the subject in hand and proceed to give it due position of importance'.[64] By the time of the third All India Music Conference (Benaras, 1919), the question of notation as the only scientific means of conveying a standard version of music to students was taken up once more. Notation was also seen as an instrument of modernity; for the organizers, it was 'obvious from the trend of modern thought and taste that if we want our Indian music to take its proper place in the musical world of today, we must standardize our notation and engraft on our ancient system the scientific method of the west'.[65]

The conferences had their share of detractors. Notwithstanding their dissent on questions of notation or on the means of grading primers and instruction books, the idea of musical reform and the importance of amalgamating music into the general system of education and of establishing a foundational basis for Indian music on modern and scientific lines, gained substantial currency. Atiya Begum summed up the mood of those present in 1919.

I am certain that we shall unite into one great force that knows no Weakening and with earnest sincerity of purpose lay before long the foundation stone of the well beloved institution that will scintillate like a guiding star throughout the ages to come and will remove all the causes that are obstructing the preservation and progress of the Aesthetic science before long ...We have wasted too much time. Let us unite and cooperate. Let us start the great campaign. Let us found the Academy for music and let the Academy control all matters belonging to music and expound its wonderful history and impart its marvelous technique to all who are desirous of knowledge and where the learned pandits will meet together and do away with the differences and where we shall hold conferences and demonstrations for the benefit of the public.[66]

These conferences, while drawing on reasonable representation from southern India, fed into the growing concern of the Madras intelligentsia to incorporate music as part of the overall educational system. Here, the Theosophist advocate Margaret Cousins, played a major role. In 1917, in response to the movement for national education, a National University was organized in Madras and Cousins was appointed member of the Senate and Board of Studies. She pressed for the inclusion of music in the existing curriculum, and with the help of leading citizens of Madras, organized a conference of Tanjore musicians in order to facilitate the drafting of a graded course of study of Karnatik music.[67]

The Tanjore conference yielded the necessary results, in that a complete syllabus of musical studies was drawn up for yearly graded instruction and examination to cover the 'acquisition of skill in the art of singing, playing on the instruments, composition and a working knowledge of western notation'. These initiatives, followed up by Cousins' visiting lectures in Mysore, to prepare public opinion for the inclusion of music in University education matured, with the appointment of a committee by the University of Madras to consider the inclusion of music as part of its syllabus. Musicians took a lead role in the negotiations. In 1925, a meeting of the musicians of Madras, presided over by Muthiah Bhagavatar, was held under the auspices of Tyaga Brahma Sabha where resolutions were passed requesting the university authorities to include music in the curriculum. In 1926, the Madras University appointed a special committee to frame the syllabus for the intermediate course.[68] Two years later, in July 1928, Queen Mary's College secured affiliation to teach music as a subject at the undergraduate level.

The formalization of music instruction within the institutional space of modern education was only one aspect of the nationalist cultural project. In south India, the project was more immediately concerned with the construction of a proper aesthetic, a canonical standard for classical music. Defining the authentic, high classical south Indian style became from the 1920s a major preoccupation with the Madras intelligentsia, one that was informed as much by the perceived dilution of standards following a proliferation of music clubs and theatre performances, as by the needs of pedagogy and instruction. To this was added the compulsions of marking out a distinct style that reflected the changing sensibilities and tastes of the consuming elite. The *Daily Express* became the mouthpiece for musical reform as it carried articles that highlighted the predicament of the patron and performer alike. The first in the series set the debate rolling when it pointedly asked the question, 'Is it not the duty of every true lover of Karnatik Music to strive to rescue it from its present neglected state and to develop it on the right lines so as to preserve ancient Indian music in its pure and pristine form and in all its glory for the benefit of posterity?'[69] The articles proceeded to lampoon the utter indifference of musicians to educate the general public to distinguish good music, the general lack of discrimination in public taste, and the failure to encourage genuine talent. The articles spoke at length about the need for a common standard that would deter performers from indulging in gimmicks just in order to please the audience. As a way out of the degeneration of standards, it was suggested that musicians and connoisseurs should confer and arrive at a consensus about acceptable standards that could be demonstrated through lectures and performances by distinguished artists.[70] Defining an aesthetic involved several aspects of performance and interpretation ranging from purity of form to the toning down of accompaniments in vocal performance. 'How often have we seen a really good musical performance incessantly interrupted by the noisiest drummer who believes in the strength of his brawny arm and goes away pounding with his might and main?'[71] Nor were these baneful accompaniments the only drawbacks for, according to the author, musicians had lost sight of the true conception of music in the rendering and interpretation of melodies. Under the circumstances, it was necessary to set up academies that would engage seriously with the agenda of music reform, undertake research, and involve artists to come to a consensus on standards and interpretation.

Even the preoccupation with the pure voice as an integral part of the emerging discourse on aesthetics was tempered by the insistence on proper training and authentic reproduction that alone guaranteed the virtues of classicism. While connoisseurs like E. Krishna Iyer exalted the virtues of the natural singing voice that women were especially blessed with, he was insistent on proper training. Rigorous and systematic training alone elevated music from being a natural art to a classical art form. In his words,

It is obvious that good music is to be sought for in a happy combination of sweet sounds and human art of refined technique, practice and presentation. When all is said anywhere and at anytime, no highly developed art can be well understood and enjoyed or properly valued without some initiation into its technique and convention, though everyone need not be an expert either in theory or in practice.[72]

Subsequently, as we shall see, the engagement with the voice, the importance of a perfect pitch or adhering to *sruti,* which the practice of Hindustani music was seen to facilitate, became more vocal. What persisted, however, was the emphasis on training and discipline—the cerebral component where, the ability to explore the melody to its fullest potential and to sing complex combination of notes to cross rhythm, was stressed time and again as an important component of classical music—in other words, music had to be both pleasing to the ears and capable of stimulating the brain.[73]

The call for reform had been sounded loud and clear. The response came sooner than expected. In 1927, at the Madras session of the Indian National Congress, a decision was taken by the Reception Committee[74] to establish a special academy in Madras to take up the cause of classical music—specifically Karnatik music—its promotion and proper dissemination. The Academy that was thus born out of a convergence of nationalist agitation and cultural self-reflection emerged as the new patron and arbiter of music. Henceforth, the Madras Music Academy would assume the onus of redefining the tenets of south Indian classical music and performance, providing it, at the same time with an altered social and institutional context.

NOTES

1. *Hindu Music and the Gayan Samaj. Published in Aid of the Funds of the Madras Jubilee Gayan Samaj,* Bombay, 1887, p. 3.
   Vishnu Digambar Paluskar (1872–1931), was arguably one of the most charismatic personalities in the history of Indian music in the late nineteenth and twentieth centuries. Born in a family of traditional keertan singers, he received his training from Balkrishna Bua of the Gwalior Gharana. Paluskar's disenchantment with his

teacher and his subsequent disappointment in the Gaekwad's court in Baroda, led him to question the existing system of musical instruction and patronage and to consider the establishment of a modern system of musical education. He established the Gandharva Mahavidyalaya in Lahore (1901) with a branch in Bombay in 1908. Paluskar was a reformer who was convinced of the need to relocate the teaching of music in modern institutional spaces and to yoke it to the larger nationalist project.

2. Sourindro Mohan Tagore, *Hindu Music*. First Published, 1882. Second Reprint, Low Price Publications, Delhi, 1994. See Preface to the First edition.

3. Addressing the anniversary of the Madras branch of the Poona Gayan Samaj in 1884, the chairman emphasized that a second object of the association was to cultivate the national music of India and of making it as in other countries, a source of amusement and a thing with which everyone should be acquainted. See *Hindu Music and the Gayan Samaj*, p. 54.

4. V.N. Bhatkhande, *A Short historical Survey of the music of Upper India. A reproduction of a speech addressed by Pandit V.N.Bhatkhande at the first all India Music Conference, Baroda, 1916*. Bombay, 1934. For Bhatkhande's biography, see S.N. Ratanjhankar, *Pandit Bhatkhande*, National Book Trust, New Delhi, 1967.

5. J.A. Dubois, *Hindu Manners, Customs and Ceremonies*. Translated from the author's later French manuscript and edited with introduction and notes by Henry K. Beauchamps, Clarendon Press, Oxford, 1897. Reprint, New Delhi, 1978, pp. 595ff.

6. Captain Thomas Williamson, *The Costumes and Customs of Modern India: From a Collection of Drawings by Charles D'Oyly* engraved by J.M. Clark & C. Dubourg; with a preface and copious descriptions by Captain Thomas Williamson. London, printed and sold by E. Orme, 1913, Plate 19.

7. H.K. Kaul, *Travellers' India: An Anthology*, chosen and edited, Oxford University Press, New Delhi, 1979, pp. 68–9ff.

8. Ibid., pp. 68–9ff.

9. Ibid.

10. In S.M. Tagore, *Hindu Music*, p. 133.

11. Ibid., p. 135.

12. Ibid., p. 136.

13. Ibid., p. 155.

14. Ibid., p. 156.

15. Ibid. Here, Jones was possibly conflating his English auditory habit with a textually unsupported interpretation of the *Natya Sastra*. * This was an allusion to the play on srutis.

16. Ibid., pp. 163–72, 193–7, 201–8.

17. Ibid., pp. 243–73.

18. Ibid., p. 266.

19. Ibid., p. 267. Col. French mentioned that Europeans rarely heard good or classical music of the Hindus. 'What is ordinarily played to them is the commonest ballads and love songs, with modern Persian and Hindustani ditties, sung by ill-instructed screaming dancing women, at crowded native durbars, marriages and other ceremonials. The late Nawab Shumsh-ool Oomrah of Hyderabad, for instance used to cause from ten to twenty sets of dancers and singers to stand up together, each set consisting of several women as singers, and a proportion of instrumental performers. All sang and played together whatever they pleased, and the clamour of different tunes, with all their varied accompaniments, was quite indescribable.'

20. C.R. Day, *The Music and Musical Instruments of Southern India and the Deccan* (1891), Reprint Delhi, 1996, pp. 1–2.

21. Ibid., pp. 5–7.

22. Ibid.

23. Anne C. Wilson, *A Short Account of the Hindu System of Music*, London, 1904, pp. 3–7.

24. By May 1901, V.D. Paluskar had founded the Gandharva Mahavidyalaya in Lahore. This was a turning point in the history of music in modern India for it was the first music school run by a middle-class musician without the patronage of the aristocracy. It was run by public support, donations and funds raised by the concerts of Vishnu Digambar Paluskar. Clearly, Paluskar's charismatic personality and passionate commitment to the advocacy of classical music made an impression on Anne Wilson.

25. A.H. Fox Strangways, *The Music of Hindostan*, first published 1914. Reprint, Delhi, 1965, p. 86.

26. Ibid., p. 90. Strangways' observations appear to reflect an arbitrary access to singers of both regions.

27. Stuart Blackburn, *Print, Folklore and Nationalism in Colonial South India*, Permanent Black, Delhi, 2003.

28. Ibid.

29. William J. Jackson, *Tyagaraja and the Renewal of Tradition*, p. 69ff. Also see vol. 34 in p. 78.

30. See P. Sambamoorthy, *A Dictionary of South Indian Music and Musicians*, vol. I, The Indian Music Publishing House, Madras, 1952. See entries on Ananta Bharati (1845–1905) who authored the *Dasamskanda Kirtanas* and the *Desika Prabhava Prakasika Kirtanas*, Also see entries on Taccur Singaracharulu (1834–92) and Chinna Singaracharulu who published several works and graded compositions in syllabic notation. Also see Ludwig Pesch, *The Illustrated Companion to South Indian Classical Music*, p. 209.

31. Sourindro Mohan Tagore, *Hindu Music*, Preface, pp. 2–3.

32. Ibid., p. 29.

33. Lokenath Ghosh, *Music's Appeal to India: An original, Instructive and Interesting Story Agreeable to the taste of both Young and Old*, H.C. Gangooly & Co., Calcutta, 1873, pp. 12–16.

34. Ibid., p. 19. Ghosh was evidently making a strong case for the efforts of S.M. Tagore and Khetter Mohan Goswami whose work *Sangit Sara* was the prescribed text of the newly founded Bengal Music School. What is interesting to note is that Tagore enlisted the support of practicing ustads in his venture and had a number of them sign a petition to the effect that they fully endorsed Khetter Mohan Goswami's work, which was based on authoritative Sanskrit and Persian texts. See Appendix in S.M. Tagore, *Hindu Music*, pp. 393–7.

35. Ghosh, *Music's Appeal to India*, pp. 20–1ff.

36. Bruno Nettl and Philip Bohlman, *Comparative Musicology and Anthology of Music*, University of Chicago Press, Chicago, 1991.

37. Ghosh, *Music's Appeal to India*, pp. 17–18.

38. The *Sangeet Prabesika*, edited by Jyotindranath Tagore, *Ananda Sangeet* pioneered by the ladies of the Tagore household and the *Sangeet Vigyan Prabesika* edited and founded by Radhika Prasad Goswami, a representative of the Vishnupur lineage are instances in point. See *Sangeet Vigyan Prabesika* (Bengali journal), no. 1, 1920. See editorial by Manmathamohan Basu.

39. *Hindu Music and the Gayan Samaj*, p. 33.
40. Ibid., Part II, p. 22ff. Address made to the Travancore Raja and the correspondence thereafter. This covered a fairly detailed interview with the ruler about the system of music and instruction prevalent in Travancore.
41. P. Sambamoorthy, *A Dictionary of South Indian Music and its Musicians*, Part I. Also see William Jackson, *Tyagaraja and the Renewal of Tradition*. Also see B. Dayananda Rao (ed.), *Carnatic Music Composers. A Collection of Biographical Essays*, Triveni Foundation Hyderabad, 1994. See entries on Veena Kuppier (1798–1860), one of Tyagaraja's most distinguished disciples and whose son Tiruvottiyur Tyagier published the *Pallavi Swara Kalpavati*.
42. B. Dayananda Rao (ed.), *Carnatic Music Composers*. See entries on Kotiswara Iyer, Muthiah Bhagavatar whose uncle was his principal patron in Tanjore his uncle was Professor of Sanskrit in St Peter's College in Tanjore.
43. P. Sambamoorthy, *A Dictionary of South Indian music and its Musicians*, part I.
44. Chinnaswami Mudaliar, *Oriental Music in European Notation*. First printed 1893. Reprint Delhi, 1982. See Introduction and p. 29. Also see P. Sambamoorthy, *A Dictionary of South Indian Music*.
45. Pamela Price, *Kingship and Political Practice in Colonial India*, Cambridge, Cambridge University Press, 1996, p. 179.
46. For a study of the entertainment media in south India in this period, see S.Theodore Baskaran, *The Message Bearers: The Nationalist Politics and the Entertainment Media in South India 1880–1945*. Cre-A Publishers, Madras, 1981.
47. P.S. Iyer, *Articles on Carnatic Music*, Madras, 1937 (These articles appeared in the *Daily Express*, Madras in 1921–2), p. 71.
48. Ibid., p. 73.
49. E. Krishna Iyer, *Personalities in Present Day Music*, Madras, 1933. See Introduction.
50. R. Ranga Ramanuja Ayyanagar, *Musings of a Musician*, Wilco, Bombay, 1977.
51. Tapati Guha Thakurta, 'Instituting the Nation in Art', in Partha Chatterjee (ed.), *Wages of Freedom: Fifty Years of the Indian Nation State*, Oxford University Press, New Delhi, 1998.
52. K.S. Ramaswami Sastri, *The Future of the Brahmin*, 26 June 1935, Madras, 1935.
53. Ibid.
54. William Jackson, *Tyagaraja and the Renewal of Tradition*, pp. 207–25.
55. V.S. Pathak, *Smarta Religious Tradition of Northern India c.600 A.D. to c.1200 A.D.*, Kusumanjali Prakashan, Meerut, 1987.
56. Milton Singer (ed.), *Krishna: Myths, Rites and Attitudes*, The University of Chicago Press, Chicago and London, 1971.
57. William Jackson, *Tyagaraja and the Renewal of Tradition*, p. 224. Also see pp. 191–2ff. For Sambamoorthy, Tyagaraja was a gifted teacher and musician whose ideals of plain living and high thinking were exemplary and worth emulating.
58. Abraham Panditar, *Karunamirtha Sagaram on Sruits: A Treatise on Music or Isai Tamil which is one of the main Divisions of Muttamil or Language, Music and Drama*, New Delhi Reprint 1984, Original 1917, pp. 218–19. See section on 'The origin of the Tanjore Mahajana Sangam'.
59. Ibid., pp. 218–37.
60. V.N. Bhatkhande, *A Short Historical Survey of the Music of Upper India*.
61. *Report of the Second All India Music Conference*, 1919. See Foreword.
62. Ibid., pp. 6–9.

63. Ibid., pp. 9–10.
64. Ibid.
65. *Report of the Third All India Music Conference*, held from 19 Dec.–22 Dec. 1919, Benaras, Publication Mudrak, Chabinath Pandey, Sri Gyanmondal Yantralaya, Kochi, 1920. See Foreword by Joint Secretary Sitaram Sah.
66. Ibid., p. 90ff. See Address of Atiya Begum. Also see Atiya Begum *Sangit of India* (Classical and Instrumental Music and Nautch), Bombay, 1942.
67. Margaret Cousins, *Music of Orient and Occident* Madras, 1935, pp. 177–8 ff. Also see P. Sambamoorthy, *The Teaching of Music*, Madras, 1966, chapter XIII.
68. Ibid.
69. P.S. Iyer, *Articles on Carnatic Music*, pp. 1–2.
70. Ibid., pp. 2–3.
71. Ibid., pp. 49–50.
72. E. Krishna Iyer, *Personalities in Present Day Music*, Introduction.
73. Contemporary periodicals like the *Ananda Vikatan* carried a segment called the 'Aadal Paadal'(Music and Dance) where Kalki wrote extensively on musical taste and concerts, evaluating performers and performances. See *Ananda Vikatan* 20 September, 1936, pp. 28–9.
74. *JMAM*, vol. I, 1930, pp. 79–81.

Consolidating the Classical
THE MADRAS MUSIC ACADEMY AND THE POLITICS OF CUSTODIANSHIP

The editorial titled somewhat self indulgently 'Ourselves', in the inaugural issue of the *Journal of the Music Academy Madras* in 1930, spelt out simply but clearly the intentions of the Academy.[1] While endorsing the growing need to make music accessible to all, the Academy was quick to introduce a note of qualification, when it stated that its primary concern was to promote 'the higher learning and practice of the science and art of music, and take steps to maintain standards of excellence'. Echoing the familiar angst of the growing 'cleavage between theory and practice', the editorial pointed out that if classical music had to be preserved and promoted, it was imperative to arrive at a proper reconciliation 'based on natural and fundamental laws'. [2]

The question of standards assumed a particular urgency in the context of newly emerging institutional spaces for music education and performance. Not only did the inclusion of music as a subject of study raise the issue of appropriate textbooks, primers, and graded exercises, the proliferation of music clubs and entertainment spaces reopened the question of declining standards, and of the construction and consolidation of a classical canon that would not brook subversion. Responding to these compulsions, the Academy found itself needing to articulate a complex agenda of singularizing the tenets of classical music, and of universalizing standards for its dissemination and performance. The emphasis on notation and technological reproduction for the preservation and transmission of music, on the one hand, and the refining of a concert repertoire in terms of compositions and of permissible melodic interpretation, on the other, gave the agenda a concrete dimension. Out of this, three things emerged: a clearer demarcation of what Karnatik music was all about, a restructuring of the actual performance within an altered material and social context, and finally the construction of new aesthetics and taste that was informed both by artistic considerations and by the self-imaging of the new patrons.

The Taskforce: Patrons and Performers at Work

Right from its inception, the Madras Music Academy worked closely with performing musicians and involved them in its organizational structure. The Academy, actually, came into its own during the annual winter conference that it organized, when musicians and scholars met to confer on issues of musical theory and technique, and to participate in concerts and lecture demonstrations before the public. For the rest of the year, it concentrated on bringing out a music journal that helped to frame a larger debate on the issue of the reform and preservation of classical music. The experts committee set up during its annual winter event, consisted of leading musicians and scholars, both amateur and professional, and was by and large well informed about the subjects under scrutiny and open to debate. There was, predictably, a correspondence between patrons and performers, and ties of caste and orientation facilitated the emergence of a consensus in the shaping of new aesthetics. Even more compelling was the shared need to establish a strong, even immutable, foundation for classical music, that would announce its distinct character and individuality, and insulate it from distortion. Leading musicians like Muthiah Bhagavatar, Tiger Varadachariar, and Ariyakudi Ramanuja Iyengar among others, who were already involved in the modernizing project either in the capacity of individual artists or as court/palace musicians, were part of the Academy's inner circle. Their interventions added weight to its decisions on technical matters relating to the delineation of melodies and modes, their interpretation, the admissible combination of notes, the rendering of compositions, the identification of authentic compositions, and so on. In 1930, Muthiah Bhagavatar, as president of the annual music conference stated candidly, that when the Academy was first started, there was an impression among the musicians that it would be an amateurish affair and would not sufficiently honour musicians or even comprehend their perspectives. Fortunately, he added, this impression was quickly dispelled and he was more than willing to take his place along with the larger fraternity of musicians as 'limbs of the Academy', and to render it all the services he could for the improvement of music.[3] In the following year, it was the Academy's turn to acknowledge its success in bringing musicians and scholars on one forum. Urging the musicians to work closely with the scholars, its representative Satyamurti observed that it was said that they (vidwans and musicians) were 'two different sets of people and that we lay people could have nothing to do with them. One of the achievements of the Academy has been to get all of them together'.[4]

This was not all mere hyperbole or self-indulgence. The alliance stood firm as musicians volunteered to give model performances, record for the radio and even persuade the reluctant traditionalists to shed their prejudice against recording, and to assume teaching responsibilities in the new institutional spaces of higher education. In the 1931 conference, Muthiah Bhagavatar commented on the democratic spirit that characterized the deliberations of the experts and that it was a matter of gratification that decisions were arrived at after free and frank discussion.

I am glad to say, that during the discussions although there were acute differences of opinion, there was complete cooperation among the vidwans and much respect for honest differences of opinion, which is so essential to the smooth working of a great institution like this Music Academy.[5]

The enterprise that united the performer with the publicist was redolent with a crusading spirit—as the 1932 editorial noted while applauding the decision of the Madras University to appoint Tiger Varadachariar as a lecturer in music—'in the elevation of Mr.Varadachariar, the Music Academy loses one of the trusted knights of the Round Table but is fortunate in securing a fitting successor in Gayaka Siromani Muthiah Bhagavatar, Palace Vidwan of Mysore, a great composer on whom the Durbar has bestowed very rich honours'.[6]

The publicists, who ran the Academy and took an active interest in its journal and annual conferences, on their part, combined their professional calling with an informed appreciation of music and a considerable knowledge of Sanskrit and classical theory. P. Sambamoorthy, for instance, who was closely associated with the Academy from the very beginning, was both a law graduate and musician by training. His scholarship so impressed Reverend H.A. Popley who ran a summer school in music in Madras, that he was appointed a lecturer in Popley's school. In 1928, when a department of music was set up in the Queen Mary's College, Madras, Sambamoorthy was appointed as its first head. In 1931, he went to Munich to study the violin, flute, and musicology.

V. Raghavan was another example of the Madras elite, who combining a professional career with a deep knowledge of Sanskrit, scriptures and classical Indian literature, brought to the project a very distinct inflection. The Academy continued to draw on the support and generosity of the rulers of Travancore, Mysore, and Ramnad as well as of wealthy businessmen like Raja Annamalai Chettiar. Using their public profile and their location within new institutional spaces, they accelerated their efforts to establish a sound foundational basis for Karnatik music, both in terms of its theoretical framework as well as performance practice. These efforts took various forms, the most important of which were a history-writing project that highlighted the individuality of the Karnatik musical tradition, and the enterprise of systematically standardizing its practice in performance and pedagogy. This fixing of certain attributes as authentic and integral to classical music and the construction of new aesthetic standards for performance that accompanied the restructuring of the concert format and repertoire, became the hallmarks of the Academy's project and were intrinsically tied to the complex self-imaging of the Madras elite, which saw itself as the ultimate custodians of India's spiritual traditions and the most qualified purveyors of modernity.

History for Classification: A Leap into the Future or Return to an Imagined Past?

The Academy's journal invited original contributions from members and readers on the history of music and musical literature (*charitra*), musical compositions (*lakshya*), and musicology (*lakshana*).[7] Its editorial committee made up of scholars and performing musicians, was receptive to new ideas and debates and did not allow consensus building to obscure critical enquiry. In 1931, when the experts met to deliberate on the project, the president reminded them that differences of opinion should not be taken personally. In his words,

Several eminent vidwans have assembled here and have been freely expressing their views for or against a particular proposition. In the course of the discussion, some experts may have to differ from others, and I would only appeal to all not to take anything stated in this Conference as any kind of personal reflection or insinuation.[8]

The Academy's journal, too, from the very first year of its publication, provided a space for criticism of the project and of the way the history of classical music in south India was being represented and how, in accordance with what was an unreliable theoretical framework, the practice of music was being jeopardized. Hulugur Krishnachar of the Bharat Sangeet Shala, was for instance, a stern critic of many of the new histories that exaggerated the distinctiveness and relative purity of the southern system as well as of the enthusiasm of the reformers in trying to invent new modes of classification and new melodies to fit in with the actual practice and rendering of compositions.[9]

For the most part, the histories of the development of the Karnatik system that the journal carried, emphasized the isolation of the Deccan from Muslim influence, the importance of the Vijayanagar court in the development of musical culture, and the convergence of devotional poetry and court sponsored musical theory in the articulation of a distinct regional style. The seventeenth century classification of 72 musical modes by Venkatamakhin was identified as the basis of the system,[10] notwithstanding prolonged and protracted debates about its utility in the deliberations of the experts committee. Professional musicians like Nataraja Bhagavatar and Muthiah Bhagavatar as well as scholars like P. Sambamoorthy were reluctant to jettison the classification scheme of 72 parent melodic modes,[11] which in their view gave the system its individuality and a solid foundational structure.

Muthiah Bhagavatar in his presidential address to the Music Conference of 1930 mentioned quite categorically that Karnatik music represented the Margi style of music (by which he presumably meant authentic) as distinct from the Desi style that he associated with the Hindustani system. The distinction was rooted in a disputed classificatory system that nevertheless appeared to organize the southern system around stricter rules. 'Govinda Diksitar and Venkatamakhin', his address pointed out, 'have settled the scientific basis of our system and have elaborately classified the ragas into 72 melakarta modes and their janya ragas. Today Carnatic music owes its features to these writers'.[12] These views found wide currency among most of the Academy's members, for whom the idea of a structural solidity and identity for Karnatik music was particularly compelling. Here, the seventeenth century classification formula was of paramount importance for 'it gave permanence to ragas and helped them preserve their identity'.[13]

The question of the melakarta scheme, and its instrumentality in the evolution of the southern musical system, did not remain confined to history writing. It was critically tied and connected to the larger issue of standardization of melodies and the authentic reproduction of compositions and song texts, which were considered essential preconditions to future instruction and transmission of the art form. It is very likely that to many members and musicologists and even composers, such a rigid system did not represent either the truest or most creative way of looking at the accumulated inheritance of melodies. But there was no doubt that a consensus had to be built about melodies, their arrangement, and how these were to be rendered. Equally, there was no doubt that in terms of actual practice and performance, the compositions of the trinity were the most useful practical guides to the understanding and interpretation of melodies. Muthiah Bhagavatar endorsed this when he pointed out that the trinity had 'familiarized the lay world with the intricacies of the science as formulated by Govinda Diksitar and Venkatamakhin'.[14] It was thus necessary to combine both these aspects under a comprehensive system and in a manner that would ensure for the future student, performer, and listener the authentic version of classical music.

The Academy responded to the challenge by inviting debate and discussions during its annual conferences, and the standardization of melodies in terms of the permissible combination of notes, their nomenclature and their relationship to the parent mode (Venkatamakhin), became the most contentious subjects of discussion. Alongside, there was the whole question of retrieving and circulating known compositions, either in manuscript form (if and when available) or in their reproduction by practicing musicians who claimed to have access to an established lineage. The exercise generated heated exchanges, and at times, the whole methodology so far employed in the modernizing project was questioned. The compulsion to standardize was complicated by the fact, that in actual performance, there was always a tendency to improvise by emphasizing or by playing down certain notes, using others that strictly speaking did not conform to the parent mode. The confusion was compounded by the nineteenth-century project of compiling and codifying the compositions of the eighteenth-century musicians, notably Tyagaraja, wherein various unlikely, and sometimes spurious, ragas had been erroneously ascribed to many compositions.[15]

The discussions elicited a wide range of views from practicing musicians and their publicists, and it was to the Academy's credit that its attempts to build a public opinion took full cognizance of what performers had to say. The inaugural issue of the journal carried three important articles, that set the terms of the debate. For P. Sundaram Iyer, who was emphatic in his advocacy of the 72 mela system, it was 'a wonder that the necessity for the very 72 modes has come to be publicly questioned by the modern skeptic reformer for queer individual reasons'.[16] Hulugur Krishnachar, on the other hand, was critical of the claims that the southern musicologists made of the classicism of the system, and particularly of the validity or even utility of the Venkatamakhin classification. He argued that several scholars of the south had, in fact, admitted that only 32 out of the 72 melas were usable and that the rest were impracticable and included only for systematizing scale building.[17] Tiger Varadachariar, a celebrated performer, outlined a third position. While lamenting the gap between theory and practice, he made a case for artistic license when deliberating on particular melodies and critiqued the suggestions of nineteenth-century musicologists, Subburama Diksitar (1839–1906) and Singacharulu (1839–92) concerning the use or omission of controversial notes. This, he said was an instance of letting 'the doctrinaire get the better of the artist'.[18]

Under the circumstances it emerged that what was necessary was the standardization of melodies after very careful consultation. In the experts committee that met in 1931, Nemam Nataraja Bhagavatar along with Ramakottaya Pantulu and S. Subramanya Sastri argued against the idea of introducing more modes,[19] or of altering the existing classification scheme, while Hulugur Krishnachar and others, recommended the adding of new melas without disturbing the system. These suggestions were not adopted and the Academy confined itself in the succeeding years, to arriving at a consensus about the features and classification of melodies. The project went ahead and, within three decades of its existence, the Academy could claim to have surveyed the entire range of melodies in use and had established a set of authoritative conventions regarding their interpretation. Its journal, however, carried the debate forward with Hulugur Krishnacahar[20] and K.V. Ramachandran[21] continuing to interrogate the standard assumptions behind the project of melodic standardization. It heated up especially in the late 1940s and early 1950s, when enthusiasts tried to promote and legitimize the popularity of rare melodies (*apurva* ragas) by linking them with a long textual tradition and with the compositions of the trinity.

The agenda before the Academy's experts committee was to fix, by consensus, the attributes of melodies, their nomenclature, and their relationship to their parent modes. The method adopted was to try to square the practice of rendering melodies with both the theoretical prescriptions conveyed in existing musical literature and, more critically, with the practical expression as conveyed through actual compositions received and sung by disciples of well-known lineages. The latter became especially significant when musical theory was not available or was garbled, and it became imperative to obtain the widest possible range of opinions and interpretations before fixing the standard with permissible deviations or usage (*prayoga*). It was here, that feelings ran high but in fairness to the Academy in its early years, it must be mentioned that there was a genuine attempt to negotiate differences and come to an agreement about practice and to give musicians and their interpretation a greater centrality. Most members of the Academy were clear, that more than a solid and elegant theory to regulate practice, it was musical interpretation by individual artists that held the key to appreciating the essence (*raga bhava*) of a particular melody, but believed that endorsing indiscriminate usage without fixing the basic arrangement was unwise. Sabesa Iyer, one of the most important musicians of the period was critical of both theory and indiscriminate endorsement of practices that were in vogue, and preferred to speak from his own training and experience. The Academy in cases of major dissent put the matter to vote and subsequently carried the resolution through, but with minor caveats that sanctioned certain usages as rare.[22]

Integral to the classification project was the reproduction of compositions and their public dissemination, and here the songs of the trinity especially those of Tyagaraja enjoyed pride of place. The latter's pre-eminence arose largely because his compositions had enjoyed such an impressive circulation from the latter half of the previous century, thanks to his disciples, many of whom had initiated a rudimentary publications project. The biographies of the celebrated saint composer, as William Jackson has argued, made him not just a musical icon but a role model of traditional values. Jackson suggests that the repetition of Tyagaraja's songs was part of the modern Hindus' response and adaptation to the changes that transformed south India, 'making a potent music in the face of change and noisy chaos'.[23] For the Academy, the accurate reproduction of the composers' songs was of paramount importance; the retrieval and examination of compositions in their manuscript as well as published form and musical demonstrations by well-known exponents, became part of a sustained drive to revive the correct version of the compositions.

The nineteenth-century publications of Chinnaswami Mudaliar, who in 1893 produced an impressive anthology of Tyagaraja's songs with the assistance of Krishnaswami Bhagavatar (considered one of the leading disciples of Tyagaraja), and of Tacur Singacharulu, came under closer scrutiny. For some time, however, these books carried the weight of their scholarship as, for example when in 1931, Varaha Narsimhachari expressed misgivings about the so-called authentic character of the composer's work as they were being sung.[24] He argued that the composer did not personally name the raga or even the mela, and that only latter day musicians classified and codified his kirtanams according to their whims under the present names of ragam or melam, and that it was essential to verify these against the versions of Singacharulu and others.

The Academy discussed at length the discoveries of fresh manuscripts and the problems these presented in terms of classification. V.K. Raghavan, for instance, commenting on two manuscripts of Tyagaraja songs, admitted that there were mistakes in the assignment of melodies in some of the compositions and that these had to be modified.

While recent musicians have not hesitated to sing a piece originally in a rarer raga, it appears, especially at the time of the first printing of the songs, the rare ragas of some pieces handed down simply as *apoorva* (rare) ragas were give names which on further examination have now to be modified.[25]

For this the evidence of manuscripts handed down within the lineage was seen as useful. In 1938, Raghavan with the help of D.V. Krishnamurti secured a palm leaf manuscript, which was in two parts, one giving the mere text of the song and the other the text with notation. While the former section was titled on the margin '*Peddu Kirtanulu*' and the latter '*Apoorvakirtanuluaadharam*', the former also carried at the beginning of each piece, the raga, and the *janaka* and *tala* while in the latter, the formulae for understanding the lakshanas and *sanchara*s of the ragas were also added. The manuscript was clearly coded—melodies misspelt, an attribute that may suggest, according to Raghavan, the perversity of the custodians. It was, therefore, quite possible that someone had fabricated names for apurva ragas when they did not exist, and only the melas were mentioned.

In 1942, P. Sambamoorthy commented on a set of manuscripts that he acquired from Venkatrama Wallajapet Bhagavatar, which recorded a number of compositions with notation, some others that were in bare text form in addition to separate references to melodies and modes. The manuscripts needed very careful reading.[26] K.V. Ramachandran was particularly critical of the tendency to increase melodies at will and by arbitrarily naming them. In a strongly worded article, he wrote that scribes had been callous in their representation of Tyagaraja's work and that the late Ramaswamy Bhagavatar of Wallajapet had admitted to him that several melodies, which had become the subject of much controversy, had been adopted from doubtful sources. It was not Tyagaraja who was guilty of such misnaming but certain editors. 'Then the blame was transferred to Narada (the puranic sage-musician) who was supposed to have given Tyagaraja a book called Swarnavam', an unnecessary invention. There was, he wrote, no need to seek this supernatural intervention when the textual tradition was able to provide all the materials on the theoretical side, while the existing practices of the Hindustani, Maharashtrian, and other traditions provided ample practical illustrations.[27]

The Academy reacted to the problem with its characteristic enthusiasm. Given the perceived urgency of standardizing and notating compositions, it invited its members to work with musicians and to publish as many authenticated and notated compositions as possible. Over three decades, the Academy sponsored a publication project that generated a huge corpus of such song texts, while facilitating their circulation in the public domain and providing teachers with a basic aid. This worked in tandem with the project of developing notation, that was seen as critical to the modern pedagogy.

Notation for Instruction

The idea of notation as a means of facilitating preservation and instruction, had interested patrons like Serfoji II of Tanjore, who under the influence of Schwartz, had experimented with the method to suit the requirements of band music. Whether this was one more instance of Serfoji's eccentric disposition or whether it was redolent with a new orientation that aimed at new orders of classification and systematization, is difficult to say. The potentialities of notation as a means of retaining the basic form of a melodic text could not have been completely lost on either the king or his subjects, even if they did not have occasion to relate it to the requirements of modern education and transmission of the art form. Eighteenth-century composers particularly Tyagaraja and Diksitar, in all probability experimented with the idea, but in a very rudimentary form as their later biographers demonstrated.

The engagement of the cultural reformers of the later nineteenth century with the idea and method of notation was very different, and was mediated by considerations of modernization and of a comparative framework of western and Indian music. Influenced by European enthusiasts who promoted ideas of modernization in which notation would serve as a scientific means of introducing order into the existing system, Indian 'reform' publicists responded by an emphatic plea for notation, which they saw as a potentially invaluable aid in the understanding and teaching of Indian music. Chinnaswami Mudaliar's *Oriental Music in European Notation* was a significant beginning as it attempted to 'redeem the treasures in southern India' through a system of notation. Mudaliar was conscious of the difficulties of notation,

no written language can reproduce the thousand variations met with in the articulation of new sounds—much less can it convey the peculiar impressions produced by gestures and other graces employed by effective public speakers.[28]

And yet it was the only available tool for reproducing and thus preserving some of India's most exquisite music that would otherwise be lost. Mudaliar's work was developed and elaborated by Subburama Diksitar, who collaborated with him to devise signs for the various *gamakas*, mainly drawing from the western staff notation. These refinements were incorporated in the *Sangita Sampradaya Pradarsini*, published in 1904.[29] In this work, Diksitar stuck to the Indian sargam notation, (Indian solfa) that made use of the first letters of the names of the seven notes in the octave, of a select number of staff notation symbols, some with and without modification. The rhythmic beats were indicated by single and double bars, symbols indicating the end of a phrase or its beginning, and those indicating the lengthening of notes, rising and falling inflection were taken directly from staff notation, while other symbols were adapted to suit the specific requirements of Indian music, especially when it came to distinguishing full and diminished versions of notes, that is, sharp and flat notes.

These efforts seem to have made a positive impression upon music reformers and publicists in centres like Baroda and Mysore, where the ruling princely states fully endorsed the idea of notation for instruction. The Mysore court in collaboration with E. Clements, the District Collector of Bellary and Chairman of the Philharmonic Society of Western India, (1913), systematically promoted the establishmen of music schools and encouraged musicians to set compositions to notation.[30] By the time of the first All India Music Conference (1916), the question of whether to have music written or not, was not an issue although the value of the preliminary attempts remained doubtful. In 1919, at the third All India Music Conference, M. Fredilis, Director of Music, Baroda State presented his views on the subject and argued that the existing books on notation were far from satisfactory and as a practicing musician, he found that 'only easy and ragas of a very light character' could be noted and when it came to noting down 'expressions of melodies, musical phrases, light and shade as sung by eminent gavayyas, they have so far failed in producing anything like a standard of Indian classical music'.[31] The conference he said had no option but to fall back on recording. He emphasized the importance of introducing a universal notation system that would enable both southern and northern musicians to play together and maintained that the western system, with the added feature of translating the names of notes with their symbols in Indian languages, was more than adequate for the purpose. 'Western notation was the most complete in the world and the only one capable of producing those musical phrases which is the very life of Indian music'.[32] Fredilis' proposals did not meet with the approval of all those present and it was decided to form a subcommittee to investigate the possibility of a viable alternative.[33]

Within the Madras Music Academy, these discussions were very closely linked to the avowed intentions of the Academy to introduce music as part of the modern system of education and for notation along with recordings, to enable a faithful representation of the art form. On closer reflection, this programme did not seem so simple or easy, and the discussions threw up the larger question of the viability of modern pedagogic methods in transmission of traditional music. There were serious misgivings about the efficacy of notation in conveying the essence of Indian music, which did not lend itself to mechanistic translation.[34] Reverend H.A. Popley initiated a debate when he contributed to the first issue of the Academy's journal an essay entitled, 'A Plea for an All India System of Notation and Classification'. This was a shot in the arm for the puritans in the Academy, for it suggested that north Indian musicians would be well advised to adopt the southern system of raga classification based on the 72 mela scheme of Venkatamakhin or at least V.N. Bhatkhande's proposals that were derived from there. Notation remained a fundamental problem and Popley urged the Academy to address it, for without a suitable system of notation, it was 'hardly possible for music in India to develop into full and rich maturity. We are hampered more by the lack of an all India system of notation than by anything else'. Following Mudaliar's suggestions, the Reverend hesitatingly recommended the adoption of the western staff notation with alterations to include key notes as well as sharps and flats. More insistently, he suggested that the notation should remain a solfa notation, making use of the initial syllables or letters of the notes, whose names were common to both systems of music. Variations could be shown by lines either above or below the notes; the lines below showing the *komala* or soft notes and the lines above *tivra* or sharp notes. The *tara sthayi* or higher register in the octave could be shown by a dot above the note and the *mandara sthayi* or lower register by a dot below the note. Popley favoured the use of the Nagari script on account of the increasing use of Hindi, thanks to the efforts of 'Mahatma's Hindi Prachar Movement', and because its letters were distinctive and easy to read in print. The sharp and semitonal flats (komala and tivra marks) could be placed at the top of each piece from which its applicability could be deduced. Regarding rhythmic symbols, he suggested that the bar stroke which had become universal be adopted while the question of how to indicate the exact length of elongated notes needed to be worked out.[35]

When making these recommendations for an all-India system of notation, Popley introduced a note of caution. He readily admitted that notation could never adequately represent all the curves and graces given to the notes and melody by Indian musicians and singers,

Notation will represent what may be called the bones of the melody. The singer will have to clothe it in suitable flesh. One of the distinctions that has been made between Indian and western music is that the former is curved while the latter is linear meaning that the former delights in all kinds of slurs and ornaments while the latter emphasizes more specially the exactness of pitch. This is of course not to be taken strictly for even in western music a great many graces are used and modern singing makes a great deal of the tremolo, but in Indian music, the curvature is very much more marked and one rarely uses a clear sharp note.[36]

He was referring to the full range of gamakas,[37] features that was not merely decorative additions to a melody but intrinsic to the melodic movement and its amplified unfolding of the melodic that are difficult to capture in notation.[38]

Popley's suggestions for notation were promoted with even greater enthusiasm by Subramania Sastry of Tanjore who going a step further, recommended the use of the English alphabet, which in his view could easily 'differentiate between sharp and flat swaras, the initial names of the swaras being used respectively as symbols denoting them'.[39] Notation, he argued, was the only effective way of preserving musical compositions, which could then be printed in the form of books, and introduced as texts in the academies. Among the specific suggestions that he made on Popley's scheme, was the use of different fonts to indicate the three octaves. He illustrated his point by notating a traditional composition as a guideline to future interventions.[40]

While the importance of notation as a means of preservation and transmission was by and large endorsed as a working principle, the debate did not end there. A section of the Academy's members saw the advocacy of notation, within a modern system of music education, as coterminous with the jettisoning of the traditional system, where the student learnt under an individual teacher and underwent a personalized musical apprenticeship, living with his teacher as part of his family, serving him, and in the process, identifying completely with the lineage that his teacher represented. Learning under such a system with an individual teacher was more in the nature of osmosis; one imbibed the notes and the interpretation of melodies by listening to the master time and again. Vaikuntaram Pandit expressed this dilemma rather succinctly when he wrote in 1932 of the glories of traditional systems that had never petrified into superstitious rules. The strength of the traditional system lay in its flexibility, and as a result, while insisting on certain principles and methods as part of the musical legacy of certain families, there was still provision for creativity and improvisation within the larger framework. In fact, the teacher let go of a student at a certain stage of his training, urging him to be introspective and evoke his own creative style. Pandit, therefore, expressed his reservations about the general tendency towards standardization and institutionalization, which inhibited freedom and spontaneity of expression and struck at the very root of Indian music that had to be saved from becoming a slavish imitation of inferior European models. He deplored the 'modern craze for perpetuation' that was antithetical to the individuality and freedom of classical Indian music.[41]

The majority in the Academy did not subscribe to this position. They were, by and large, committed to the introduction of Indian music as a subject of study in the University of Madras. P. Sambamoorthy, whose reputation as a musicologist and music teacher was by this time well established, expressed his satisfaction that Indian music was on the way to finding its rightful place in the scheme of studies in schools and colleges, and hoped that the day was not far off when music as a subject would be made compulsory for all boys and girls' schools, and appropriate training colleges would be instituted to handle the business of instruction.[42] On his own initiative, he embarked on a systematic project of publishing compositions and teaching material, which drew largely on the earlier models of Subburama Diskitar. In fact, in 1942,[43] when the Academy passed a resolution recognizing the need for an adequate scheme of notation, the committee appointed for the purpose, consisting of P. Sambamoorthy, C.S. Ayyar and Venkatrama Iyer, was specifically instructed to evolve its system on the basis of symbols adopted in the *Sampradaya Pradarsinin* of Diksitar.

The formation of the committee and the brief that it was given had been prefaced by C.S. Ayyar's persuasive advocacy of the Pradarsini, in which he specifically addressed the issue of gamakas and a set of symbols[44] he had evolved. This resolution constituted a definitive step in restructuring the actual transmission of music and in ensuring its preservation in a particular form. The resolution makers were fully cognizant of the distinctive orientation of Indian classical music that lent towards individual improvisation and could not be trapped within rigidly notated absolutes. On the other hand, they were equally concerned with the requirements of modern instructional methods that could facilitate the transmission of music among a wider section of the population and thereby conform to the larger all-India social campaign. It was in the emphasis on educational reconstruction and the place of music within the modern system of education that the Academy's nationalist profile was marked.

In keeping with the agenda of the All India Music Conferences, where the question of music in modern education was raised time and again, the Madras Music Academy expressed its commitment to the cause of musical education in no uncertain terms. Its intervention came at a number of levels. The most important of these related to the setting up of a Teachers Training College to provide for an appropriate faculty for the university where a music department had been introduced in 1931, and also for the Chidamabaram Music College that had been set up under the patronage of Raja Annamalai Chettiar. In January 1931, a subcommittee consisting of important musicians as well as educationists, framed and recommended a scheme for a one-year course in vocal training in the Teachers Training college. The college, thanks to the Academy's efforts, was able to enlist the sustained cooperation of its musician members who also performed to raise funds for the college. Within a short time, the college established its reputation as the premier teaching institution—a fact that the Academy and its publicists emphasized in their attempts to emerge as the sole arbiter of standards.[45] U. Rama Rao, in his 1932 presidential address to the annual music conference of the Academy, commended the efforts of the Teachers Training College while expressing misgivings about the private music schools that had mushroomed in Madras, and granted certificates to students who attended short-term courses. 'This', he said, would

create a caste distinction among trained musicians, there being three kinds of passports for service—one granted by the University after a term of lectures and examinations, another by the Music Academy with a longer and more intensive study, training and examination, and third by institutions in the city with a very limited training and course of instruction.[46]

He appealed to the educational authorities 'to note this and see that inferior training is not permitted and that certificates granted by those schools are not recognized'.[47]

The following years saw successive batches of students graduating both from the Teachers Training College and from the University of Madras. Margaret Cousins remarked on the distinction accorded by the University of Madras to its first woman graduate in music, Kalyani Sundaram. 'When one remembers', she wrote, 'that all music was taught orally and individually, only until about ten years ago, it will be seen that this change to class teaching and the placing of Indian music within the purview of standardized examination is in the nature of a revolution.'[48] The Academy's role in this revolution was fundamental. Its members maintained very close organic connections with the university's music department and, over time with the consolidation of the Academy as the principal arbiter of musical standards, it is easy to see how the connection was institutionalized. The Teachers Training College was increasingly recognized as a model for similar institutions; on 26 December 1933, the Academy adopted a resolution to the effect that it would facilitate the promotion of mofussil centres of model institutions on the lines of and in the methods adopted by the Teachers College for the purpose of giving instruction on Karnatic music.[49] At the same time, the 1933 conference recommended that such institutions should 'follow the syllabus that may from time to time be prescribed by the Experts Committee'.[50]

Articulating an Aesthetic

The creation of standards related, at one level, to the actual methods and tools of teaching and, at another, it was concerned with the articulation of an aesthetic conception more immediately linked with actual performance. If in promoting music as part of the new national system of education the Madras elite deployed the rhetoric of modernization, the creation of a new aesthetic invoked the trope of tradition, especially its spiritual dimensions, and proceeded thereafter to rework it in a manner that suited the somewhat eccentric reflexivity and self-representation of the middle class and the artistic notions it engendered.

P.S. Iyer in the 1930s and C. Subrahmanya Ayyar in the 1940s represented both these aspects of the modernizing programme of developing an appropriate aesthetic for music for performance and pedagogy. P.S. Iyer, who laboured during the 1920s to make music part of an educational curriculum, was emphatic in his assertions about the establishment of proper training schools for professional musicians so that they could be trained to disseminate music scientifically to their students in schools and colleges. In 1919, when the Government of Madras with a view to the introduction of music in schools called for a draft scheme and syllabus and appointed a committee, P.S. Iyer suggested that for proper instruction, 'trained teachers shall be appointed after the teachers themselves have undergone a course of training in a musical school. It will be of no use if professionals are to undertake this task'. For Iyer, modern training centres and handbooks of grammar were indispensable tools for proper dissemination and without which, the art was threatened with irreparable damage.[51]

Subrahmanya Ayyar on the other hand, was more tuned to the actual process of listening to music, which generated its own aesthetics and which was not easily reproducible by mechanical devices. As he said, 'music is neither like the written language of poetry nor like the finished statue in marble to be read or gazed on and enjoyed by anyone at any time. One has first of all, listen to music'. At the same time, Ayyar while developing his views on musical criticism and aesthetics invoked classical texts to point out the traits that musicians and performers had to eschew. These traits were not only related to vocal deficiencies or unimaginative interpretation of melodies, but also applied to mannerisms, facial contortions and mispronunciation. As he observed, 'I wish ardently that the present day vocalists reform and eradicate these ugly features which are very prevalent today'. He also observed that some of them were so naïve that even when Tamil weeklies carried satires and caricatures of their gimmicks or *cheshtai* as these were known, they believed that the photos were a matter of advertisement for their renown in music.[52]

The construction of a new performance aesthetic for classical music was as much the product of individual initiative as it was of a collective adherence to an ethically driven artistic identity. What primarily marked the new aesthetic impressed was the foregrounding of the solo vocalist performer and the relative scaling down of the accompanying ensemble, whose role in musical entertainment had been more enhanced in the context of theatre. The use of multiple percussion and other accompanying instruments was part of a more robust and popular theatre mode that had entered into the domain of classical music and created a controversy. It remained for the Academy to step in, address the issue and here, it followed the earlier reformist opinion widely expressed in the articles that the *Daily Express* had carried in the 1920s. These had identified the practices that corrupted performance of classical music, namely, the excessive use of the percussion instruments and the tendency to execute complicated combination of notes (*swara prastara*) in the three octaves without much heed to melody or to the content in the compositions.

The editorials of the Madras Academy's journal repeated the same kind of arguments. 'The great need of the day,' the 1932 editorial reminded its reading public 'was the maintenance of a high standard of music and appreciation. The craze for mechanization has invaded the realm of music where it is playing great havoc. If vulgarization of the art is to be perceived, an effective organ which will serve as a corrective is necessary'.[53] The editorial reaffirmed the Academy's ideal, which unlike that of some singers, was 'aesthetic' and 'cultural', and not 'sensual'. This necessarily meant that the emphasis of performance had to be on the development of the melodic potential through the compositions of the trinity, who embodied the finest traditions of devotion and music. The next year, the journal carried an article by one of the members of the experts committee, G.V. Narayanaswami Iyer who came up with a sociological explanation for the declining standards and changes in popular taste. The breakdown of the *gurukula* system, the democratization of music in the sense of its appropriation, albeit duly modified, by theatre and subsequently cinema, and the proliferation of summer schools that gave a crash course in some sort of music were all part of a changing social context, where the moral economy of the temple and the court had been replaced by that of the market. This meant that music was no longer a spiritual pursuit but an article of trade, and that both organizers as well as performers had a different relationship with the art form and no qualms in compromising standards. While the former in order to boost ticket sales brought to the stage 'all kinds of monstrous combination of unusual instruments, the aspirant singer with just six weeks training in summer schools was ready to take the stage'.[54]

The editorial scathingly attacked the degeneration in public taste and the impurities that had crept into classical music. In particular, the obsessive fascination for rhythm that had no time for the introspective treatment of melody that was after all the essence of Indian music. Raga, the editorial commented had been dethroned, and tala had usurped the supremacy.

The practice of mathematical swara permutations had frozen up the fountains of creative joy of the emotional spirit. This mechanical attitude of the singer has had its reaction upon public taste. A singer has come to be esteemed less for those exquisite touches of melody that move even non-sentient beings than for the number of swara avrittas with which he can overwhelm the drummer. No more is heard the soft and restful rendering of the great passion mode with graceful glides and long drawn notes, the favoured haunts when the spirit of raga forever dwells. The art of Melody is gone, that of the drum succeeded.[55]

Efforts were accordingly made by the Academy to cultivate public opinion against such practices and articulate an aesthetic that balanced the accompaniment in relation to the musical essay of the solo vocalist. Model concerts[56] demonstrating melodic delineation and the singing of compositions in accordance with what the canonical principles of the Academy were presented. The validity of swara singing[57] was debated, some arguing that this was a relatively new practice as far as performance was concerned, while others argued for its retention in a modified manner. The foregrounding of the solo performer and the relative sidelining of the *pakkavadyam* was an important shift in the aesthetic conception, which was quickly internalized as the standard presentation practice and remains so to this day.[58] Whether this was intended to create a dyad between separate genres of music or whether the dominating presence of percussionists was a reminder of a parallel between different genres of music and that the Academy wanted to distance classical music from these, is not clear. Were the aesthetic reasons for their intervention, according to their own prescriptions, not convincing? What is certain is that the Academy wished to construct a modern format for classical music with an identifiable style that represented a refinement of existing performance practices and worked on a new conception of balance between melody and rhythm, that would by its interpretation of melodies and the authentic rendering of compositions bring out the transformative potential of music in its spiritual and sacral dimensions.

In the articulation of the new aesthetic that emphasized the individual voice, the violin as an accompanying instrument played, according to

Amanda Weidman, a critical role. The travels of the violin from being a common fiddle to that of a classical instrument was complete by the late nineteenth century, when amateur enthusiasts picked up the instrument and appreciated its ability to mimic the human voice. As music shifted to the concert hall, the violin became the perfect accompaniment facilitating what Weidman calls the figuration of the performer's voice.[59] Weidman skillfully demonstrates how the violinist was expected to give the vocalist's sound a greater presence and in the process become critical to canon formation. The violin was undoubtedly, in the case of south Indian classical music, an audible determinant of the new aesthetics, but it is important to remember that the alignment of instrument to voice was not a new idea; the same period saw references to the *nadaswaram pani* as being the most perfect referent.

The working out of the new aesthetic involved the organization of both concert format and repertoire. How an actual concert was to be organized in terms of time, selection of compositions, and presentation became important issues for consideration. The context in which these issues were debated was provided by the need in the late 1930s and 1940s, for a new performing space, for the newly articulated musical canon. The key elements constituting the 'classical' in terms of structure, was the repertoire, a range of compositions that framed melodic movement or raga singing in definitive terms and were set to identifiable rhythmic cycles. These compositions included older forms such as varnams that were recognized as essential exercises for relaxing the voice and preparing the performer for the concert to follow, kirtanas (particularly of the trinity) and love songs such as padams and javalis (traditionally associated with court and temple dancers). There was also the improvisational aspect of classical music, referred to as *manodharma sangitam* that included free and inventive melodic elaboration using either single syllables or small phrases for the purpose.

What the concert format was expected to demonstrate was sound theoretical knowledge within an effective practical performance, the standards for which the Academy was in the process of establishing. The construction of a new performing aesthetic was framed within a limited or truncated duration of concert time—the general opinion being that the duration of the habitual concert was too long.[60] Within this shortened time frame, it remained for the musical fraternity to devise repertoires that would demonstrate both authenticity of a performer, musical lineage, as well as his expertise in rendering musical compositions with full understanding of their underlying theoretical basis.

It was found necessary to accommodate a variety of other genres that the Academy identified as applied music, namely: compositions associated with religious dance and operatic music. Padams and javalis belonged to a category, which until the 1930s was virtually the community property of a hereditary social class of female dancers known as devadasis and their male kin. There was also a growing corpus of nationalist songs and modern devotional poetry associated with theatre, which deployed classical melodies and enjoyed immense popularity. It remained to bring these into the regular concert structure in a manner that enhanced the performing repertoire without undermining its classicist dimension. The Academy was successful while making a distinction between classical and light classical music, in endorsing a composite performing idiom that bore the stamp of refined men and sensibility.

Figure 2: Patrons and Publicists. Published in *Ananda Vikatan*, 6 January 1935. Courtesy: Roja Muthiah Research Library.

The chief architect of the concert format or *kacheri paddhati* was Ariyakudi Ramanuja Iyengar[61] who was early in noting that expansive recitals and relaxed listening for long hours belonged to a past era, and what was needed was to quicken the concert tempo with shorter performances and a balanced selection of compositions. The decision to sing 'miscellaneous' pieces in a variety of languages, he said was not a traditional practice, but a modern innovation that was in keeping with the nationalist temper of his times. On the other hand, the decision to stay with the medium and fast tempo, in marked contrast to the slower movement adopted by musicians in the north, became an important marker of the Karnatik style, the preservation of which was tied up with notions of a distinct cultural expression if not a separate identity. In 1947, Semmangudi Srinivasa Iyer speaking in favour of a shorter duration mentioned that discriminating people were beginning to feel that the average concert was too lengthy for proper assimilation and absorption.[62] Ariyakudi, however, insisted that the kacheri had to incorporate a specific selection of musical compositions like the varnam which helped in voice relaxation and include a variety of both melodies and rhythms, and that alone would keep the torch of Karnatik music alive.[63]

The construction of the dyad between classical and non-classical in the dissemination of the new style and aesthetic, through modern educational institutions and the All India Radio Broadcasting had serious implications for traditional performing communities, whose presence and participation in the new cultural economy of modern India became increasingly tenuous. Simultaneously, in the context of the anti-brahmin political agitation in south India that was largely mediated through language, the very notion of the classical and its upper-class custodianship came under attack. Not surprisingly, the new institutions of power and patronage became contested spaces, as they became agents in the reform process.

Broadcasting Music

To record or not to record remained a difficult question for performers but not for their publicists. From the very beginning, the use of technology to reproduce and consolidate the authentic classical tradition was an idea that found widespread acceptance among the reforming elite. Not only was broadcasting seen as an invaluable instrument in strengthening the taste for classical music, it was also seen as a disciplining institution. As Narayana Menon observed in 1950, 'Broadcasting has given our musicians the quality of precision and economy. The red light in the studio door is a stern disciplinarian. Broadcasting has also given the musicians a clearer sense of proportion and a clearer definition of values that matter in music.'[64] The observation was a telling index of how central broadcasting and its politics became in the consolidation of the classical tradition, more so in the first half of the century than private commercial recordings. The latter was seen as purely dictated by market variables of demand and supply and thus inappropriate for executing the reformist agenda.

Figure 3: The President of the Academy with the office-bearers, the President of the Music Conference 1932 and other *vidvans* assembled therein. Courtesy: *Journal of the Music Academy Madras.*

But not so radio broadcasting, whose agenda worked in close tandem with that of institutions like the Madras Academy and its counterparts elsewhere in the country. The anxiety to present and preserve pure music was evident in the first official report that came out in 1940, which observed that in India, 'the whole art of music has largely fallen into the hands of prostitutes and mirasis and that from this association, has sprung a general feeling that there is something inherently immoral in the music itself'.[65] More importantly, the report went on to state that the situation with regard to Karnatik music was different. To start with, 'there is strictly speaking no Carnatic light music. Carnatic music has preserved a close link with tradition'.[66] What the report presented was not accurate and verifiable ethnographic material, nor an older rhetoric that had gained extensive currency, but proof of the success of the music reform movement in Madras that had been able to use the channels of radio to promote its version of the tradition. For musicians and their middle-class sponsors, radio broadcasting was a desirable channel of patronage, that was capable of assuming custodianship of the tradition in its revived incarnation. The Madras Academy enthusiastically promoted musicians to perform for the All India Radio, thereby hoping to disseminate as widely as what they considered authentic art music.

The Indian Broadcasting Corporation was inaugurated on 23 July 1927. Prior to this, a number of amateur radio associations had enjoyed permission to broadcast on very low power in various parts of India and had been granted a proportion of license fees. In 1926, the idea of a regular service took shape in the form of an agreement between the Government of India and the Indian Broadcasting Corporation, under which a license for the construction of stations at Bombay and Calcutta was granted. In Madras, a club was formed on 31 July 1924 called the Madras Presidency Radio Club with the Governor of Madras as its patron. In its first year, the club purchased a 20-watt transmission, which it used till 1927. When the Government of India stopped giving proportionate license fees to the various radio clubs in consequence of the formation of the Indian Broadcasting Corporation, the club ceased functioning and handed over its transmission to the Madras Corporation, on condition they took up the broadcasting service. In 1929, a broadcasting license was obtained and service began on 1 April 1930.[67] Five years later, the Government of India decided to create a broadcast monopoly as a department of the central government.[68]

The broadcasting of music was not a high priority subject for the British Government in India. However, it assumed the responsibility of creating good taste. Some serious constraints stood in the way of articulating a consistent and coherent approach to programming. As a preliminary report stated,

in Broadcasting, many accepted standards fail. The ear divorced from the eye makes new demands. The infectious enthusiasm of an audience is absent. In the intimacy of the listeners' home, the great singer so popular at music conferences has after all not so good a voice, the orator who so easily sways a crowd becomes a bellowing nuisance, the academician who holds so many degrees is unexpectedly dull and tedious. The honours of broadcasting go only to those who can present their material effectively whether through some happy combination of voice, manner and material or through a flair for devising programmes in a way which captures the listeners though such people are rare and rarity (while it lasts) combined with the immense daily output of broadcasting must produce an average below that of the concert hall, stage or the film. A concert of one hour, a film of three demands months of preparation but broadcasting must somehow manage itself for 365 days and nights every year.[69]

The report clearly identified the eccentricities and ephemeral nature of public taste as a major impediment in designing programmes that were sustainable over a length of time. 'No one opinion is unanimous in matters of taste. Thus the programme maker is in a dilemma, he cannot follow his own convictions and opinions since by doing so, he will impose one man's taste and alienate the majority, yet the method and choice must ultimately be his decision and responsibility'.[70] The programmer was handicapped further by the absence of standard guidelines; he could hardly rely upon letters or fan mail as a barometer while advisory committees, however constituted, disagreed almost as a principle.

Broadcasting music was clearly a tedious proposition, and all the more so because Indian music did not conform to clear standards. The authorities in charge of broadcasting argued that only music duly standardized and reformed could constitute the chief source of entertainment. Implicit in this was the will to endorse the standardized version of classical music as nationalist institutions like the Madras Academy espoused, as well as the decision to restrict broadcasting space to those whose credentials were vouchsafed for by the Academy. From the very beginning, the authorities, depended upon the cooperation of the Madras Academy for ensuring a steady supply of performers and prevailing over prejudices of some professional musicians against singing for the radio.

The annual report of the Madras Broadcasting Corporation for 1931–2 registered the cooperation it had received from the Madras Academy on these counts. It emphasized the educational potential of radio broadcasting and maintained that 'properly directed', radio music could have nothing but 'beneficial effects both in the art and in the artist' and that its power could always be used 'for the gains of the public and the musician'.[71] In fact, from 1931, the Academy, in accordance with its intentions of showcasing model performances to consolidate the new aesthetics in classical music, supplied information on a regular basis to the radio authorities about front ranking musicians for the Sunday performances.[72] The experts committee that met in the annual music conference emphasizing the importance of such relays; noted that it was useful to get experts to share their knowledge with a large audience by singing in the radio.[73] The partnership worked well; for the broadcasting authorities, there was no doubt that the Academy's help had been instrumental in improving the standard of music.[74]

For the Academy, the radio was an indispensable vehicle for transmission of the correct version of traditional music. At the same time, it held out prospects of a public space for middle-class performers. By encouraging young and aspiring musicians, men and women to sing for the radio, the Academy simultaneously deployed the medium for the presentation of classical music. Their agenda had necessarily to compete with popular demand, and it remained for the Academy and the broadcasting authorities to evolve a balanced approach to the problem. In 1940, for instance, commenting on the progress of broadcasting in India, the programme authorities admitted that it was difficult to adopt a standard and that the pressures of public opinion were exceedingly diverse and only a part of the public would 'demand that all prostitutes and mirasis should be excluded from the microphone and in fact that the employment of singers should be deregulated by their morals'.[75]

This comment was particularly relevant in the case of northern India, where the practice of some musical genres were specialized by courtesan communities, but who were barred from participating in the music reform movement. In the case of south India, the Academy did not explicitly institute pogroms against performing communities like the devadasis, who had long been associated with the performing arts or deny their cultural capital. By the first decades of the twentieth century, the community had already languished and was subsequently compelled to respond to the changing social and economic situation in south India in the context of the anti-nautch agitation that had gained momentum in the 1930s and 1940s. The Academy attempted to 'domesticate' the performers and their art—women performers were urged to come forward and lead respectable married lives and in association with the mainstream. Exceptional artists like Jayammal and Balasarasvati were invited to present their performances in the annual conferences of the Academy but these inclusions were insufficient to expand the parameters of the newly articulated classical canon. While senior artists like Veena Dhanammal and Nayana Pillai, two of the most outstanding artists and teachers of the decade refused to record for either private companies or the radio,[76] others like Salem Papa, Bangalore Thayi, the Enadi sisters, and Bangalore Nagaratnam responded more enthusiastically to commercial recordings than the radio.[77]

After independence, the radio became even more of a disciplinarian and the self-appointed custodian of classical music while the traditional performing community had meanwhile, all but disappeared. In 1954, B.V. Keskar, the Union Minister for Information and Broadcasting emphasized the services of the Madras Academy in canonizing develop- ments in the music world in the 'right direction', in providing a platform of thought in matters musical and rued that something similar had not occurred in Hindustani music.[78]

Keskar's comment, even if it reinforced stereotypes of southern exceptionalism, was a legitimate testimony to the success of the Academy in having consolidated the classical tradition within the emerging spaces of modern communication and education. Retrieving a past from a corpus of musical practice that had been dispersed in the nineteenth century and imagining around it a present and framing the composite within the emerging disciplines of history and musicology, the Academy had been able to develop both a compelling nationalist narrative of the arts and an aesthetic conception with powerful hegemonic claims. The inner logic of the new aesthetics, necessarily marginalized those performing communities whose social identity and functions were no longer compatible with the sensibilities of middle-class actors and social engineers, who through a network of nationalist institutions such as the Madras Academy in music and Kalakshetra in dance, effectively constructed the 'classical' canon and defended it in the successive decades.

NOTES

1. *JMAM*, vol. I, no. 1, Madras, 1930, pp. 1–2.
2. Ibid.
3. *JMAM*, vol. II, no. 1, Madras, 1931, pp. 72ff. Sir Muthiah Bhagavatar's address in Tamil.
4. *JMAM*, vol. III, nos 1 and 2, Madras, 1932, pp. 74–5.
5. See Muthiah Bhagavatar's concluding speech at the Madras Music Conference of 1931. *JMAM*, vol. III, nos 2 and 3, Madras, 1932, p. 147.
6. *JMAM*, vol. III, nos 3 and 4, Madras, 1932. See editorial, pp. 1–2.
7. *JMAM*, vol. I, no. 1, Madras, 1930. The editorial committee consisted of T.V. Subba Rao, Tiger Varadachariar, W. Doraiswami Iyengar, T.L. Venkatrama Iyer, P. Sambamoorthy, and E. Krishna Iyer.
8. *JMAM*, vol. III, nos 2 and 3, Madras, 1932, pp. 143ff.
9. Hulugur Krishnacharya, 'Introduction to the Study of Bharatiya Sangita Shastra', *JMAM*, vol. I, no. 3, Madras, 1930, pp. 10–12.
10. Somarao Tatti, 'History of Karnatak Music', *JMAM*, vol. I, no. 1, 1930, pp. 2–6. P.S. Sundaram Iyer, 'Music of South India and Govinda Diksitar', vol. I, no.1, 1930, pp. 55–6ff. Pandit S. Subramanya Sastri, 'Some Anomalies of South Indian music', vol. I, no. 2, 1930, pp. 101ff. and 'Venkatamakhin and his Twelve Notes', *JMAM*, vol. II, no. 1, 1931, G.V. Narayanaswamy Aiyer, 'South Indian Music: Past and Present', *JMAM*, vol. I, no. 2, 1930, pp. 244ff and 'The Soul of South Indian Music', *JMAM*, vol. II, no. 1, 1931, pp. 16–19ff.

11. See the Report on the Music Conference of 1932 (30.12.32) in *JMAM*, vol. IV, no. 4, 1933, pp. 129–31ff.
12. Muthiah Bhagavatar's address, *JMAM*, vol. II, no. 1, 1931, pp. 72ff.
13. N.S. Ramachandran, 'Melakarta Ragas in Practice', *JMAM*, vol. III, nos 1 and 2, 1932, pp. 8–9ff.
14. See Muthiah Bhagavatar's address. *JMAM*, vol. II, no. 1, 1931, p. 72.
15. The proceedings of the Madras Music Conference of 1932 (reported in the 1933 issue) are particularly revealing. These not merely illustrate the manner in which the Academy conducted its business but also reflect the importance it attached to the question of standardization of melodies, modes and compositions. Those assembled were familiar with the practice of music and showed no hesitation in expressing their views freely and frankly. See *JMAM*, vol. IV, no. 4, 1933, pp. 104–5ff, 106–49.
16. P.S. Sundaram Iyer, 'Music of South India and Govinda Diksitar', *JMAM*, vol. I, no. 1, 1930, pp. 53–6ff.
17. Hulugur Krishnachar,'Introduction to the Study of Bharatiya Sangita Shastra', *JMAM*, vol. I, no. 1, 1930, pp. 8–25.
18. Tiger Varadachariar, 'A Note on Hindola and Allied Ragas', *JMAM*, vol. I, no. 3, 1930, pp. 235–6.
19. *JMAM*, vol. III, nos 1 and 2, 1932, pp. 72–4ff. Proceedings of the 1931 Music Conference.
20. Hulugur Krishnachar, 'The Ragas (Lakshya) and their features (Lakshana) before and after Tyagaraja's Time', *JMAM*, vol. XIX, 1948, pp. 114–47.
21. K.V. Ramachandran, 'Carnatic Ragas and the Textual Tradition', *JMAM*, vol. XXI, no. 1, 1950, pp. 99–104ff. Also see p. 107 for his essay on 'Apurva Ragas of Tyagaraja's Songs'.
22. Most of the disagreement was related to the usage of certain notes in melodies— and whether these were permissible by convention and how important it was to consider practical demonstrations before coming to a formulaic convention. As T. Sabesa Iyer (a practicing musician and attached to the Tyagaraja lineage) put it, 'If we are going to solve problems of music on the strength of books and speeches, it is not possible to come to any correct conclusion. We must hear these usages practically sung by musicians in the course of an alapana or pallavi and then we can arrive at a reasonable decision', p. 104. The experts committee generally put the matter to a majority vote. See *JMAM*, vol. IV, 4, 1933, pp. 104–5ff, 106–49. However, R. Ranga Ramanuja Ayyangar had a different take on the proceedings of the experts committee and referred to vote canvassing. In his view, 'On the whole, the set up smacked of politics and bureaucracy rather than dedication to values', See *Musings of a Musician*, Bombay, 1977, pp. 28–9.
23. William Jackson, *Tyagaraja and the Renewal of Tradition*, pp. 130.
24. V.V. Narasimhachariar, 'On the Nomenclature of the 72 Mela Ragas', *JMAM*, vol. III, nos 3 and 4, 1932, pp. 167ff.
25. V. Raghavan, 'Two Manuscripts of Tyagaraja's Songs', *JMAM*, vol. XVIII, nos 1–4, 1947, pp. 133–44.
26. P. Sambamoorthy, 'The Wallajapet Manuscripts', *JMAM*, vol. XIV, nos 1–4, 1943, pp. 86–9ff.
27. K.V. Ramachandran, 'Carnatic Ragas and the Textual Tradition', and 'Apurva Ragas of Tyagaraja's Songs'.

28. Chinnaswami Mudaliar, *Oriental Music in European Notation* (first published 1893), Cosmo, Delhi, Reprint, 1982 (ed.) Gowri Kuppuswamy and M. Hariharan. See Introduction.

29. S. Ramanathan, 'The Indian Sa Ri Ga Ma Notation', *JMAM*, vol. XXXII, nos 1–4 pp. 82–7.

30. *Selections from the Mysore Palace Records*, vol. I, Mysore, 1993, p. 64. See letter from Laxman Rao Heblikar dated 17 June 1915 to his Highness asking him to send over Bidaram Krisnappa for the district collector Mr Clements benefit. Clements wished to familiarize himself with the principal ragas. *Government of Karnataka Selections from the Records of the Mysore Palace*, vol. I *Musicians, Actors and Artists*. Divisional Archive Office, Mysore, 1993.

31. *Report of the Third All India Music Conference*, Benaras, 1920, pp. 25–6ff.

32. Ibid., p. 26.

33. Ibid. The proposals were not well received by many of the delegates present. Some of them were of the opinion that western notation was by no means perfect to express the delicate graces of Indian music, others felt that there was sufficient material in Sanskrit texts which could form the basis of a simple notation system and yet others who claimed that no notation system could satisfy the requirements of professional singers.

34. There was a common Indian misconception about western notation, one shared no doubt by many not very musical Englishmen that it represented a set of modern mechanized instructions rather than the description of a musical idea open to interpretation by educated and artistically puissant musicians, like the script of a play in which conventions and their inversions are more or less understood by large numbers of patrons and players. It must have been a perplexing question and the debates around notation reflect this confusion.

35. H.A. Popley, 'Plea for an All India System of Notation and Classification for Indian Music', *JMAM*, vol. I, no. 2, 1930, pp. 91–8.

36. Ibid., pp. 92–3.

37. Gamakas are contours and expressive details given to a note (swara) beyond its mere pitch definition. These can be subtle or obvious, long and short sliding approaches from various directions, undulations, note clusters rapidly produced about the salient notes and include inflexions that touch frequencies other than the apparently specified notes.

38. Ibid.

39. S. Subramanya Sastri, 'A Plea for a Rational System of Simplified Notation', *JMAM*, vol. II, no. 4, 1930, pp. 192–4.

40. Ibid., pp. 192–8.

41. 'Indian Music' by Vaikuntrama Pandit, *JMAM*, vol. III, nos 3 and 4, 1932, pp. 89–92.

42. *JMAM*, vol. III, nos 1–2, 1932, p. 228ff. For history of Teachers Training College in Madras. Also see report of the Madras Music Conference of 1932 in the 1933 issue. Vol. IV, no. 4, p. 92 for Tiger Varadachariar's address. His address expressed some of his misgivings about modern teaching methods for music.

43. *JMAM*, vol. XIV, Parts I–IV, 1943, p. 20ff.

44. Ibid.

45. *JMAM*, vol. III, nos 3 and 4, 1932, pp. 228ff. 'History of Teachers Training College'.

46. For U. Rama Rao's address, see *JMAM*, vol. IV, nos 1–4, 1933, p. 87.

47. Ibid.
48. Margaret Cousins, *Music of the Orient and Occident*, Madras, 1935, pp. 179–80.
49. *JMAM*, vol. V, nos 1–4, 1934, pp. 106–7.
50. Ibid.
51. P.S. Iyer, *Articles on Carnatic Music*. Printed at the Kamala Press, Tirupapuliyur, 1937, pp. 157–58.
52. *An Artist's Miscellany on Society, Religion and Music* by Kumara guru C. Subrahmanya Ayyar. Published by R. Venkateshwar & Co., Madras, 1946, pp. 94–5. Both Iyer and Ayyar worked with the Madras Academy which attempted to balance the requirements of pedagogy with the new performing aesthetic, which had to validate traditional interpretations of music while presenting it within a new format.
53. G.V. Narayanaswamy Iyer, 'The Mechanization of South Indian Music', *JMAM*, vol. IV, nos 1–4, 1933, pp. 134ff.
54. *JMAM*, vol. IV, nos 1–4, 1933, See Editorial titled 'Decline of Taste'.
55. The Madras Music Conference of 1931 took up this issue. On the sixth day of the Conference (30 December 1931), one of its members Satyamurti mentioned that the Academy had been requesting vidwans to give model performances in front of larger audiences. He also used the occasion to mention that the experts committee members were keen on scaling down the accompaniments or *pakka vadyam*. See *JMAM*, vol. III, nos 1–2, 1932.
56. *JMAM*, vol. V, nos 1–4, 1934, pp. 105ff. Proceedings of the 1933 Music Conference.
57. One has to recall a recent interview that the late Semmangudi Srinivasa Iyer gave about his experiences and his perception of aesthetics. 'Mridangam', he said, 'should merely keep the beat like the Hindustani tabla,' and though he encouraged violinists with bhesh and shabhash, he disliked long essays by them.
58. Amanda Weidman, *In the Kingdom of the Voice* (forthcoming).
59. A resolution was passed by the Madras Music Conference on 29 December 1933 to the following effect: 'In the interests of the development of music it is necessary that no musical performance including Kalakshepams exceed three hours in duration'. See *JMAM*, vol. V, nos 1–4, 1934, pp. 105–6ff.
60. For the innovations introduced by Ariyakudi in the concert format, see Ranga Ramanuja Ayyangar, *Musings of a Musician*, pp. 12, 21–2. Also see V.V. Sadagopan, 'Ariyakudi Ramanuja Iyengar', *Sangeet Natak*, vols 3–6, 1966–7 in vol. 3, pp. 63–79.
61. Presidential Address by Semmangudi Srinivasa Iyer and the Opening Address of the XXI Music Conference of 23 December 1947. See *JMAM*, vol. XIV, no. 1, 1948, pp. 3–10.
62. 'The Concert Tradition' by Ariyakudi T. Ramanuja Iyengar, *Sri Ariyakudi Ramanuja Iyengar Commemoration Volume*. Sri Ariyakudi Ramanuja Iyengar Centenary Commemoration Society, Madras, 1990, pp. 13–14.
63. Quoted in David Lelyveld, 'Upon the Subdominant Administering Music on All India Radio', in Carol A. Breckenridge (ed.) *Consuming Modernity Public Culture in Contemporary India*, Oxford University Press, New Delhi, 1996, p. 53.
64. Broadcasting in India P&J 4348, Report on the Progress of Broadcasting up to 31 March 1939, pp. 21ff.
65. Ibid.
66. *JMAM*, vol. IV, 1933, pp. 164–5ff, p. 187.
67. David Lelyveld, 'Upon the Subdominant', p. 52.

68. P&J 4348, Report on Broadcasting in India, See section on programming.
69. Ibid.
70. Annual report of the Madras Corporation Broadcasting Service of 1932–3, *JMAM*, vol. IV, 1933, p. 187.
71. *JMAM*, vol. II, no. 4, 1931, p. 248ff.
72. *JMAM*, vol. III, nos 1–2, 1932. See Satyamurti's comment, p. 74.
73. The Madras Broadcasting Service Annual Report for 1932–3 mentioned, 'It will be noticed that the standard of music has considerably improved through the kind cooperation of the Madras Music Academy who have specifically requested their experts to help us in the selection of artists. We have also to thank the Madras Music Academy for having helped us overcome the prejudice some of the professional musicians had against singing in the radio.' *JMAM*, vol. IV, nos 1–4, 1933, p. 188.
74. Ibid.
75. L/P and J/8/117 Collection 104, A Government of India's Reports on Development of Broadcasting in India 1940, See (P&JB406) No. F/2/6/40 July 15, 1941. Also see (P&JB406) Broadcasting in India upto March 1939, pp. 21–2.
76. Indira Menon, *The Madras Quartet. Women in Karnatak Music*, Roli Books, New Delhi, 1999, pp. 78–9.
77. Ibid., pp. 66–74.
78. B.V. Keskar's opening Address to the Madras Music Conference, *JMAM*, vol. XXV, Parts 1–4, 1954, pp. 5–6.

On the Margins of the Classical
LAW, SOCIAL REFORM, AND THE DEVADASIS IN THE MADRAS PRESIDENCY

Nineteenth century social reform in south India was fixed firmly on the body of the devadasi who became the site of multiple definitions, imaginings, and contestations. Viewed as both the bearer of artistic skill and tradition, and as the purveyor of immorality and dissolution, deified as the servant of god who never bore the stigma of widowhood and, at the same time, reviled as the common whore whose powers of seduction snared the misguided householder,[1] the devadasi became the principle site for the debate between tradition and reform. If educated native opinion condemned the practice of dedication of young girls to temples as criminal, and the devadasis as 'depraved in manners and dissolute in morals',[2] there was also a tacit, even unconscious endorsement of the devadasi as the signifier of auspicious energy and grace.[3] Added to this was the legitimately and widely shared impression that the devadasi community was especially proficient in the arts. Squaring up these apparently irreconcilable attributes and attitudes proved to be a complicated process, the strains of which surfaced in course of the late nineteenth century social reform movement and the cultural project spearheaded by the Madras elites.

While the social morality of an important section of nationalist opinion informing the nineteenth century programme of social reform related to temperance and the anti-nautch campaign, saw the devadasi as a prostitute adopting extreme measures to preserve her languishing resources, there was a countervailing tendency to see her as the embodiment of a more complex idea that had informed the earlier moral economy. Implicit in the characterization of the devadasi as a *nityasumangali*,[4] one who never had to undergo the shame and opprobrium of widowhood was a celebration of old traditions and myths. This convention saw the devadasi as a legitimate custodian of traditional religion and of artistic skills and graces, who was permitted to express her sexuality in a space that was denied to the wife of the householder. To the socially responsible modern subject, such a construction was unsupportable and it came under attack from the social reform movement that deployed colonial legislation and reformist propaganda to redefine the devadasi. At the same time, the nationalist cultural project of the Madras elite to reclaim and define an appropriate artistic heritage for the emerging nation, directly impinged on traditional networks of patronage, skills and transmission, and detached traditional communities of performers from their context as well as from their art. Law, social reform, and the cultural project worked in unison from the late nineteenth century to create new standards of morality, new idioms of cultural expression and standards of aesthetics and performative practices. The combination was potent and served to dislodge the devadasi from the stage and push her into the wings as a relic to be retrieved by a sensitive artist or a diehard researcher with his or her own specific agenda.

Historical Roots of the Devadasis

The reconstruction of the devadasis on the basis of textual and epigraphic sources, European as well as indigenous, has tended to emphasize their location within the temple as part of a long-standing ritual tradition, their access to a range of artistic skills, notably music and dance and their proximity to political authority either the ruler or a local potentate or even a commercial magnate of some importance. Both their ritual status within the temple as well as their connections with notables made the devadasis public women, a feature that surprised and shocked European observers in the eighteenth century. Abbe Dubois, the French bishop who visited India in the eighteenth century, was particularly dismissive in his judgment but ironically came up with a description that was intuitively accurate in locating the devadasis' historical roots in a complex matrix of cultural values and symbols. Describing a religious procession in which the devadasis figured prominently, Dubois observed:

The procession advances slowly. From time to time, a halt is made, during which time, a most frightful uproar of shouts and cries and whistling is kept up.

The courtesans who are present in great numbers in these solemn occasions perform obscene dances, while as long as the procession continues, the drums, trumpets and all sorts of musical instruments give forth their discordant sounds. On one side, sham combatants armed with naked sabers are seen fencing with one another, on one side, one sees dancing in groups and beating time with small sticks, and somewhere else, people are wrestling. Those who have nothing to do shriek and shout so that the thunder of the great Indra striking the giants would not be heard by them. As for myself, I never see a Hindu procession without being reminded of a picture of hell.[5]

What is striking about this description is not so much the obvious fact that Dubois was a prudish missionary whose sensibilities were easily offended, as the centrality of performing women in a ritual that was redolent with symbolic connections. In the case of the southern procession that Dubois witnessed, the symbols used, the sequence of words and acts expressed in what one might call in Stanley Tambiah's words, 'multiple media',[6] formed part of an older tradition of performing activity that invoked symbols, sounds and images to ward off evil, and ensure the strength and vitality of the ruler and his realm. Thus the French missionary's observations intuitively placed the devadasi procession within an older context of bardic performance and courtesan culture; an interface that was particularly complex in the Tamil country.

Saskia Kersenboom Story's study of the devadasi tradition brilliantly captures the emerging cultural landscape of early Tamil society and polity, which accommodated a central role for bardic activity and women performers—whose presence was seen as critical in supporting the life essence of the king.[7] According to her, the virali and *pattini* (bards) who find mention in classical Sangam poetry (100 BC–600 AD) were the earliest prototype of the devadasi, whose incantations had a magical power with the potential to empower the king. The bardic tradition waned in the succeeding centuries but did not entirely die out. On the other hand, in the period of settled politics associated with the establishment of the political power of the Pallavas in the seventh century AD, a synthesis between bardic Tamil culture and Brahmanical traditions found expression in the coalescence of a ritual performing community within the temple precincts. As this amalgamation of the Tamil and Brahmanical traditions evolved in the eighth and the ninth centuries, the status and persona of the ritual woman was reconstituted and she became part bard, part courtesan, and part ritual servant in the temple.

The multifaceted character of the devadasi was reinforced in the period of Chola rule (AD 850–1279), the high noon of Tamil political expansion, when the temple emerged in this period as one of the principal sites of political articulation. Extensive grants to temples and the main-tenance of a huge temple hierarchy became markers of political status, and resulted in the accretion of new forms of property rights validated and legitimized by the state. Women or dancing girls wedded to the deity—literally servants of god—constituted an important part of the establishment and enjoyed not only ritual status for their indispensability to temple worship, but also acquired material wealth and a hereditary claim to property. An inscription of AD 1004 reveals that about 400 dancing girls were attached to the Brahadiswaram temple at Tanjore, lived in free quarters, and were allowed to enjoy tax-free land out of the endowments.[8]

In addition to the impressive corps of dancing girls in temples, there were court dancers attached exclusively to courts. However, royal courtesans enjoyed a special relation with the temple as principal donors and patrons, a connection that went some way in keeping the devadasi category fluid and in enlarging the artistic repertoire of the community as it congealed into a definitive performative cum ritual role. Under the rule of the Vijayanagar kings, and their successors, the Nayakas, artistic developments attained new heights while the distinction between temple dancers and court dancers was maintained.[9] An extraordinary richness of artistic developments in this period particularly in the sphere of music and dance necessarily enlarged the repertoire of the devadasis, or at least of those who were attached to temples of status and distinction. Ritual songs common to the entire community were combined with sophisticated forms derived from the culture of the court.

While, the ritual location of the devadasi was connected with the idea of her power as a medium in warding off malign influences—an idea that persisted right through the eighteenth and nineteenth centuries, when their ritual services continued to be solicited even though their economic base had been considerably reduced—the artistic inheritance and temperament of the community continued to respond to new changes coming in the wake of early colonial rule. On the one hand, the community developed a genre of songs associated with the cycle of quotidian worship in the temples and with social events like weddings and childbirth, and on the other, the more artistic among them specialized in the rendering of padams and javalis that accompanied dance and drama. From nineteenth century accounts, it appears that some families had emerged as custodians of particular artistic styles and established in due course lineages of transmission.[10]

The visibility of the devadasis in the eighteenth and nineteenth centuries underscored their continuing relevance to the moral economy of early colonial India, even as it generated tensions and contradictions that affected the organization and status of the community. How the community was reconstituted in terms of caste and profession, how skills were transmitted within the community, and how it evolved identity markers in the context of the colonial state's interventions are the questions that merit attention. How did the colonial state reinforce, modify, or erase, as the case may be, the existing definitions and perceptions of the community?

Devadasis: Caste or Profession?

The term devadasi literally means servant of god. As such, it entered the domain of European classification of south Indian temple dancing girls from about the eighteenth century, when observers attempted to describe and define women attached to temples and thereby to construct a specific caste category. Subsequently, the British colonial state and the Indian elite applied the term to all females throughout India who were married to a deity or symbol of the deity. Francis Buchanan in his journey from Madras through Mysore, Canara, and Malabar (1800) referred to dancing women and their musicians forming a distinct caste, having broken away from the larger weaving caste of Kaikolars.[11] Membership of the community of dancers attached to temples, however, was not determined by birth alone, and members of the caste could and did enlarge their numbers by the purchase and donations of female children. Buchanan referred to the fact that the male members of the community, the *nattuvans* could and did purchase 'handsome girls of any caste whatever that he can procure'.[12] Here, Buchanan was reflecting on an established caste practice that involved donating female children to temples on recovering from illness or relief from other misfortune. Once inducted into the group, the children were taught to sing, play an instrument and dance, and thereafter become eligible for temple service and the emoluments that came with it. The emphasis on artistic education was important in investing the community with a clear identity marker, and gave rise to the idea that being a devadasi was in fact a way of life. Equally conspicuous was the fact that the devadasi never entered into a marriage bond and was free to maintain independent sexual relations. Buchanan mentions in this connection that most of the patrons happened to be high-caste brahmins. This was seen as aberrant sexual freedom on the part of the devadasi by European observers who were confounded and tended to describe them inevitably as prostitutes. Dubois, the French missionary came up with the most severe indictment. 'And in fact they are bound by their profession to grant favours to anybody demanding them in return for ready money.'[13] Subsequently, colonial writers followed in this vein and categorized devadasis as prostitutes, scarcely going beyond the idea of the stylized concubinage relationship these women entered into with upper-caste males.

The twin notions of dedication to temples and the sanction to liaise sexually outside the confines of marriage were built into the developing ethnographic discourse; by 1871, the preliminary census report of Madras town and presidency described dancing girls—the *dasis, bhogams* as a prostitute class, who were to be found 'in every large town and village, where there are temple endowments'.[14] The report disapproved strongly of the traffic in young girls

avowedly with the object of training them as prostitutes for the use of a particular class or community and that Hindu parents should be permitted to devote their daughters of tender years to the services of the temples or in plain language to prostitution is not a creditable state of things either to the Government or the people concerned.

Two decades later, the 1891 census continued to refer to dasis and bogams as singers and dancers attached to temples and functioning as professional prostitutes.[15] In 1892, Fred Fawcett in a paper published in the *Journal of the Anthropological Society of Bombay* took a more informed view when he described the dedication of *basavis* in Karnataka and mentioned that in most places, basavis were not considered inferior to married women and that their children were considered legitimate. What informed the dedication of basavis was the powerful appeal of the idea of eternal wifehood—nityasumangali—the guaranteed route to women's salvation since as the wife of god, she could never be widowed.[16]

Edgar Thurston and K. Rangachari described at length the artistic profile of the community, when they put together the ethnographic study of castes and tribes in southern India and posited the notion of the community having coalesced into a specific caste by the eighteenth century. They had their own laws of inheritance, customs and rules of etiquette, and panchayats to oversee their functions. A critical component in the constitution of the community was their expertise in the performing arts. According to Thurston, most of the devadasis were recruited from Vellala and Kaikola castes and subsequently entered a regimen of professional training in music, dancing, and other related arts of entertainment. Music and dance were taught to them by male members of the caste, the nattuvans who functioned as accompanists in the temple orchestra—the chinna melam. Nattuvans married within the community and even affixed to their names titles such as Pillai and Mudali, the most common titles of the Vellala and Kaikola caste.[17] Although devadasis themselves did not technically undertake the business of instruction, it would appear that there was some movement in the exchange of skills and repertoire between professional male musicians and individual devadasis attached either to temples or to individual courts. This was certainly true in the late nineteenth and twentieth centuries, when a number of women singers and performers migrated to centres like Madras[18] and Mysore, and interacted with a number of male artists. Their reputation as custodians of artistic knowledge was universally recognized. Thurston referred to the point time and again, that the dancing girls and their allies the *melakkarans* 'are practically the sole repository of Indian music, the system of which is probably one of the oldest in the world'.[19]

If the idea of the eternal wifehood was the single most important determinant in the construction of the devadasi's social and ritual identity, the access to artistic skills was what gave her and her community a set of coordinates to organize what Amrit Srinivasan calls a devadasi way of life, a *vritti*, or *murai* and not so much a jati.[20] Though the office of the devadasi was hereditary, it did not confer the right to work without adequate qualification. The artistic capacity of the devadasis gave her the respect of society that was essential for her livelihood not to speak of her self-esteem. Without her art, as Saskia Kersenboom Story argues, she was always vulnerable and liable to 'sink back into the level of a mere nityasumangali with or without legislation that criminalized the institution'.[21]

The Community in Transition

The break up of indigenous polities in south India in the first half of the nineteenth century and the gradual dissipation of the Tanjore principality, divested traditional communities like the devadasis of their immediate social context, and materially affected their economic status. The temple and the court ceased to provide them with the larger ceremonial setting and access to material support. Their ritual status and social accomplishments, however, enabled some of them to switch over to individual patrons, a move that was still possible in the mid-nineteenth century. In fact, even in the last decades of the eighteenth century, substantial numbers of dancing girls seem to have migrated to the new city of Madras, where they were attached to temples and city notables.[22] Their access to education and their status as public women had, in an earlier period, enabled them to liaise effectively with officials. Buchanan, for example, referred to their role as cultural ambassadors;

They must also receive every person traveling on account of government, meet him at some distance from the town and conduct him to his quarters with music and dancing. In ordinary sets they are quite common, but under the Company's government, those attached to temples of extraordinary sanctity are reserved entirely for the use of native officers, who were all Brahmans, and who would turn out from the set any girl that profaned herself by communication persons of low cast, or of no cast at all such as Christians or Mussulmans. Indeed, almost every one of these girls that is tolerably slightly is taken by some officer of revenue for his own special use and is seldom permitted to go to the temple, except in his presence. The women very much regret their loss, as the Mussulmans paid liberally.[23]

Devadasis were asked to perform in marriage ceremonies and even in state processions where the presence of the melam was an integral part of the social honours or mariyadai that the potentate sought after. This was an entrenched practice and part of kingship and persisted right through the nineteenth century. Pamela Price in her work on the Marava state of Ramnad in the nineteenth century points out, that ritual performances like *Navratri* celebrations with sword fighters, performers, musicians, and dancers were critical as visual statements of variable honour and status. In Ramnad, devadasis also enjoyed proximity to political power and some of them could make substantial claims especially during succession disputes.[24] In 1830, for instance, a complicated situation arose when on the death of Raja Ramaswami Setupati, his wife Parvatavardhini faced the claims of Kunjara, a wife of her father-in-law and whose grandson was put forward as a claimant to the throne. Parvatavardhini's lawyers argued that Kunjara was but a concubine and that her mother was the daughter of a devadasi, who in theory could not marry and produce legitimate offspring. This logic appealed to British officialdom, in whose eyes, the daughter of a devadasi could not be a proper wife for a zamindar. The ultimate fallout of this testimony was the banishment of devadasis from Ramnad palace at the end of the nineteenth century, a period when law and social reform combined to bring the community under greater scrutiny.[25]

The emergence of Madras as an important metropolitan centre encouraged the movement of professional musicians and dancers into the new city. The English East India Company Records of Madras speak of certain areas where dancing girls had taken up residence—the Kachali pagoda street for instance, built sometime in 1725 and adjacent to the Company's old garden, had been assigned to dancing girls.[26] The eighteenth-century Sanskrit text, *Sarvadevavilasa* waxed eloquent about the courtesans and their patrons.[27] In the succeeding decades, the movement of women performers into the city continued, George Town becoming the nucleus of their settlement. The legendary Veena Dhanammal's mother, Kamakshi Ammal migrated to Madras where she found a patron in Krishnaswami Mudaliar.[28] There were others like Coimbatore Thayi, the Enadi sisters, and Bangalore Nagaratnam who established their artistic credentials as they negotiated the changes that came in the wake of social relocation. This assumed several forms. Acquiring a patron was one. The main patrons were upper-caste men.[29] Literary representations of the devadasis in the twentieth century tended to be harsh as they dwelt on the theme of the dasi's snares and the ways in which she seduced young brahmin men—the Madras minors[30] and extracted all that she could from them. An alternative trope was the reclamation of the dasi women either by marriage or by devotion. Referring to a very successful dramatic production in Telugu in the 1930s entitled *Vipranarayanan* which spoke of the love passion of the dasi Devadevi for the Alwar guru Vipranarayanan and her subsequent transformation as the ultimate devotee, the critic Kalki Krishnamurti elaborated on the histrionic talents of the artistes who enabled the audience to suspend moral judgments on either the passion of Devadevi or social reform issues.[31]

Modern education was another resource, but this was not an unequivocal choice—the reasons being both the ambiguity if not hostility of middle-class educated elite to the idea of allowing their women to share the school space with the community as well as the community's appraisal of modern education that left them little time to focus on their traditional skills.[32] The community also appears to have organized themselves into joint families, the control of which rested with the dancing women themselves, and not with the other members of the household.[33] Those not specifically attached to temples provided entertainment in official functions as well as social events until the ban on the nautch closed this source of livelihood.

The social relocation of the devadasis in Madras and elsewhere in southern India was not an easy process. To the material pressure deriving from an erosion of the older moral economy that resulted in a shrinking patronage for temple-based activity and ritual, were added the pressures of western educated opinion and an aggressively reformist judiciary. Both these developments targeted the devadasi community, redefined it, and in the process, set the stage for a reconstitution of the art form that was associated with it. Shorn of its ritual importance and saddled with a new legal definition, the community had little room for manoeuvre with the result that, barring a few exceptions, an entire repertoire of artistic expression was subordinated to the compulsions of the 'classical' project as conceptualized by the Madras elite.

The politics of reform in the mid-nineteenth century did not augur well for the community. Sita Anantha Raman's work on female education in the Tamil districts draws attention to the resistance of high-caste Hindus to the inclusion of devadasi children into the new educational system being envisaged by the colonial authorities. In 1868, the colonial government gave in to the pressure, exerted by the colonial elites, and agreed that the newly proposed school in Madras would be open to girls of all castes but drew the line to include only 'those of a respectable social station'.[34] The debate resurfaced in the 1870s. In 1877, the government withdrew its ruling against the devadasis by allowing them into local board schools. Almost immediately, there were loud cries of protest from both officials like W. Robinson, who pointed out that educated Indian opinion would never endorse this move and that their fear about their children becoming corrupted by children of the dancing girls class, was not entirely absurd and by no means unreasonable.[35]

By the end of the century, the community, which was constantly being subject to a process of social and legal reappraisal, was no longer in a position to relocate themselves within the newly emerging modern spaces of education and empowerment. Even the more established artists among the community—who were known for their skills and expertise, the family of Veena Dhanammal for example—saw only a limited value in modern education.[36] Those who did not pursue a career in the arts were even less inclined to consider the benefits of modern education. Those who were able to acquire a legal husband remained locked in traditional notions of family and religion. For example, Muthulakshmi Reddy, the veteran reformer, who herself came from a devadasi background had this to say of her mother, Chandrammal:

My mother though pious, religious and loyal to my father was always telling him that my education should be stopped and that I should be married. She would often weep that I was not married and sometimes openly quarrelled with my father on that account. My mother could never see any value in the education of girls.[37]

Reddy, of course, was writing at a time when the heat was on against the community and the combination of law, social reform and changing notions of marriage undermined the basis of the devadasi's existence.

Law, Social Reform, and the Devadasi

Recent historical scholarship on the devadasis has emphasized the role of the judiciary in transforming their legal definition between the nineteenth and twentieth centuries.[38] Kunal Parker has argued that a reformist judiciary, backed fully but silently by the colonial state, represented dancing girls as prostitutes and how this construction was organized round Hindu legal norms that designated all female sexual activity outside marriage as prostitution or unchastity as well as around new notions of marriage. Kay Jordan, on the other hand, works out the details of the judicial encounter, foregrounding in the process—the principal features of the emerging colonial and Indian discourse on devadasi related legislation. What is more than evident from both these works is that, until the late 1860s and 1870s, the judiciary tended to recognize the customary law of the community but endorsed the 'immoral' nature of their profession. The resultant ambiguity meant that in the second round of official intervention, there was an attempt to enforce more effectively the laws that were in place, especially those around the Indian Penal Code of 1861, which in theory did not prohibit adoption by a devadasi or prostitute. The issue was complicated further by the reluctance of the government to initiate reform measures in matters that were semi-religious and likely to offend the sensibilities of the ruled. It preferred the courts to do the job—to apply or exempt devadasis from the general laws against prostitution. The strategy paid off—as the westernized Indian elite began to press more urgently the cause of reform and aggressive legislation aimed at devadasi dedication.[39]

The legislative initiative was framed within the larger context of the social reform movement that became prominent in the Tamil and Telugu districts of the Madras Presidency from about the 1870s and 1880s. Kalpana Kannabiran traces the origins of the devadasi abolition movement in the Madras Presidency to the social reform movement started by Kandukuri Veerasalingam in the Telugu districts in the 1830s. Focusing on women's emancipation, he was concerned with social hygiene: conjugality and sexual relationships, education, religious practices as well as government corruption.[40] By the last decades of the nineteenth century, social reform movements as well as colonial discourse about prostitution combined to make the devadasi issue an agenda for social reform. The social reform movement, was in its early stages inspired by Brahmo Samaj ideals and subsequently by the Theosophists.[41] Spearheaded largely by upper-caste elite groups, it focused principally on the issues of female education, infant marriages, and widow remarriage, which in its broader scope touched on the status of the devadasi and the validity of child dedication to temples that was seen as being complicit in child prostitution. The movement was distinguished by several discrete voices; there were leaders like Virasalinga Pantulu, an advocate of the Brahmo Samaj who attacked casteism as well as those elements in Hindu tradition that inhibited women and restricted their space. Sharing his passion for female education but not for Brahmo doctrines, were Justice Muthuswami Iyer, G. Subramania Iyer, and Madhav Rao, who were committed to the Theosophical movement and preferred a moderate approach to both strategies of reform as well as conceptualizing a revived tradition.[42] This view championed social purity and temperance, issues that were endorsed by the National Social Conference, established in 1887 as a social wing of the Indian National Congress. Both these demands very centrally affected the status of the devadasis and nautch women as performing artists. The demands for social purity led to an immediate clamour for the abolition of the nautch altogether, while, in the long run, it informed the making of a new and puritanical-ethical aesthetic as far as the art forms of dance and music were concerned. Within the National Social Conference, the upper hand remained with the reform party. Through its official mouthpiece, *The Indian Social Reformer*, it advocated the cause of rationalism, organized dinners for remarried parties, held inter-caste dinners, and inaugurated the anti-nautch movement.

Anti-nautch discourse articulated by *The Indian Social Reformer* tended by and large to emphasize the centrality of companionate marriage and the pernicious effects of practices such as the dedication and free sexuality associated with devadasis, and the nautch on the youth and on the sacrality of marriage as an institution. *The Indian Social Reformer* carried graphic stories of how young and impressionable bridegrooms got sucked into unsavoury liaisons with nautch women, whose powers of attraction they could barely resist. Krishna Sarma, writing in 1899, suggested that the practice was especially prevalent in Trichinopoly, where, he found the youth enamoured by the nautch girls. 'Our young men are so handy that a moment's notice will do to gather them at any nautch party.' At the same time, the practice of arranging a nautch was ubiquitous with rich and poor alike, even though the consequences were unpredictable and occasionally disastrous. Illustrating his argument, he pointed out that in a recent marriage celebrated in the house of a 'professional prostitute patronizer', the bridegroom was so taken up with the ravishing dancer, that he 'lost his tranquility, his mental equanimity', and spent all his time in the house of the prostitute. Sarma had no doubt that this practice had to be stopped and he exhorted his readers to consider, 'how many good wives have been by its influence (i.e. nautch women and their art) separated from their husbands and made to live a life of extreme misery?'[43]

The reformers showed little interest in either the artistic endowments of the community or their material pressures—their focus was squarely on cleaning up the moral tone of public life, and in a small way, on reclaiming the field of performance for respectable middle-class women. They scoffed at the arguments that some of their opponents came up with, and which bore strange resonance with Lord Dufferin's sentiments about the Indian National Congress. For the protagonists of the devadasis, the institution's chief function was that of a safety valve invented by the wisdom of their ancestors to contain the superfluous animal passions which existed in every society and, which if let loose would lead to the destruction of family life.[44] The reformers condemned these arguments as superfluous and expressed their outrage at the idea that it was at all necessary to 'dedicate a class of women to a life of promiscuity in order to maintain the purity of our mothers, sisters, wives and daughters'.[45]

Taking the cue from the demands of social purity and temperance, the anti-nautch movement picked momentum from about the 1890s, when reformers demanded the de-legitimization of nautch entertainments accompanying public events.[46] Venkataratnam Naidu, a principal leader of the National Social Conference, was especially vocal in denouncing a variety of 'pastimes ranging from that hideous sin engendered by vice and practiced in solitude to the watching of nautch dancers and urged men to sign a pledge that they would avoid indecent practices, impure thoughts and nautch dances'.[47] In 1893, a public meeting was organized at Madras Christian College, where the principal Dr Miller (who was part of the reception committee for Prince Albert's visit and had endorsed the entertainment provided), was obliged to preside and where Subramania Iyer, the editor of *The Hindu* took a leading part in the proceedings. A memorial was drawn up demanding the abolition of such entertainment. The *Madras Mail* took up the cudgels for reform but official British opinion remained ambivalent. It was predictably hesitant to interfere in a matter of public entertainment, where the moral character of the performers did not come into question.[48]

Following on the heels of the *Madras Mail*, came *The Hindu*, equally relentless in representing reformist Indian opinion. When the National Social Conference met in 1894, Venkataratnam Naidu introduced a resolution condemning nautches, and prophesied hopefully that Indian dancing and music would benefit when they were purged of immorality.[49] Other instances of solidarity followed suit. In May 1905, E.L. Thornton, the Collector of Trichinopoly, issued a circular to his subordinates advising them not to arrange nautch parties because his sympathies were with the movement. Local zamindars like the Raja of Ramnad, were sufficiently impressed by the moral position of the Anti-nautch movement in seeking to distance themselves from the practice. Speaking on the occasion of a public debate on the nautch parties organized by the diwan of his state, Bhaskar Setupati, went on record publicly proclaiming his opinions on the issue. In a letter to the *Madras Mail* (dated 5–6 May 1894), he observed:

I have been asked by a few friends about the entertainment given to me by Virasamy Naidu on the night of the day before yesterday and about a nautch there, and I, therefore, consider it necessary to write to you (concerning) all that happened in order to avoid unwarranted news spreading about. Mr.Virasamy invited me to dinner at his new house and I accepted on the condition that I was not to be entertained by a nautch. When I got to the house, I saw a nautch was going on in the hall and hence I stopped outside refusing to enter the room. Messrs. Robert Fischer, and Sundaram Iyer who were the only persons in the hall came out and shook hands with me, learning that I refused to go into the hall. I was taken upstairs where I dined while the nautch was kept up in the hall below. After the nautch, I was again asked to enter the hall, and on refusing to do so, the nautch was stopped. I then went into the hall and was entertained by a fiddler and by my own songster. When I left, the song was again commenced. These statements will be borne out by my host, Messrs. Fischer and Sundaram.[50]

The anti-nautch campaign drew considerable support from a wide spectrum of opinion; for some, it was only a campaign against obscene social practice that offended the moral sensibilities of the educated elite,[51] for others, it became part of the larger emancipatory discourse for women, reinforcing the judicial initiative in Madras that was being organized around the re-conceptualization of temple dancing girls in terms of patriarchal Hindu norms and the construction of a Hindu community around marriage. In fact, reformers extensively publicized marriage as a strategy to bring devadasis into the mainstream. C. Sankaran Nair, in his presidential address to the National Social Conference in 1908, mentioned quite enthusiastically that efforts were being made to reclaim dancing girls and that a number of marriages had taken place.

The heads of many of the families of that caste have taken a vow to give their girls in marriage and to discard their customary life. Of one community whose hereditary profession is prostitution the members have resolved to lead ordinary married life. This was only to be expected as there are graduates amongst them and many boys of that caste are receiving English education.[52]

The offensive gained momentum in the subsequent years, and the central government came under pressure between 1912 and 1914, following public debate in England in response to Amy Wilson's publications (1903, 1909) on devadasi reform. It was in this period that Indian legislators like Manackjee Dadabhoy took the initiative and instituted protective measures for minors, including the case of the dedication of young girls to temples. Nothing came out of the debates— British officials were against new legislation and recommended the enforcement of existing laws while reform-minded Indians supported reform legislation even while endorsing their advocacy of Hindu religion. Even after the war, and the Montague–Chelmsford Reforms that structurally altered the government and increased Indian representation in the legislative councils, the official British position remained conservative. The bill that was passed in 1924 avoided mentioning the devadasis. The government defended its stand by arguing that the general provisions of the bill were adequate to address the issue without going into the specificities of the subject. The bill had little effect; the Madras High Court continued to come up with conflicting judgments and the inefficacy of the law was all too apparent.[53]

It took the severe indictment of an American journalist Katherine Mayo and the crusading zeal of the Madras legislator, Muthulakshmi Reddy, the first woman legislator in the Madras Legislative Council to force the issue. In 1927, Reddy resumed the debate as she proposed that the government take steps and legislate a stop to the practice of dedication. Reddy spoke in many voices—as a doctor apprehending the spectre of disease and death, as an enlightened social reformer who questioned the basis of such acts as dedication, and as a woman who brought with her the cooperation of other devadasis, who had by this time, formed several associations.[54] Addressing the council in 1927, she stated:

I beg to move this resolution which stands in response to the wishes of all the women's associations in the presidency who feel that this practice of dedicating young girls or young women to temples for immoral purposes as a slur on Indian womanhood and a great wrong and injustice done to the innocent young of the country and in response to the incessant demands of the enlightened sections of those aggrieved communities themselves, whose rightly developed moral sense naturally revolts at the practice of such a notorious custom prevalent among the enlightened of their community and who in their persuasive method and educated propaganda work among those illiterate, are unable to suppress this vice without further legislation, and above all in deference to my own personal conviction that in the cause of humanity and justice we can no longer delay this piece of beneficial legislation, a reform by which we can rescue thousands of young children from a life of immorality suffering disease and death resulting from infection with venereal disease.[55]

Reddy insisted that marriage among the girls was becoming popular and that, thanks to social reform associations, many were being rehabilitated as nurses, teachers, and handicrafts tutors.[56] She stressed in her resolution before the council that there were many in the community who had found and made suitable mates, and who 'made faithful wives and model mothers' which to her was proof of 'what healthy associations and change of surroundings' could do even for adult women.[57] The resolution was voted and passed even though ambiguities remained. For instance, it was more in the nature of a recommendation rather than a law, further, it involved neither criminal penalties nor the redistribution of rights and properties. In fact, C.P. Ramaswamy Ayyar, law member, reminded legislators that in the past, land endowments had been made to support legitimate temple service by devadasis. If devadasis were no longer dedicated to fulfill their temple obligations, the question of these properties and the control vested in them would have to be addressed.[58]

How did the community respond? In the first place, in its dislocated and straggling condition the community was deeply stratified. Not all women belonging to the community functioned as temple servants, and not all of them were in the practice of receiving dedicated girls. Some among them had entered marriage while others had single patrons who looked after their families. A few were recognized as excellent artists who enjoyed a unique inheritance while a good many others were performers, whose skills were solicited by drama companies and commercial recordings. Their response, therefore, to the politics of social reform and legislation was bound to be fractured. Established artists who had access to important patrons and reform-minded citizens participated in music concerts; the case of Madurai Shanmukavadivu, the mother of the legendary singer M.S. Subbulakshmi is a well-known instance. An established veena artist, Shanmukavadivu had influential friends in Madras, including Veena Dhanammal, while her patron Subramania Iyer was deeply interested in music and provided the necessary contacts. There were others who did not command the same resources or skills and felt threatened by the changing circumstances. In their protest in Madras[59] in 1929, they claimed that both law and religion had sanctioned their custom, and that legislation affecting their customs would amount to a deviation from the religious neutrality so long espoused by the colonial government. They complained about the impact that the new legislation would have on their earnings, property rights, and cultural life—describing themselves as the guardian angels of music and dance who, laboured without government support, and attached themselves to 'these arts with a devotion that bears comparison with the ardour of the pundit reading his vedas in preference to modern pursuits'.[60] Muthulakshmi Reddy dismissed these representations as baseless and as the work of a misguided few. She maintained that a large section among the community championed the cause of reform and had formed themselves into associations in the presidency.[61]

The representations of the devadasis did not cut ice either with the reformist brahmin elite or with the Justice Party and the Self-Respecters.[62] In fact, in 1927, when the Congressmen Satyamurthi and Swami Venkatachalam Chetty opposed the proposed amendment to the existing Hindu Religious Endowment Act, the Self-Respecters were outraged. They spoke out against the degraded lives the devadasis led and condemned the system, which perpetuated sexual slavery. They were even able to persuade some influential women among the community to embrace the political creed of self-respect. Moovalur Ramamrutammal was a notable example of this conversion as she came up with a novel *Dasigal Mosavalai* (1936)[63] that graphically illustrated the terms in which the debate relating to the devadasis had been framed in the century. From 1928, it was only a matter of time before the practice of dedicating girls was legally abolished in 1947.

The Cultural Project: Disinheriting the Devadasi?

What remained now was to divest the devadasi of her artistic heritage and reclaim her repertoire for the nation as part of its cultural heritage. The campaign against the devadasis, therefore, naturally entered the new cultural project undertaken by the Madras elite who were in the process of recasting the tradition of music and dance, secularize it, and make it accessible to the middle class. Clearly, the intention was not to be diverted by the more trivial and flamboyant elements in the devadasi repertoire but to focus on those lineages, whose artistic inheritance were identified as exceptional and worthy of incorporation in the classical repertoire that the Madras Academy was assembling. Also, the importance attached to the enabling of middle-class women to learn music meant that it was critical to legitimize the practice of public performances by women, and not leave it entirely to traditional performing artists, whose status was ambiguous.

In the first two decades of the twentieth century, women from the devadasi community were the only women performing Karnatik music in public. The most distinguished musical family was that of Veena Dhanammal, traditional performers who had migrated to Madras in the mid-nineteenth century. The family evidently had access to musical training of a high standard, especially from Subbaraya Sastri and accumulated over time a rich repertoire of kritis, javalis, and padams. They developed an individuated conception of musical aesthetics; Dhanammal in particular, articulated this with uncompromising perfection. She adopted the veena as her chosen instrument and underwent rigorous training under Sattanur Panchanada Iyer (a disciple of Diksitar) and Tirumalachar of Saidapet. This meant that she brought to her art an impressive range of styles and compositions as well as her own conception and imagination. For instance, it is said that she preferred to play without accompanying percussion lest it drown the gentle sound of her instrument.[64] By the 1920s, Dhanammal had become a household name in Madras.

The Enadi sisters were equally impressive. Like Dhanammal, they were able to receive musical training from established lineages; Patnam Subramania Iyer was their teacher. The sisters who sang together and specialized in singing kritis and javalis adopted a distinctly slower tempo in their rendering. Dhanammal was a great admirer of their javali singing and was able, after much persuasion, to get Rangaiya Enadi to teach her daughters Rajalakshmi and Lakshmiratnam a few pieces from their repertoire. From the fragments of information that we have of these contemporary women artists, it is clear that they specialized in certain genres traditionally associated with dance music and adopted a distinctly different approach to melodic delineation. According to Indira Menon, what distinguished the Dhanammal school was the tempo or *kalapramanam* that was slow, deliberate, and controlled; a sensuous delineation of the melody, and one that played down excessive use of note combinations of swara prastharas. Dhanammal's individual aesthetic conception was in marked contrast to the dominant style being popularized by male musicians.[65]

Performers like Dhanammal, the Enadi sisters; Dhanakoti Ammal, and Madurai Shanmukavadivu responded positively to the opportunities that Madras offered in the first decades of the twentieth century. In addition to the support of individual patrons, there was commercial recording to which most of the performers responded enthusiastically. Male musicians saw recording itself as derogatory, and consequently it is no surprise that many more women from the devadasi community were recorded in the 1920s and 1930s.[66] Established musicians acknowledged their talent and expertise and even sought to learn from them, though for professional reasons, they often kept this association a secret.

The agenda of the nationalist cultural project was challenging—both for the performers as well as for the new patrons. On the one hand, associations such as the Academy could not but be aware of the artistic wealth and authority of the best in the community, while on the other hand, the imperative to enable middle-class women to function as singers and performers with unquestioned respectability necessarily required the erasure of the devadasis and the values they represented. The National Social Conference did not make a distinction between women of talent and lineage, and more ordinary entertainers. In 1927, K. Natarajan in his address on 'Forty Years of Social Reform' came up with a telling comment. Speaking of the obstacles to social reform, he mentioned that a very good friend of his who had 'something like a passion for music' referred to the great proficiency attained by some of the dancing women, and that he bitterly reproached social reformers as being instrumental in extinguishing this class of artists. For the speaker, this was of no consequence at all for it was only by eliminating the nautch girl that the study and practice of music by women leading respectable lives could be facilitated. For the Madras Music Academy, the issue was more complicated, for it was an association of musicians and scholars who had a deep appreciation of the art form that had to be balanced with the considerations of social morality and of broadening the practice of music within the middle class. Right from the beginning, therefore, especially in the case of music, the Academy invited seasoned performers to perform in its annual concerts (Veena Dhanammal in the 1932 conference) and even to honour them with titles.[67] In the same spirit, the Academy responded positively to Shanmukavadivu's request to provide her daughter a forum to display her musical talent.[68] However, the Academy did not find it necessary to invite these artists to participate in the experts committee whose deliberations remained a closed affair. Equally significant was a restructuring of the concert format that played down the genres that were associated with the community.

By 1938, it appeared that the music of Dhanammal, the style and tradition she represented, was already a thing of the past and a subject of nostalgia. A tribute to the veena maestro by S.Y. Krishnaswamy in that year mentioned how with her demise, a type of music had become extinct, and which 'apart from its individual excellence, mirrored a civilization' that was 'fast receding into memory'. The author spoke of an age when sabhas and modern style associations had not come into prominence and when 'entertainment by courtesans was part of the social amenities that the rich had indulged in. It had not died out in response to the purblind Puritanism of a later decade'. What distinguished Dhanammal's music besides her prodigious talent was a scrupulous adherence to melody and grammar, a stately style, and an extensive repertoire that she could demonstrate, given the absence of constraints of time and place. Clearly, then here was a veiled allusion to the effects of modern musical reform that had ironed out diversity and difference.[69]

The overriding compulsion to relocate the practice of music within the middle class, combined with the gradual eclipse of the devadasis, thus explains why their repertoire was not adequately presented. The welcome address by U. Rama Rao in 1931, emphasized the importance of stimulating a 'scientific' interest in music among middle-class families. 'We are trying', he said, 'to resuscitate the art (of dance) along with the sister art of music and make it flow along healthy channels'.[70] The operative word was healthy, which in effect, meant a deliberate deletion of explicitly erotic aspects, particularly in the dance form. This project was successfully executed by Rukmini Arundale. In the case of music, this angst was not so evident, except the allotting of a smaller niche for padams and javalis, the specialties of the community in the concert repertoire.

Implicit in the construction of the classical–non–classical dyad that we spoke of earlier, was a redefinition of the artistic status of the community and the music that it employed. In 1933, E. Krishna Iyer, one of the most passionate advocates of dance and music, stated that the art required not only to be 'rejuvenated but also to be overhauled to have real appeal. As it is, it is mostly confined to erotic songs'.[71] He identified some specific compositions, with erotic overtones, to be eschewed. In 1944, the Madras Academy even invoked the need to jettison 'unsastraic mudras' not in consonance with the true feeling of the song.[72] Further, it stated that not all padams were suitable for performance. Here, what was being suggested as inappropriate for public consumption had nothing to do with explicitly artistic standards, but with the compulsions of a new morality that had to be juxtaposed with the emerging cultural project. With the fine-tuning of the concert repertoire, or kacheri, the Academy was able to incorporate those padams and javalis as part of their repertoire but with the understanding that these represented the lighter aspects of the tradition. It was the kritis, and that too of the trinity, that carried with it the weight of classicism, tradition, and artistic merit. It was this domain that had to be protected and preserved and was more readily identified as the preserve of the male vidwan. In 1932, P.S. Sundaram Iyer, a member of the experts committee, in his enthusiasm for foregrounding the classical version of Tyagaraja's compositions, did not shy away from making a distinction between 'music of the vidwans' and that sung by 'women'.[73]

This is not to suggest that the Academy was not receptive to the richness of the devadasi repertoire, or even to the talents of younger singers from the community who were wooed in the 1930s by stage and screen. But, while it continued to extend support to traditional women artists, and honour them for their services to classical music, it never lost sight of the need to consolidate the retrieved classical tradition and locate it within the middle class. An important adjunct of this project, as far as women performers were concerned, was to domesticate traditional performers, and bring them within the fold of classical music.[74] Nor was this confined to traditional artists but as Amanda Weidman has argued, the process of such domestication was part of the new politics of voice that was played out in the 1930s.[75] It was during the 1930s and 1940s that an entire discourse developed around the 'natural' voice that made women's music closer to the universal language of art, and subsequently fed the newly emerging notions of ideal womanhood. E. Krishna Iyer was among the first to comment on the natural qualities of women's music, which, thanks to a spate of gramophone recordings in the 1920s and 1930s, created an impressive following. The emergence of M.S. Subbulakshmi as a child prodigy reinforced the mystique about the perfect voice and its ability to convey sublime devotion. To this was added the ideal of domesticity, with 'classical music as the soundtrack for the modern marriage and the modern home'.[76]

M.S. Subbulakshmi's career, which was as much the manifestation of an exceptional talent as it was the creation of her husband, epitomized the workings of the 'middle-class' cultural project of the Academy. The need to consolidate the classical as the special preserve of the middle class, as a feature of brahmin sociability was never lost sight of. It was not mere chance that the image of M.S. Subbulakshmi was fashioned in a very special way and that her music became so appropriate to the expressive needs of the brahmin community in the city. The rendering of Sanskrit hymns that became an integral part of the quotidian listening schedule of middle-class brahmin homes as well as temples, the projection of a certain concert etiquette and persona that emphasized above all the singer's subjective absorption with personal devotion, and the stress on charity concerts, all served to make her the ultimate cultural ambassador and a role model for middle-class south Indians in the fifties and sixties. The cycle was complete; the traditional artist had been appropriated by the logic of the nationalist project while the stage was now made free for the new middle-class female singer.[77]

This is not to suggest that there was only one dominant voice type that captured the aural imagination of the consuming middle class or that alternative conceptions of music and voice did not find reflection in the public scene. Even as M.S. Subbulakshmi became the sought after voice, which was symptomatic of an innocence, a sublime and evanescent quality that conveyed the inchoate sensibilities and aesthetic longings of the middle class, there were other women singers whose music and musical scholarship enabled to position themselves quite centrally in the social world of performance. D.K. Pattamal is the best illustration in point. As Kalki Krishnamurti, the popular critic, observed in his weekly round-up of the arts and music scene in Madras in 1936, there was among music lovers, a sharp disagreement about women performers and their ability to perform classical music to full potential. There were those who argued that women's voices alone had intrinsic sweetness, while there were others, who treated women performers with barely veiled derision, suggesting that their approach was amateurish, their voices falsetto and nasal, and they made a complete mess of rhythm. Pattamal, however, bridged the gap as she brought to her performance a rare mélange of sweetness, solidity, rigour, and emotion all held in perfect balance to produce a music that stirred the senses and stimulated the intellect.[78] It seemed fitting that as embodiments of two distinct social classes, M.S. Subbulakshmi and D.K. Pattamal should have fulfilled in their own individual ways, the two major imperatives of the nationalist cultural project.

NOTES

1. Krishna Sarma, writing for *The Indian Social Reformer* in 1899 was eloquent in his critique of the nautch and nautch women. 'How many more dear youths of our land', he asked 'suffer from being caught in the snares of such women', *The Indian Social Reformer*, vol. IX, no. 37, p. 208, May 14, 1899. Interestingly, Ramamrutammal, the author of the *Dasi's Snares* and a staunch advocate of the Self-respect campaign deployed the same rhetoric in condemning the institution of the devadasis and their cunning in seducing the young brahmin lads. See K. Srilatha (ed. and trans.), *The Other Half of the Coconut: Women Writing Self-Respect History, An Anthology of Self-Respect Literature (1928–1936)*, Kali for Women, Delhi, 2003.

2. In 1877, a renewed debate occurred over the inclusion of devadasi children in local board schools. Official European and high caste Indian opinion voiced their disapproval of the idea of including these children in local schools. The *Indian Native Opinion* observed, 'This fear (of educated girls turning out to be wicked) absurd as it may be as regards the influence exerted by wholesome intellectual and moral education is by no means unreasonable when the girls are exposed to the danger of mixing with girls of the dancing class, who from their earliest years, and long before they are physically fit for prosecuting their infamous trade, are depraved in manners and dissolute in morals'. Quoted in Sita Anantha Raman, *Getting Girls to School: Social Reform in the Tamil Districts 1870–1930*. Stree, Calcutta, 1996, p. 36.

3. This idea is best expressed and elaborated by Saskia Kersenboom Story who prefaces her work with the question, 'Can a Devadasi wear toe rings?' 'Of course she can for she is *nityasumangali*'. Implicit in the question and answer is the idea that as the servant of god, the devadasi's sexual energy was yoked to the temple deity and thereby rendered benign and external to the norms of householder society. Cast in such a role, she enjoyed the privilege of eternal wifehood. See Saskia Kersenboom Story, *Nityasumangali: Devadasi Tradition in South India*, Motilal Banarasidass, Delhi, 1987. See Preface.

4. Ibid.

5. Abbe Dubois, *Hindu Manners, Customs and Ceremonies*. Translated from the Author's later French manuscript and edited with introduction and notes by Henry K. Beauchamps, Clarendon Press, Oxford, 1897. Delhi, Reprint, 1978, pp. 604–5.

6. Stanley Tambiah, 'A Performative Approach to Ritual' in *Proceedings of the British Academy*, London, pp. 113–69.

7. Saskia Kersenboom Story, *Nityasumangali*.

8. This is mentioned in P. Subramanian, *Social History of the Tamils*, Sundeep Prakashan, New Delhi, 1999, pp. 82ff.

9. Saskia Kersenboom Story, *Nityasumangali*.

10. Veena Dhanammal's family is a case in point. Dhanammal's grandmother for instance, had access to the rich repertoire of compositions that she learnt from Syama Sastri and his son Subbaraya Sastri. Dhanammal's contemporary Dhanakoti Ammal too had similar access. See Indira Menon, *The Madras Quartet*, Roli Books, New Delhi, 1999, pp. 53–64. Also see Ranga Ramanuja Ayyangar, *A History of South Indian Classical (karnatik) Music*, pp. 289ff.

11. Francis Buchanan, *A Journey from Madras through the Countries of Mysore, Canara and Malabar in three volumes*, London, 1807, vol. II, p. 266.

12. Ibid., p. 268.

13. Dubois, *Hindu Manners and Customs*, pp. 584–6.

14. *Census of the Town of Madras 1871*, printed by H. Morgan at the Fort St George Gazette Press, Madras, 1873. See *Report on the Census of the Madras Presidency, 1871*, Madras 1874, p. 167ff.

15. *Census of India, 1891*, vol. XIII, Madras. *Report on the Census*, pp. 273, 347.

16. Fred Fawcett, 'On Basavis: Women Who Through Dedication to a deity Assume Masculine Privileges', *Journal of the Anthropological Society of Bombay*, vol. II, 1892, pp. 326ff, 336, 346–51.

17. Edgar Thurston and K. Rangachari, *Castes and Tribes of Southern India*, Indian reprint, Delhi and Madras, 1987, vol. II, pp. 124–52.

18. Indira Menon, *The Madras Quartet*, pp. 38–40, 56–7ff.

19. Edgar Thurston and K. Rangachari, *Castes and Tribes of Southern India*, vol. II, pp. 128–9.

20. Amrit Srinivasan, 'Reform and Revival: The Devadasi and her Dance', *Economic and Political Weekly*, 20(4), 1985, pp. 1869–76.

21. Saskia Kersenboom Story, paper presented to the Barbara Stoler Miller Conference, Columbia University, February 2004.

22. *Sarvadevavilasa*. See Introduction also pp. 31–2, 37 where Manga is mentioned as among the foremost of the courtesans (ganika).

23. Buchanan, *A Journey from Madras through the Countries of Mysore, Canara and Malabar in three volumes*, vol. II.

24. Pamela Price, *Kingship and Political Practice in Colonial India*, Cambridge University Press, Cambridge, 1996, pp. 68–9, 70–5.

25. Ibid.

26. H.D. Love, *Vestiges of Old Madras*, vol. II, pp. 419–21ff.

27. *Sarvadevavilasa*. See Introduction, pp. 31–47.

28. Indira Menon, *The Madras Quartet*, p. 56.

29. Sita Anantha Raman, *Getting Girls to School*, p. 36.

30. K. Srilatha (ed. and trans.), *The Other Half of the Coconut*, pp. 93–176.

31. *Ananda Vikatan*, 20 January 1935, pp. 24–5.

32. Sita Anantha Raman, *Getting Girls to School*, p. 36ff, 111–12.

33. Kunal M. Parker, '"A Corporation of Superior Prostitutes": Anglo-Indian Legal Conceptions of Temple Dancing Girls 1800–1914', *Modern Asian Studies*, vol. 32, 3, 1998, pp. 559–634.

34. Sita Anantha Raman, *Getting Girls to School*, pp. 34–5.

35. Ibid., pp. 36–7.

36. Ibid., p. 112.

37. Ibid., p. 209. Also see autobiography of S. Muthulakshmi Reddy, *A Pioneer Woman Legislator*, Madras, 1964, p. 9. Reddy speaks of her mother being continuously depressed and resenting the fact that none of her daughters had married.

38. Kunal Parker, 'A Corporation Superior Prostitutes'. Also see Kay Jordan, *From Sacred Servant to Profane Prostitute: A History of the Changing Legal Status of the Devadasis in India 1857–1947*, Manohar, New Delhi, 2003.

39. Kay Jordan, *From Sacred Servant to Profane Prostitute*, pp. 84–104.

40. Kalpana Kannabiran, 'Judiciary, Social Reform and Debate on "Religious Prostitution" in Colonial India', *Economic and Political Weekly*, 30 (43), 1995, pp. 59–69.

41. Colonel H.S. Olcott and Madame Blavatsky founded the Theosophical Society in New York in 1875. Adhering to its aims of promoting brotherhood, of promoting interest in Aryan culture and religion, the leaders visited India and established contacts in Tirunelveli and Tuticorin in 1881. Their ideas appealed to upper-caste brahmins and non-brahmins as well as to sections of the westernized elite whose disenchantment with imperial rule persuaded them to take a closer look at the Theosophist agenda of promoting Indian civilization and values. In 1882, the Madras branch of the Theosophical Society was established with Raghunath Rao as President, Muthuswamy Chetty and Srinivasa Rao as Vice Presidents and T. Subba Rao as Secretary. See R. Suntharalingam, *Politics and Nationalist Awakening in South India, 1825–1891*, Rawat Publications, Jaipur–Delhi, 1980, pp. 292–301.

42. Sita Anantha Raman, *Getting Girls to School*, p. 123. She argues that leaders like Madhava Rao and Justice Muthuswamy Iyer were revivalists with a difference. They were convinced that reform had to come from within. Without advocating either an open attack on all tradition or an implicit compliance with immoral customs, these men advocated extensive propaganda.

43. *The Indian Social Reformer*, May 14, 1899, pp. 208ff. Correspondence by Krishna Sarma.

44. *Fortieth Indian National Social Conference*, Madras, 1927. See presidential address by K. Natarajan, pp. 11ff.

45. Ibid.

46. Until the latter half of the nineteenth century, nautch was still considered to be a prestigious but expensive form of hospitality. Such dances were provided in honour of the visit of the Prince of Wales in 1875 and of his son Prince Albert in 1890. The Bishop of Calcutta is said to have protested against such performances but Lord Lansdowne, the Viceroy had replied somewhat glumly that the proceedings had been fairly decorous. See Kenneth Ballhatchet, *Race, Class and Sex under the British Raj: Imperial Attitudes and their Critics*, Weidenfeld and Nicolson, London, 1980, p. 157.

47. Ibid., pp. 157–8.

48. Ibid., pp. 158–9.
49. Pamela Price, *Kingship and Political Practice*, pp. 155–8.
50. Quoted in Pamela Price, *Kingship and Political Practice*, pp. 158–9.
51. In 1900, M. Ramachandran published a booklet entitled 'The Devadasi' where he referred to the institution of the devadasis and to the practice of dedication as a national blot, a social scandal. He extolled his countrymen to take immediate action. He admitted that reform could not come from those who had their self-interests tied up with the temples, 'for nearer the Church, the farther from God'. See M. Ramachandran, *The Devadasi* Secretary, Aryan Mission, Conjeevaram, June 1900.
52. C. Sankaran Nair, Presidential Address to the Madras Conference. See *The Madras Congress and Conferences*, Madras, 1903, p. 18.
53. Kay Jordan, *From Sacred Servant to Profane Prostitute*, pp. 93–104.
54. Reddy criticized the temple authorities and the Hindu public for endorsing a 'criminal, unholy and anti-social act, an act productive of the most virulent diseases to the individual and the community, and the practice of which demoralizes the individual in every way, as a hereditary right and caste dharma'. Government of Madras, *Proceedings of the Madras Legislative Council*, vol. XXXVIII, p. 513. Also see Muthulakshmi Reddy, 'Why Should the Devadasi Institution in the Hindu Temples be Abolished?' A bill to prevent the dedication of women in hindu temples in the Presidency of Madras. Act 1929. Chintadripet: Central Cooperative Printing Works Ltd., n.d. See also Appendix in her autobiography. *A Pioneer Woman Legislator*, Madras, 1964, pp. 138ff.
55. *Proceedings of the Madras Legislative Council*, vol. LI (nos 1–10), Madras, 1930.
56. Muthulakshmi Reddy, 'Why Should the Devadasi Institution in the Hindu Temples be Abolished?'
57. *Proceedings of the Madras Legislative Council*, 1930, p. 514.
58. Kay Jordan, *From Sacred Servant to Profane Prostitute*, pp. 119–27.
59. See Kay Jordan, *From Sacred Servant to Profane Prostitute*, pp. 127–30.
60. Government of Madras, Law Department, (General), Proceedings, December 20, 1927, G.O. 4079. In essence, the devadasis argued that they were religious artists and that their legitimate vocation was threatened by the proposed legislation. They objected that: 'No one would think of annexing the lands of a family because some one of its members offended the ethical conscience of the public, and we are not in the hands of Bolshevic legislators'.
61. Muthulakshmi Reddy, 'Why Should the Devadasi Institution in Hindu Temples be Abolished?' The devadasi women's associations mentioned are Coimbatore Manimekalai Sangam, Andhradesa Devadasi Sangha, Devadasi Association in Tenali Taluq, Devadasi Association in Repalle Taluq, Devadasi Meeting in Tanjore, Tinnevelly Women's Association Proceedings signed by a number of devadasis.
62. V. Geetha and S.V. Rajadori, *Towards a Non-Brahmin Millennium: From Iyothee Thass to Periyar*, Samya, Calcutta, 1998, pp. 386, 396.
63. K. Srilatha (ed. and trans.), *The Other Half of the Coconut*.
64. R. Ranga Ramanuja Ayyangar, *History of South Indian (Carnatic) Classical Music*, pp. 289ff. Also see T.V. Subba Rao, *Studies in Indian Music*, 1962. See section on Dhanammal. Dhanammal is supposed to have learnt padams from one Balakrishnayya, a blind musician.
65. Indira Menon mentions a remark that Dhanammal's grandson recalled when he tried to impress her with a javali. 'How can a thadian (robust male) like you sporting long moustaches sing a love ditty like this?' she snapped, p. 62.

66. Indira Menon, *The Madras Quartet*, pp. 67–70. Also see Michael Kinnear, *The Gramophone Company's First Recordings, 1889–1908*, Bombay, 1994, pp. 115–22.

67. *JMAM*, vol. XXIV, 1953, p. 42. For titles conferred on Jayammal, Veena Dhanammal's daughter. The Academy recognized the richness of her repertoire that included the compositions of the trinity, padams of Ksetragna and javalis and acknowledged Jayammal as the bearer of Dhanammal's style. In the 1930s, the Academy regularly invited Dhanammal to perform in its annual music conference.

68. Indira Menon, *The Madras Quartet*, pp. 128–30.

69. *The Indian Review*, Madras, November, 1938, pp. 735ff. 'Veena Dhanammal: A Tribute by S.Y. Krishnaswamy'.

70. U. Rama Rao's Welcome address in *JMAM*, vol. II, no. 1, 1931, pp. 208ff.

71. E. Krishna Iyer, *Personalities in Present Day Music*, with a Foreword by S. Doraiswamy Iyer, Madras, 1933, pp. 98–9.

72. Lakshmi Subramanian, 'Gender and the Performing Arts in Nationalist Discourse: An Agenda for the Madras Music Academy, 1930–47', *The Book Review*, 23(1–2), 1999, pp. 81–4.

73. P.S. Sundarama Iyer at the Madras Music Conference of 27.12.31. *JMAM*, vol. III, nos 1–2, 1933.

74. T. George, *M.S.: A Life in Music*, Harper Collins, New Delhi, 2004.

75. Amanda Weidman, 'Gender and the Politics of Voice: Colonial Modernity and Classical Music in South India', *Cultural Anthropology*, 18(2), 2003, pp. 194–232.

76. Ibid. The success of Saraswati Bai, a brahmin performer of the harikatha was a major shift in attitudes. E. Krishna Iyer, commenting on the reception that Saraswati Bai enjoyed in the 1930s mentioned that the world of music had become liberal and that there was an enhanced appreciation of women's music, which had a more natural feel. Thanks to gramophone recordings, women artists had achieved a certain measure of popularity. Additionally, there was the novelty factor that fostered the idea of child prodigy, a status that suggested certain isolation from the world and a selfless devotion to music. The idea gained ground in the wake of the meteoric rise of Subbulakshmi generating a new discourse about the 'natural' voice, and its ability to express bhakti. The emergence of Saraswati Bai, the first brahmin·woman exponent of the harikatha was an important, moment in the circulation of Karnatik music outside southern India. M.S. Ramaswami Iyer, who introduced the commemoration volume on Saraswati Bai in 1939, specifically mentioned that Bai had achieved a rare miracle in popularizing southern music in the north. In the words of a poet who was present on one such occasion, 'In North, Southern music lay hid in sight. God ordered "Let Bai sing" and all was light'. See *Smt. C. Saraswati Bai. Commemoration Volume issued on the occasion of the unveiling of her portrait at the Jagannath Bhakta Sabha Egmore*, Saturday, 16 December 1939. The volume carried extracts from the *Bombay Gazette* dated 10.12.1913, from the *Hindu Prakasan* 14.2.1913 and the *Amrita Bazar Patrika* dated 7.10.36.

77. Amanda Weidman, 'Gender and the Politics of Voice', pp. 196–232.

78. *Ananda Vikatan*, 4 October 1936, 'Pattamal Pattu' (Pattamal's music), pp. 29–32.

Contesting the Classical
THE TAMIL ISAI IYAKKAM AND THE CONTEST FOR CUSTODIANSHIP

The Tamil Isai Iyakkam (Tamil Music Movement) developed as an auxiliary element of the Tani Tamil movement. It cannot be detached from the larger issues of Tamil separatism and the non-brahmin movement that inflected the course of political agitation in the Madras Presidency from about the latter decades of the nineteenth century. Recent writings on the Tamil movement have demonstrated its complexity and emphasized the multiple strands in its constitution, none of which were the exclusive preserves of specific caste groups or interests.[1] What was central to the movement in its various incarnations of anti-Brahmanism, Tamil separatism, and assertion of self-respect, was an abiding commitment to the Tamil language as the vehicle for political and social empowerment. It was a commitment that transcended the bounds of nationalism, one that assumed proportions of devotion, passion, and sacrifice and, at the same time, held out prospects of genuine empowerment for its speakers. The compulsion to celebrate Tamil as the essential expression of an exceptional identity was not merely a political strategy to rally underprivileged groups of non-brahmin society under a banner of difference but also an ongoing psychological drive to invoke a collective memory and a unique inheritance. The issue was not one of a mimetic playing out of linguistic nationalism; it was as Sumathi Ramaswamy suggests,[2] about the crystallization of passion and practice centred around language. Language devotion defined the identity of the modern Tamil subject—in whom it generated a range of responses, the subjectivity of which were derived from the myriad imagings of the language while inducing the development of discourses of love, labour, and life for the language. It was *Tamilparru* or devotion that determined true Tamil identity, but this was of necessity conceived in multiple imaginings that inevitably produced a splintering among representatives.[3]

The celebration of language thus acquired a special edge in the discursive search for Tamil identity and the attendant programme of social and political empowerment in the closing decades of the nineteenth century. It was only a matter of time before the logic of the new discourse entered the domain of culture, its practice, patronage, consumption, and custodianship, all of which by the first quarter of the twentieth century had already become significant issues in the emergent nationalist agenda. This chapter investigates the issues of cultural custodianship and consumption in the context of the Tamil separatist movement, to identify the points of convergence between the nationalist and the regional cultural projects, and to understand the limited impact of the Tamil movement in reclaiming the site of neo-classical culture. More specifically, it looks at the case of classical music, which had emerged as one of the more significant emblems of the nationalist cultural project that directly and elaborately engaged with the performing arts, both as an aesthetic inheritance and as a social network of practitioners and traditional performing communities. The delineation of the project involved not just the retrieval of an artistic tradition and the repositioning of communities of performers associated with it but also the hegemonic prioritizing of a particular version of musical practice as 'classical', with strong if not wholly, Brahmanical overtones. How inclusive or exclusive this was of indigenous Tamil traditions that claimed a non-Sanskritic and non-Brahmanical identity became a key question in the debate that broke out between the Madras Academy and the Tamil Isai Sangam.

The Project and its Publicists: The Southern Experience

Of the many streams of nationalist thought, one concerned itself specifically with the cultural foundations of nation building. The logic of nationalist thought, as Partha Chatterjee has argued, dictated the demarcation of a distinct domain of sovereignty within colonial society. This was the inner domain 'bearing the essential marks of a cultural identity', and its distinctiveness and difference had to be protected and nourished in order to enshrine the already existing sovereignty of the nation.[4] The essential feature of this cultural inheritance was this difference, which necessarily had to be located in a whole range of expressive legacies—language, visual arts, and cultural heritage in the form of relics or living practices, as in the case of music and the performing arts. Partha Chatterjee uses the term 'classicization' to describe the elevation of select aspects of culture, specifically as part of a deliberate and negotiated process of national culture formation. A classicized tradition is one which has been 'reformed, reconstructed, fortified against charges of barbarism and irrationality', and hence made palatable for the tastes of middle-class people and appropriate content for a nationalized cultural identity. Writings on public culture in recent years have tended to emphasize the emergence of a visual and aural vocabulary for the nation and how this worked to forge a sense of community as the basis for participation in the public sphere as well as for the articulation of nationalist rhetoric.[5] Music and the performing arts, in so far as their discursive history was concerned, were critical elements and self-professed publicists, participants,[6] and custodians came forward to initiate a project of retrieval and revival. One cannot overstate the self-conscious-ness of the project and, as in any engagement with an aesthetic experience, the distinction between a rhetorical overlay and an individual, subjective orientation or a collective invocation was not always easy to figure out.

A growing interest in classical music among the middle classes, combined with a need to articulate the richness of India's cultural legacy, produced a richly textured critique on the tradition of the performing arts. From about the last quarter of the nineteenth century, in several quarters of India, the new consumers and patrons, the urban educated elite, initiated projects for the revival of the performing arts, especially classical music. The efforts of notables like Sourindro Mohan Tagore in Bengal and the collective initiative of the members of the Gayan Samaj in Poona, typified the beginnings of a more or less spontaneous, India wide, educated metropolitan cultural project that assumed, over the years, explicitly nationalist overtones. The need of the hour lay in retrieving the tradition, re-examining, and reconstituting it in the name of artistic standards and authenticity. These new standards were largely determined by the social and intellectual imperatives of middle-class elites. For instance, there was the need to transform the social base of the tradition and to validate its authenticity by seeking a strongly grounded textual lineage and stressing the spiritual aspects of the tradition. The imperative of relocation was not simply a question of patronage, of who consumed classical music and dance, or the changing locus of the arts from the temple and the salon to the modern concert hall or urban soirée, but one of ownership. The tradition belonged to the nation—it was part of the national legacy and as custodians of the nation's heritage, the newly empowered middle-class elites were responsible for its preservation and dissemination.

In the Madras Presidency, the onus of responsibility for the newly emerging cultural project lay with brahmin publicists who dominated the public life of the city. Their non-brahmin associates, drawn from affluent sections of the trading and landed classes, tended to share common concerns as far as social reform and civic interests were concerned as well as of cultural tastes and patronage in the field of arts. This did not, however, counter the social and ritual divide between brahmin and non-brahmin, especially in the context of growing non-brahmin consciousness in the closing decades of the nineteenth century. For the greater part of the century, the balance lay very much with the brahmin elite. With their access to western education and professional standing, they came to represent their civic and political concerns as nationalist and, at the same time, ground the nationalist sentiment in a remembered and sanctified past, in which culture and its recovery played a central role. Their agenda was considerably informed, as we have seen, by Oriental assumptions and by Theosophist inputs that exalted the Aryan legacy and celebrated the vigour and merits of the 'mighty brahmin' caste performing the ultimate feat of sacrifice, of giving to the nation the power of their past.[7] These sets of interventions enthused a generation of publicists to reconnect with their heritage and, as individual appreciation of music acquired a symbolic aura of epiphanic dimensions, an overpowering need to initiate a collective endeavour of preservation and representation developed.

The question of the brahmin's self-image was equally important, and entered in an oblique way into the cultural project, especially as it related to the reconstitution of classical music. As V. Geeta and S.V. Rajadorai observe, the community, captivated by Besant's rhetoric of culture, caste, and nation, came to 'view her ideas as so many mirrors which returned to them flattering images of themselves and fortified them in their self-appointed roles of patriotic reformers and modern Hindus who would usher in a brave new world of glory and prosperity'.[8] Exemplars of simple living and high thinking, they were best placed to balance the virtues of modernity with the wisdom of tradition and to stand forward as the custodians of India's civilization. Deploying a discourse, largely derived from Theosophist propaganda,[9] and which emphasized the virtues of merit, intellect, and self-discipline. they saw themselves as natural leaders and eminently capable of providing an appropriate language of symbols for the nation. As K.S.R. Sastri observed in his address to the All India Brahmin Conference in 1935, 'Its aim is to weigh on the brahmin community so that it may realize itself by embodying the ancient culture and applying it in national service as an integral part of the modern Indian nation'. The brahmin was eminently qualified to assume a central role in national regeneration, to guide spiritual and secular life for 'they had never exploited the community by priest craft' and had always 'tried to realize higher ends by following the principles of renunciation'.[10]

It may be of some interest to note that European music was a particularly powerful signifier of difference for the British. It was frequently invoked as a measure of European cultural superiority, having the virtues of genteel mobilization, dignity, and scientific principles of organization. It would seem likely that, to some degree, the passionate embrace of indigenous art music as a pillar of the national identity was a proud response to this chauvinism. The rather Confucian notion of disciplined and refined music being essential to the health of the state and nation came naturally enough to empire and nation builders alike.

And how vital were the performing arts, especially music, in this pool of nationalist symbols that emphasized the spiritual and the secular? In the case of south India, very central; for music, its patronage, protection, consumption, and representation became critically tied up with issues of self-definition, taste,[11] and ideals of individual and collective behaviour, especially for the brahmin community, which constituted a major element in the composition of the colonial middle class in the Tamil districts of the Madras Presidency. The very organization of the musical tradition, as it had historically evolved, came into play directly supporting the brahmin's claim to custodianship and facilitating the drawing of boundaries between neo-classical and light classical, high culture and popular culture. Moreover, music as the most audible emblem of India's spiritual and artistic expression—essentially the language of bhakti— had the potential to emerge as the most effective autonomous domain of cultural difference in which the self-appointed leaders of the nation could inscribe their aspirations.

The south was especially qualified to assume the responsibility for laying out the cultural topography of the emerging nation—it was seen to have preserved the vital essentials of India's ancient traditions. The association of high-caste brahmin musicians with musical knowledge and practice, made it easier for later brahmin publicists to emerge as spokesmen for retrieving and recasting the tradition. At the same time, the collapse of traditional sources and sites of patronage, and the dissemination of music in new urban centres, meant that the city elites became the most important patrons and consumers of classical music—a development that not only generated a genuine passion for the tradition but also fostered a sense of responsibility for it. This is not to suggest that their non-brahmin counterparts did not have an equivalent affinity with and appreciation of music. In fact, it was among the notable families of Chettiars and Pillais not to speak of zamindars and rajas of local estates and princely courts of Mysore, Vijaynagaram, Mysore, and Travancore, that classical music continued to enjoy substantial patronage. A closer look at the world of literary and performing culture in the second half of the nineteenth century in south India also suggests the interconnectedness of Brahmin-Pillai-Chettiar scholarship and cultural transactions. However, it would appear from the autobiography of U.V. Swaminatha Iyer that scholars engaged in Tamil studies were not always receptive to music and musical concerns—K. Minakshi Sundaram Pillai, the celebrated Tamil teacher, was supposedly critical of Gopalakrishnan Bharati's work. What is equally striking about Iyer's life story is the circulation of Tamil songs and kirtanams, which according to him, disappeared only in the last decades of the nineteenth century.[12] Clearly, with the articulation of the nationalist cultural project by the Madras elite, there was a self-conscious attempt to reclaim a particular style and genre as classical with the attendant particularizing markers, namely composition in Sanskrit and Telugu, the principal musical languages of the tradition. This highlights a shared continuity with the lineages of the celebrated saint composers of the eighteenth century, namely Tyagaraja, Diksitar and Syama Sastri, and a renewed emphasis on the spiritual aspects of musical expression. The result was the emergence of a cohesive discourse around music and musical reform that involved questions of content, style, language, and etiquette.

In the context of the Hindu revivalism that the Theosophical Society promoted in south India, the issue of musical reform and entertainment was inevitably tied up with Brahmanical culture and leadership wherein, notions of religiosity, custom, and scriptural erudition were stressed. In 1903, referring to the increasing popularity of kalaksepam or harikathas, which as we have noted were one of the most significant mediums for creating a listening habit in Madras, Natesa Sastri, the celebrated folklorist, wrote scathingly of its practitioners, none of whom in his opinion had any real knowledge of the scriptures. 'Most of the *Bhagavatars* are self-styled and having managed to get a smattering knowledge of a few Puranic tales, they make *Kalaksepams* of those tales, not on religious occasions but invariably during the *rahu kala* (considered an inauspicious moment) of a Sunday evening.'[13] Sastri urged the religious associations in Madras to come forward and clean up the act, to encourage only the really erudite among the professionals. In his words, 'A great deal of responsibility lies on the leaders of the Hindu community in this matter and if only they introduce wholesome reforms in the field of popular education, a great deal of good might in time be expected by the people'.[14]

If Sastri was keen on emphasizing the religious aspect in the harikathas, his musical minded colleagues, were intent on improving the quality of entertainment therein, and in demarcating the domain of classical music from that of harikatha and subsequently Tamil drama and cinema. It was in this context that the Madras Music Academy in 1944, passed two important resolutions one, urging the representation of at least two members of the Academy in the Film Censors Board to help preserve the purity and standards of classical music employed in cinema, and the other, appealing to film producers and musical directors to maintain the purity and standards of classical music.[15] This was the product of an ongoing debate about the erosion of classical standards. In 1938, S. Ramamurthi referred to the stir and confusion that the Tamil talkies had created in the music world. The talkies had produced such a demand for light music 'with no supply worth the name in the market'. An inevitable consequence of this boom was the emergence on an unprecedented scale, of plagiarized versions of classical songs, especially of Tyagaraja.

Apart from the incongruity of the devotional music of the saint composer being made to do duty, though in a different linguistic garb, in intriguing and even amorous situations in the popular pictures. This questionable method has brought down the high standards of classical art and is responsible for much of the musical malnutrition of the public taste observable everywhere today.[16]

There should be, the author argued, 'a clear marked distinction between high classical and light music and one should not trespass on the domains of the other'.[17]

The anxiety of the Academy to preserve classical purity was especially pronounced as it had laboured for more than a decade to put in place an identifiable classical music tradition. The construction of a classical music repertoire, the positioning of certain compositions as the core elements in the repertoire, the relegation of Tamil songs and other dance related compositions such as the javalis, padams, and *tillana*, to a lesser status in the artistic hierarchy on grounds of its sensual content and non-classical resonance, was very much part of the brahmin sponsored project of recasting the classical tradition and claiming its custodianship. This was not entirely the case with the more affluent non-brahmin publicists who did, at a later stage, question the hegemonic nature of the nationalist cultural project, though their identities were not necessarily at stake in the maximal versions of Tamil Isai.

Embodying tradition and as a responsible beneficiary of modernity, the nationalist Tamil brahmin considered himself eminently qualified to retrieve and recast the tradition as the nation's authentic inheritance.[18] By articulating an influential discourse that simultaneously adopted the categories of tradition and modernity and by implementing a project that firmly located the practice and patronage of music within the middle class, the new publicists assumed custodianship of the performing arts. The strength of the project and its sustainability remained to be tested in the context of the alternative anti-brahmin discourse that developed in the latter decades of the century. In the contest that followed, the nationalist paradigm held firm; the brahmin elite as represented in academies and associations such the Madras Music Academy, seemed to have the upper hand. The domain of classical culture remained very much with them, a convergence that was not without serious implications for the art form as well as for some of its traditional practitioners, like the devadasis and the temple oduvars, a class of temple singers who chanted and sang eulogies in praise of deities and who were well versed with traditional Tamil hymns and devotional compositions.

While the cause of the devadasis did not find resonance with the politics of the non-brahmin movement, the case of the Oduvars was different. Seen as the principal vehicles of Tamil culture and specialists of Tamil poetry and music, the community and its inheritance, became central to the articulation of an alternative classical tradition, put forward by the protagonists of Tamil devotion. The Oduvars, specialized in Tevaram songs[19] (religious hymns associated with the Nayanars of the seventh to ninth centuries), which were largely recitative and set to a specific number of melodies without too many embellishments and did not in all probability figure in the traditional concert of the courts. The Oduvars themselves claimed to be the living custodians of traditional melodies or panns as they were known in the Tamil country, and were closely connected with the nattuvan and nadaswaram performers of the temple orchestra or peria melam.

The *Tevaram*, as the scripture of the Tamil Saiva sect, enjoyed a unique significance. The process of actual compilation of the hymns of three celebrated Saiva saints, namely Tirunanacampandar, Tirunavakkaracar, and Cuntaramurti was completed only in the eleventh century, when the term Tevaram was used to designate the poetry. Indira Peterson's work on the Tevaram demonstrates skillfully how the canonization of the Tevaram actually worked itself over time, and how by straddling diverse categories in religion, literature, and culture, it promoted a unique mode of communal solidarity. Saiva devotion travelled through a network of shrines and sacred places in the peninsula, especially in the Tamil country and expressed as a living tradition by ritual specialist chanters—the Oduvars who sang selections from Tirumurai texts during ritual worship and on public occasions.[20] The emotional appeal of Tevaram especially for Saivite groups like the Chettiars and Pillais who, as patrons of the language as well as of large Saiva Sidhanta maths, may explain why they were especially vocal in espousing the cause of Tamil Isai over Karanataka Sangeetam of the Music Academy variety and also why their advocacy did not strike the same chord with other non-brahmin groups for whom the investment in Tamil Isai, did not have the same resonance.

The Madras Music Academy did not in its initial years venture to speak on behalf of the community of Oduvars, or include their repertoire in any significant way in its determining of the contours of the tradition. The case of the nadaswaram, the lead instrument in the peria melam, became the exception with the emergence of its most outstanding performer T.N. Rajaratnam Pillai (1898–1956), and was an important determinant in raising the status of the peria melam musicians.[21] But this did not apply to the Oduvars who had to wait for the protagonists of the Tamil Isai to take up their case.

As a performative genre, Tevaram appears to have undergone several changes long before the nineteenth century. Peterson suggests that even by the eleventh century, musicologically, the Tevaram tradition had been reconstructed and that, thereafter, the pann tunes had been replaced by Karnatik raga scales. However, Tevaram singing remained distinctive and was identified by what Peterson describes as the *viruttam* style where the Oduvar might select two or more verses from a hymn and render them in a set tune developed from a raga scale and regulated by a basic rhythmic pattern. Even if the Oduvar tried a few grace notes, the basic melodic delineation remained simple. The viruttam style was entirely improvisational and free in terms of both melodic and textual form—the textual line could be violated as the Oduvar took the license to repeat

one line of the verse many times and glide over others.[22] To what extent
the performative tradition continued in the early twentieth century is
difficult to assess—the impression one gets is that of a ritual performance,
which was positioned below that of scriptural chanting by the brahmin
priests. It did not seem to have an independent artistic existence that
commanded a space in the emerging classical music and entertainment
scene, or one that was factored into by musicologists, connoisseurs, and
reformers.

By the end of the 1930s, it seemed as though the classical project,
initiated by the Madras Academy had achieved a consensus. It had
successfully enlisted the cooperation of the musicians, defined standards
of performance, printed primers, retrieved old and rare manuscripts,
initiated discussions on guidelines for efficient transmission, and
established a concert format. Even if it was evident that the project was
largely informed by the middle-class brahmin elite and their moral and
aesthetic sensibilities, and was only barely representative of other
identities or ancillary traditions, the success of the Academy in establishing its credentials as the prime arbiter of classical music, and in
establishing a space for middle-class performers, including women
seemed unchallenged.[23] It was at this stage, that misgivings began to
surface and the project faced its first serious challenge in the form of the
cultural claims of the Tamil music movement, the Tamil Isai Iyakkam
that was, in part, the cultural adjunct of the non-brahmin movement
running counter to mainstream Congress politics, its ideology and social
base, but that soon acquired a momentum of its own as an independent
cultural imperative struggling to redefine the classical in the realm of
music.

The Non-brahmin Movement
and Tamil Separatism

The non-brahmin movement, from its inception in the first decades of
the twentieth century to its subsequent radicalization under E.V.
Ramaswamy Naiker (or Periyar as he was more popularly known), drew
on an ideology of difference from both the brahmin community that had
traditionally dominated civil society and from the mainstream national
movement articulated through the Indian National Congress. Emerging

as a political force in the first quarter of the twentieth century, the movement mobilized substantial sections of the non-brahmin population to question the brahmin oligarchy, to contest the unequal basis of the caste system or *varnashramadharma*, and to establish the vitality and autonomy of indigenous Tamil culture free from the alien influences the Aryan/brahmin inheritance. The movement was in its first stages dominated by the Vellalas (high-caste agricultural groups), the Chettis and Mudaliars (commercial castes), and a sprinkling of other castes and communities constituting itself as the Justice Party, contested and won the elections to the Madras Legislative Council in 1920 and 1923. Subsequently, the party floundered and its distancing itself from the *Adi Dravida*s (untouchables and depressed castes) robbed it of much of its earlier dynamism. It remained for Periyar to reconstitute the party on more inclusive and radical lines and push the demands of Tamil regionalism and separatism more stridently.[24]

Central to the ideology of non-brahmanism was a new conception of history and a new engagement with Tamil language and literature that identified them as the most critical markers of identity. Emerging narratives of non-brahmin identity articulated through tracts and pamphlets from the latter decades of the nineteenth century, posited a new history and historical sensibility that was aggressively assertive of its Tamilness and scornful of Aryan influences in Indian culture. Inspired by the discovery of Tamil classics and the antiquity of the Tamil language, enthusiasts like Sundaram Pillai (1855–97), J.M. Nallaswami Pillai (1864–1920), K. Subramania Pillai (1888–1945) and Purnalingam Pillai projected through their writings the existence of a primordial Tamil past.[25] Their enterprise not only enabled the production of an alternative historical tradition that stressed the uniqueness and distinctiveness of Tamil society and religion, but also fostered a deep and self-conscious love for the language. The exaltation of classical Tamil and the simultaneous emergence of a modern secular Tamil for political communication, produced an extraordinary phenomenon of language devotion—what Sumathi Ramaswamy calls Tamilparru. This soon became the vehicle for political articulation as well as social empowerment.[26] Brahmins were not entirely absent in this engagement—but there was an important difference. For the non-brahmin aspirants, language became the principal vehicle for articulating an autonomous racial and political identity—even a nation—whose sacral order was occupied solely by Tamil from which all members claimed, shared descent. What this meant in political terms was the establishment of the absolute rule of

Tamil through the exclusive use of Tamil in the political apparatus and administration. It was in this context that the Tani Tamil and Tamil Isai movements originated, and in time, assumed a special significance. Working on the premise of a self-respect that could be secured only by jettisoning the stranglehold of Brahmanical culture expressed through Sanskrit, the Tani Tamil movement aimed at cleansing the language of all loan words and alien accretions, while the Tamil Isai movement concentrated on popularizing Tamil musical compositions to thereby establish Tamil as the principal language of classical music and dance. M.S. Purnalingam Pillai for instance, in his pamphlet *Tamil India* spoke of the distinctiveness and antiquity of Tamil music.[27] These narratives of Tamil identity produced a keener appreciation of the Tamil language and inspired a section of Tamil intellectuals and ideologues to stake a claim for a parallel Tamil musical culture.

The Tamil Isai Iyakkam and the Custodianship of Culture

Literally, a movement for Tamil music, the Tamil Isai Iyakkam[28] may be dated to the late 1920s, when senior publicists and patrons like Sir Raja Annamalai Chettiar, Dhanamugam Chettiar, Sir Muthiah Chettiar, Chidamabaram Nada Mudaliar, Sir C. Rajagopalachari and Kalki Krishnamurti, spoke for the need to patronize and popularize Tamil songs and to document the indigenous Tamil tradition of music as it was represented in classical Sangam literature. It was part of the larger discourse on Tamilparru but reflected more than any other strand, the myriad imaginings of Tamil devotion. Brahmin poets and litterateurs, even some senior musicians, like Musiri Subramani Iyer, Dandapani Desikar, M.K. Tyagaraja Bhagavatar, C. Saraswathi Bai among others,[29] joined ranks with Tamil Isai advocates, for whom language devotion was identified with Dravidian separatism, to espouse the cause of Tamil songs, and subsequently to contest the basis on which the classical music tradition had been reconstituted in the recent past. Initially, the movement remained open-ended. Its guiding light Raja Annamalai Chettiar was a true connoisseur of classical music, and a generous patron of the Madras Music Academy, who frequently spoke out against linguistic chauvinism. Subsequently, however, the movement was hijacked by a more vocal segment, who expanded the scope of debate to the consideration of an 'alternative' tradition proposing the exclusive use of Tamil compositions in concerts and the retrieval of an older musical tradition that was unique to the Tamil country. Ironically, the modalities of the project, defining and delineating the Tamil Isai tradition, and its conceptual frame were largely derivative; it followed in almost all essentials, the Academy model. Like the Madras Academy, the Tamil Isai worked on a history project that stressed the exceptionalism of the Tamil legacy, making it the foundation stone for Karnatik music, involving traditional practitioners like the Oduvars during their deliberations and endeavouring to situate Tamil music in new institutional spaces of modern education and musical entertainment, thereby staking claims to custodianship over an alternative tradition of classical Tamil music and culture. And yet the project failed both in terms of developing a popular base for its consumption as well as of challenging the hegemony of the nationalist cultural project. For, embedded within the larger project of Tamil promotion was the problem of multiple imaginings and the need to negotiate with modernity, which made it almost impossible to singularize the local, at the expense of the national, not to speak of the global.

The Tamil Isai movement was launched in 1929,[30] when Annamalai Chettiar founded the Minakshi College in Chidambaram, which later became Annamalai University in 1932. He endowed a music school in the premises of the university that by the 1940s had instituted an academic degree programme centred on Tamil music, the first in south India. The university's affinity with Tamil music had earlier been made evident in 1936 when the Vice Chancellor, Srinivasa Sastri, organized a music conference, where it was resolved that Tamil songs should be included in greater numbers in public concerts and incentives should be held out to encourage original compositions in Tamil. These early efforts did not bear fruit as performers continued to follow the kacheri format popularized by the Academy which gave Tamil songs only a minor slot. The raja and his associates did not lose heart and persisted in their efforts to organize the first Tamil Isai conference in Madras (14–17 August 1941), in which a number of resolutions were passed to give the movement a comprehensive agenda to work on. The conference was convened under the auspices of Annamalai University and concluded with a number of concerts including those of Musiri Subramania Iyer, Papanasam Sivan and K. Minakshi Sundaram Pillai. In his inaugural address, Annamalai Chettiar pointed out that it was not his intention to denigrate compositions in other languages, all of which had a legitimate place in the repertoire, but to bring out the richness of Tamil musical traditions and encourage the popularization and dissemination of Tamil compositions. He de-linked the issue of Tamil Isai from the programme of linguistic chauvinism, and linked it instead with the larger question of aesthetic expression that was ideally conveyed through one's mother tongue. He drew attention to the fact that despite the centrality of lyrics in Indian music, many of the singers, not to speak of the listeners, did not always understand the languages in which the music was rendered. The conference lasted four days and came up with the following resolutions.[31]

1. The conference requests the executive authorities in charge of institutions for the advancement of music to give prominence to Tamil songs in preference to songs in other languages which might be taught if necessary, but only to a very small extent (Forty per cent Tamil, forty per cent Telugu and the rest in other languages).

2. The conference requests music associations (*sangeetha sabha*s) and music academies to arrange concerts in such a way that songs are in Tamil, and that only a minor portion of the concert was devoted to songs in other languages.

3. The conference requests patrons and lovers of music to support the cause of Tamil songs.

4. The conference would at an early date approach the authorities in charge of radio stations to arrange their programmes intended for the people of Tamil Nadu in such a way that Tamil songs predominated.[32]

These resolutions had the support of select musicians like Musiri Subramania Iyer, Papanasam Sivan (composer), K. Minakshi Sundaram Pillai, all of whom took part in the conference and the accompanying music concerts, but they did not go down well with the wider musical fraternity. The Madras Music Academy, while endorsing the decision to encourage and popularize Tamil compositions, did not take kindly to the suggestion of pruning the classical repertoire or of introducing the language issue in the field of classical music, which in its opinion, drew from a wide range of inspirations and cultural influences. It was not merely that the bulk of the compositions were in Telugu or Sanskrit— the languages favoured by eighteenth century composers like Tyagaraja, Dikshitar, or Syama Sastri—it was also a question of introducing divisive regional and linguistic considerations into the larger realm of the south Indian classical tradition. An editorial in *The Hindu* dated 2 September 1941 said it all.

It is one thing to wish the encouragement of the composition of great music in Tamil, those who give a fillip to this wholly laudable object by constituting prizes, holding competitions, and soon, will be doing a needed and valuable public service. But it is as futile as it is dangerous to try to affect this by laying a ban on the singing of songs composed in other languages. There is no room for protection in music. Those who think that compositions in Tamil will be stimulated by compelling singers to sing only Tamil pieces little understand the way in which the creative imagination in music or in any other art functions.[33]

The editorial stressed the openness and dynamism of classical music in the south—a tradition that had produced Tyagaraja, the Telugu saint composer, and had its foundations set by the Kannada saint Purandaradasa and creative inputs in Tamil and even Marathi. It was only when singers sang from an inner compulsion that creativity and vitality could be retained not because the 'box office or self-constituted custodians of Tamil autonomy demanded it'.[34] The editorial warned against the pernicious nature of the movement, which did not abide by artistic considerations and was bound to debase popular taste. In a similar but more humorous vein, the popular weekly *Ananda Vikatan* carried a piece on the controversy in the form of a dialogue between Tamil and Tyagaraja. It made the point that while genuine outpourings could only be in the mother tongue, no music lover could dismiss the composer's songs, for the music that it embodied, was that of Tamil Nadu and a universal bhakta. There was thus no question of dislodging Tyagaraja who belonged to the traditional lineage of Tamil Alwars and bhakti saints.[35] In a sense, the argument typified the sentiments of brahmin stalwarts like Kalki Krishnamurti (who wrote the piece) and musicians like Ariyakudi, Musiri, and Dandapani Desikar, all of whom had a lively interest in popularizing Tamil compositions without compromising their adherence to the Karnatik tradition as they had received it. The Academy followed suit in 1941, when it convened its annual winter concert. In the presidential address to the conference, Venkataswami Naidu (Principal, Maharani College, Vijayanagaram), reminded the members that the extensive use of one language was detrimental to the cause of music and that a very special responsibility had to be shouldered by his fellow Tamil musicians, (by which he meant members of the Madras Music Academy) who happened to be 'the custodians of the rich treasures of Carnatic music. As trustees they are above parties. On them rests the sacred duty of preserving and handing down intact their rich heritage of Telugu and Kannada songs'.[36]

The message was unambiguous. Ariyakudi Ramanuja Iyengar, speaking on the eighth day of the 1941 Academy conference, came down strongly on the protagonists of the Tamil Isai movement, whose agenda clearly compromised aesthetic considerations for those of linguistic pride and chauvinism. Iyengar stressed the point that he was opposed not to Tamil, but to the idea of musicians being coerced to sing Tamil songs exclusively. As an artist, his concern was aesthetic not political, and from the point of view of music, pure and simple, he found the controversy deplorable. Music had a language of its own that transcended the language of words. Further, he reminded his critics that Tamil songs had been accommodated in the new concert repertoire which was in vogue, and that he along with some other musicians had adopted the practice of singing Tamil compositions. The language controversy, therefore, had no place at all in the field of aesthetic music.[37] Moreover, the Tamil Isai Iyakkam was too limited a conception when compared to the grand classical project that nationalists had embarked upon. For Ariyakudi there was never any doubt that Tamil songs like Tevaram and *Tiruppugal* were recitative verses and not full-fledged musical compositions like the kritis of the trinity. They could be sung only as miscellaneous pieces and could not inform the basis of the classical music culture, which besides being inclusive of multiple genres was firmly structured round the musical contribution of the trinity.[38]

Raja Annamalai Chettiar continued to defend his position. In fact, even before the music conference of the Academy, the Raja addressed a gathering on the occasion of Tyagaraja's birthday celebrations in Madras in October 1941.[39] He argued that the Tamil Isai movement had been misrepresented in the press and that baseless fear and prejudices were informing the opposition.[40] Language in his view, was central to music—the presence of a rich tradition in vocal music testified to this. It was only proper for Tamilians to take pride in their language and to take on the project of preserving and developing compositions so that both the performer and his audience could achieve complete identification. The raja's supporters, many of them front ranking musicians with strong affiliations to the Madras Academy, maintained that the intention of the Tamil Isai was in fact not to oust Telugu songs from the repertoire, but to give Tamil audiences the fullest access to Tamil music. Under the raja's initiative, Tamil Music Conferences proliferated[41] where Tamil songs, both contemporary and traditional were sung. Performers were encouraged to take part in these proceedings and demonstrate their enthusiasm and musical skill in order to disseminate a wider appreciation for Tamil music. Those who responded to the call were both professional musicians and bhagavatars who had lent their support to the Madras Academy project, and stage singers and traditional performers from the Oduvar community.

To what extent the raja's patronage of Tamil music provided an alternative definition of the classical or even a more intimate and local aural legacy is debatable. For, classical music traditions, from the closing decades of the nineteenth century, had filtered down to the Tamil stage providing the rudimentary melodic basis for the music of film and drama.[42] It went to the credit of bhagavatars, stage singers, and theatre artists that many of the Tamil songs were set to scores with an appropriately classical melodic form. The interaction between stage singers, like S.G. Kitappa for example, and artists like T.N. Rajaratnam Pillai, Govidaswamy Pillai, Gopalakrishna Iyer was creatively alive[43] and resulted in the emergence of a repertoire that effectively served the interests of stage music and later on film music, but could not effectively claim the space of the classical. Actually, the reverse happened; Tamil songs were partially integrated into classical concerts and sung in the second half representing a lighter variation of the classical tradition.[44]

The Tamil Music Conferences became a regular feature and were not confined to Madras city. The year 1941 alone saw conferences proliferate in Devakottai, Tirichirapalli, Madurai, Pudukottai, Kumbakonam, Dindigul, and Tirunelveli.[45] The conferences drew on the support of stalwarts like Kalki Krishnamurti and musicians such as Dandapani Desikar, Tiger Varadachariar, Chitoor Subramania Pillai, and C. Saraswathi Bai, and reiterated the importance of popularizing the Tamil compositions. The inaugural address to the first Tamil Music Conference in Madras (14–17 August 1941) observed that it was in Tamil Nadu alone that songs in the mother tongue were being relegated to a lower slot.[46] In the Trichinapally conference of 1941, it was suggested that the All India Radio Station be instructed to take active steps to promote the cause of Tamil Isai and that the local Tamil Association act as a liaising agency.[47] The issue was kept alive but did not seem to make an appreciable dent in the structure of the classical music concert perfected under the aegis of the Madras Academy.

The movement gained further momentum in 1943, when the Tamil Isai Sangam was formally established in Madras (December 1943) and organized its first twelve-day conference on 2 December 1943.[48] A number of musicians including N.C. Vasanthakokilam, M.K. Thyagaraja Bhagavatar, and G.N. Balasubramanian took part in the conference and spoke on behalf of the movement. While these efforts supported the popularization of Tamil compositions and gave professional classical musicians an opportunity to set their melodic framework, they did not provide a basis for developing an alternative classical tradition. The musicians who were sympathetic to the movement did not, at any stage jettison their classical training which was strongly grounded in the lineage associated with the trinity. As Tiger Varadachariar explained in a letter to *The Hindu* dated 6 September 1941, that the object of the Tamil Isai movement was not to reject compositions in other languages but to give Tamil speaking audiences an opportunity to appreciate Tamil songs.

The Tamil Music Conference is not against Thyagaraja's kritis (compositions) being taught in schools and colleges, nor against these being sung in public conferences. The resolution of the Conference was only to speed up the pace in which Tamil songs will be composed and sung in the Tamil country.[49]

It was when the Tamil Isai movement tended to bring musicians to their line, that the issue became contentious. In 1941, the Madras Academy passed a resolution endorsing the opinion of the conference of experts at the Academy that it should be the aim of all musicians and lovers of music 'to preserve and maintain the highest standards of Karnatik music and that no consideration of language should be imported as to lower or impair that standard'.[50] The realm of the classical thus remained within the jurisdiction of the brahmin elite represented by associations such as the Madras Academy, and dominated by the repertoire that it had developed and refined over the years.

The preoccupation with Tamil as the only legitimate vehicle for musical expression, gave way in the early fifties, and extended to the larger question of researching into an alternative musical tradition that had found currency in Tamil Nadu since very early times and had found expression in a huge corpus of devotional and religious hymns such as the Tevaram songs. These were sung in temples and were in the form of recitative music without embellishment and set to a limited range of specific melodies said to have originated during the Sangam centuries and known as panns. A committee for investigating the history and practice of panns was instituted by the Sangam which held its first major conference in 1960.[51] Reporting on the thirteenth meeting of the Tamil Isai Research Committee in 1960, the president of the Sangam, T.M. Narayanaswami Pillai reported that the earlier emphasis on singing Tamil songs only, had been a self-defeating exercise and it was to strengthen the Tamil Isai movement that the research committee had been organized to 'establish the antiquity and authority of Tamil Isai, to investigate its scientific form, to protect and preserve whatever has survived and to research in an orderly way the various proofs that could re-connect the broken strings of the old, traditional Tamil music and to facilitate the renaissance of Tamil Isai'.[52] The continuity of the tradition, albeit fractured, was in part due to its practice by traditional singers associated with temples and temple rituals. Here, the movement came face to face with the issue of traditional performing communities, whose cooperation was envisaged as absolutely essential, but whose induction in the exercise of retrieval was, as we shall see, severely compromised by the nature of the Tamil Sangam's agenda, and by the absence of an organic connection between the practice and its patrons.

The Tamil Isai and the Traditional Performer

The Non-brahmin movement under E.V. Ramaswamy Naiker engaged only briefly with the issue of the traditional performer and the brahmin appropriation of the domain of classical music. Periyar was not entirely sympathetic to the issue of language devotion—in fact, he preferred to keep the issues of language exclusivity and Dravidianism separate.[53] For him, the questions of self-respect, social justice, and empowerment were critical and were predicated more on the subversion of the existing social and political order than on the singularity of language and the devotion that it generated. In fact, he was extremely critical of Tamilparru, especially of its celebration of the divinity and antiquity of Tamil. He deplored the extravagance and expenses incurred in the Tamil Isai conferences, referring to Sir Annamalai Chettiar and his supporters as garrulous fellows, who were guilty of perpetuating what he referred to as a useless *bhajanai* culture that only perpetuated social inequities.[54] His dilemma was, as Sumathi Ramaswamy points out, that Tamil devotion threatened his vision of a Dravidian nation that would incorporate all Dravidians of south India and not just Tamil speakers. Indeed, by the 1950's, he went to the extent of urging Tamils to give up their obsessive infatuation with the language and embrace English even in the intimate space of their homes. So while he took up cudgels on behalf of the dispossessed and degraded, he de-linked the Tamils as far as possible from the passions of the tongue.[55]

On the issue of music and traditional performers Periyar commented briefly in a couple of articles in the *Kudi Arasu*, a Tamil daily that he edited. For instance, he drew attention to the plight of the Senguttar community. This was a community of musicians and ritual performers who were skillful with wind instruments generally considered polluting by the brahmins and were part of the peria melam (temple orchestra). Their skills remained unacknowledged and as a rule drew little attention or appreciation. Periyar condemned the brahmin arrogance and the shabby treatment they meted out to their non-brahmin counterparts, notwithstanding their obvious talents.[56] His pronouncements, however, did not attempt to suggest an alternative cultural dispensation. The same ambivalence characterized his approach to the devadasi issue. There was never any doubt in his mind that the system had to be abolished for it had evolved within the abominable brahmin imaging of the cultural and religious universe. The corollary issue of relocating their artistic skills did not figure with him. In any case Periyar had very little to say about the virtues of classical culture—Tamil or otherwise. High Tamil literature or the imagined Tamil past only earned his scorn, for he believed that all of it was tainted with ritualism, casteism, and Brahmanism, and celebrating it would only perpetuate Dravidian enslavement.

But the Tamil Isai Sangam had other ideas. It did espouse the cause of the traditional performing communities but not as part of a social reform campaign, more as a means to project the richness of a 'classical' Tamil tradition that they wanted to revive and consolidate. The Oduvars, as custodians of recitative music in the temples, were central to this project and their participation in the Tamil Isai project was considered essential. Thus in the 1960 Pann conference of the Tamil Isai Sangam, the sponsors encouraged the community to come forward to express their experience and offer their comments. The conference also provided a forum for professional musicians, musicologists, and litterateurs whose participation was expected to provide a framework for further research and intervention. In so doing, the conference implicitly endorsed the broad theoretical imperatives that had informed the nationalist project to begin with, and in the process, accepted all those standards and markers of classicism that the Madras Academy had set out—the theory-practice problematic, the stress on textual authenticity, and the obsession with classification. What they failed to do as effectively was to build a genuine popular base for the alternative tradition that could become the vehicle for a shared expressive experience, and facilitate, a larger circulation of tastes and sensibilities and common affinities of social and cultural identity. Instead, it was the Madras Academy and their protégé musicians who accommodated and incorporated a whole range of Tamil songs into their concert repertoire, giving them a wider circulation through commercial recordings and incorporating them into their own aesthetic project. The cassette culture from the late seventies testified to this phenomenon as Tamil devotional songs entered in the daily mill of worship in brahmin homes, and as amplified accompaniments to wedding receptions not to speak of the homes of Non Resident Indians for whom they offered an almost mystical resonance of the culture they had left behind.

The issues that came up for discussion in the Tamil Isai Conference on the pann were the definition and antiquity of pann, the numbers of pann that could be documented and the styles in vogue. The word pann found in traditional Sangam texts, it was concluded, referred to melodies as well as certain compositions set to specific melodies sung by Oduvars as part of the daily ritual and worship in temples. By and large, the songs sung on such occasions were Tevaram hymns of the medieval period. Traditionally, these were specific to rituals like waking the deity up, or putting the deity to sleep. For the conference authorities, it was important to establish the uninterrupted continuity of the tradition on the basis of textual references, to come to a consensus on the appropriate style of rendering them, and to examine the unique development of the pann tradition independent of the larger classical tradition of raga music.[57] They were almost entirely replicating the agenda of the Madras Academy but there was a significant lack that had to do with the ties of sociability and significance that classical music of whatever version, had in the personal experience and self-definition of the subject consuming Tamil Isai.

The deliberations of the research committee were revealing and produced interesting results. It was largely established musicologists and musicians whose intervention set the tone for the debate and incidentally put the traditional practitioners as well as the protagonists of Tamil Isai on the back-foot. Ariyakudi Ramanuja Iyengar, in consequence of his personal energy and interest in popularizing Tamil compositions within the established Karnatik framework, presided over the 1960 meeting.[58] At the same time, the Sangam[59] could not but draw on the support of the established musical fraternity without which the existing musical material of the Oduvars could not be brought under a rational scheme of classification. Iyengar's address, while endorsing the richness and antiquity of the Tamil musical tradition, alerted the organizers to the importance of research in order to determine the position of notes and the structure of the melodic arrangement that the panns represented. It was not enough to go by just what the Oduvars sang.[60] The Oduvars themselves who were present were asked to share their expertise on panns, their classification, and their currency. Practical demonstrations formed an important part of the conference, which battled to establish a proper basis for the tradition they sought to invoke.

The debates centred around two principle issues of classification and standardization of panns. While, there was a general agreement about the antiquity of pann traditions in the Tamil country and the rich repertoire of mystical and devotional songs (Alwar and Nayanar hymns), it was found difficult to establish historical references to the tradition between the eleventh and the late nineteenth centuries. It was also found that the Oduvars had learnt their Tevarams purely in an oral tradition and they confessed that they did not strictly adhere to the conventions. What the conference authorities sought were definitive conclusions as to the number of panns, their nomenclature, their structure in terms of note combinations used, and the times and occasions in which they were to be sung. Confusions abounded—for instance, day melodies were often sung at night and vice versa.

The Oduvars debated the issues but confessed that it was not possible to reach any definite conclusions on any of these questions. The number of panns itself was a source of contention—some early twentieth-century publications gave their number as twenty-four, others maintained that it was twenty-seven. Velayudha Oduvar, among the more articulate of the members present suggested that there were 24 panns in all—twelve panns specifically set as daytime melodies, nine as night time melodies and three that were meant for all times of the day. He, however, admitted that the method of singing them had changed, while maintaining that this was admissible and that such 'transgressions' were part of artistic license.[61] Subbaya Desikar disagreed and maintained that the practice of singing daytime and evening melodies were scrupulously maintained in some of the temples that he knew and frequented.[62] Practical demonstrations did not resolve the issue and some members like S. Rasan mounted a scathing attack on the Oduvars, who 'escape the responsibility when they say that my father sang in this manner, my grandfather in that manner and my guru in yet another manner'.[63] Rasan took a highly critical view of the Oduvars and their failure to apply critical methods to preserve tradition.

The discussion on the structure and nomenclature of certain panns proved to be acrimonious but desultory in terms of results. While Rasan and others urged the committee to discuss the matter in the context of Tamil literature, Oduvars like Subbaya Desikar maintained that as a living tradition, some deviations were bound to occur. Ariyakudi Ramanuja

Iyengar and P. Sambamoorthy, on the other hand, representing expert musical opinion, urged that recordings of available specimens as sung in temples be made available immediately and greater care taken to ascertain the melodic features of the panns before fixing their nomenclature. It was evident throughout the proceedings that the deciding voice lay with the experts and, P. Sundaresan addressing the assembly of Oduvars proclaimed, 'we are researching into the antiquity and tradition of *pann*. Then we will come to an evaluation and if we find that these apply to your music, and then we applaud you, we will express our gratitude for having preserved the tradition. If we find that your tradition goes against the proven grammar, we request you to correct yourself'.[64]

Figure 4: Musiri, Seetha, and Balasarasvati in a scene from *Tukaram*.
Reprinted from *Sruti*, May 1999.

The comment was telling for it reflected the Sangam's dependence on the professional musicians to help map the alternative tradition. By this, it locked itself into the conceptual structure set out by the Madras Academy, and failed to rework it on its own terms or independently of the markers of the classical tradition that the Academy experts had spelt out. In this sense, the Sangam could not work without these experts, or indeed consider the larger problems of the community of traditional performers. They were driven by the need to define the tradition in fixed terms, and in the process, fell back on the same evaluative standards that the Academy had set out and elaborated having no substantive, independent musical criteria of their own. For even as experts quibbled over texts, representation, and the deviations in practice, the very space and dynamics of worship within which the traditional community had participated, had undergone an immense transformation. Most temples had dispensed with the practice of songs, and while the question of litany in Tamil (Tamil *arcanai*) became a political issue that even engaged the attention of Periyar, the question of Tamil music did not command the same attention. The community dissolved—in fact, in an interview that I had some years ago (13 October 2000) with a senior Oduvar who enjoyed the patronage of the Tamil Isai Sangam, I was told that in 1960, there were hardly fifty Oduvars left, most of them had no desire to carry on with their traditional calling and had taken up new sources of livelihood. He shared his artistic appreciation of the old stalwarts of Karnatik music and admitted that the politics of patronage had needlessly reinforced what was an artificial divide.[65]

What is, in fact, striking about the attempted revival of Tevaram singing, both within and outside the patronage of the Tamil Isai Sangam, was the manner in which it modelled itself on the Brahmanical tradition. Peterson describing her field experiences with the Oduvars, mentions that the Oduvars internalized the idea of the Tevaram as the Veda, they were constantly reminded that they were like brahmin initiates, and that they were meant to memorize the scriptures (in their case the Tevaram) like the classic *adhayayana* of the Vedas.[66] This had two consequences; on the one hand, it remained a limited and local Tamil sectarian confined to a specific domain of experience and communal feeling. On the other hand, it failed to develop an expansive social base and thereby lent itself to appropriation by the larger fraternity of musicians and tradition makers, who purported to speak on behalf of a larger and more inclusive tradition.

The Tamil Isai Sangam so failed to develop an adequate forum for Tamil music, that its activities were increasingly confined to seminars and workshops about classical literature on pann and a limited engagement with teaching Tevarams, while as far as public taste and its identification of classical music was concerned, the repertoire and the format designed under the aegis of associations such as the Madras Music Academy, became even more firmly entrenched. Musicians singing under their auspices picked up effectively elements of the Tamil Isai, popularized Tamil songs, traditional, devotional, and nationalist, and effectively incorporated them in their own vision of an archetypal classical Indian form.

The protagonists of the Tamil Isai, notwithstanding extensive public support from the ruling government, failed to carve out an independent space for the Tamil Isai tradition either in terms of creating and expanding a popular audience for its consumption, or of fostering opportunities for an effective relocation of the traditional performing communities. This failure had as much to do with a limited conceptual framework that eventually deferred to the norms of the nationalist paradigm and the categories of classicism it imposed, as it had to do with the fact that at no time did the Tamil Isai confer on classical music the central role in the articulation of an expressive space for Dravidian identity that the brahmin elite of Madras city gave it to for themselves. For the brahmin community, the consumption of classical music became an integral element in their cultural self-definition, a marker of status and taste and a cementing agent of a collective identity and presence that had no longer the same visibility in active political life.

Conclusion

The Tamil Isai movement had begun with its devotees stressing the unique legacy of their cultural inheritance—there was nothing so exalted as their language, nothing sweeter than their music. Yet they ultimately failed to give back to Tamil music its exceptionalism or to its practitioners a genuine performative space in postcolonial India. Robbed of its social context, the Tamil Isai looked for its way either in seminars sponsored by the Sangam or in carefully orchestrated concerts organized by the same association celebrating the richness of its repertoire. Invariably these concerts were dance recitals, dance dramas, and *Kuravanci*s that celebrated the exploits of the unique Tamil war god Murugan and made use of melodies that were identified as indigenous. The performers were for the most part brahmin middle-class women whose adherence to Tamil Isai as a political statement was marginal. Similarly, the rendering of Tamil songs by professional and amateur musicians remained a minor adjunct of their larger commitment to the classical agenda constituted by nationalist publicists, and subsequently, by the nation state. The latter's success lay in the fact that that they had been able to streamline a set of aesthetic components that had an all-India relevance, and did not get bogged down by considerations of the local. The Tamil Isai movement, despite its full share of individual, state support, and patronage, failed to develop an original and viable framework to support the alternative tradition, and to create a strong popular base for its consumption.

Having failed to plot a marked space in the domain of high culture for Tamil Isai, the movement shifted the emphasis of its activities into the field of popular culture, cinema, and devotion, with local temples playing pre-recorded Tamil songs as part of the daily fare. The community of Tamil devotees was essentially shot through with difference, which meant that any effort to singularize and homogenize a language or a unique tradition remained half-hearted and limited. Had the promoters of Tamil Isai jettisoned the nationalist framework of classification and textual authenticity, and embarked upon a programme of rehabilitation for the traditional practitioners—the Oduvars and devadasis—and given them an alternative forum for expression, an important strand of an older tradition might have been preserved and nurtured. Instead, the Tamil Isai, barring occasional efforts to project a more authentic version of the dance forms as a challenge to Rukmini Arundale's initiative, could not sustain its efforts to establish the independence of a distinct Tamil tradition.[67] The debate continued to resonate in the domain of public culture and found its representation in films portraying the age long conflict between the classical and the local. Tamil Isai did not carry for its projected protagonists the same expressive potential as classical music did for its passionately engaged and largely brahmin advocates, and it moved over to films and popular culture, where it was destined to undergo further transmutations.

NOTES

1. Sumathi Ramaswamy, *Passions of the Tongue*, University of California Press, Berkeley, 1997. See also V. Geetha and S. Rajadorai, *Towards a Non-Brahmin Millennium. From Iyothee Thass to Periyar*, Samya, Calcutta, 1998. Eugene Irschik *Politics and Social Conflict in South India: The Non-Brahmin Movement and Tamil Separatism, 1916–1920*, University of California Press, Berkeley, 1969.
2. Sumathi Ramaswamy, *Passions of the Tongue*. See Introduction, pp. 8–9.
3. Ibid., pp. 245–6.
4. Partha Chatterjee, *The Nation and its Fragments: Colonial and Postcolonial Histories*, Oxford University Press, New Delhi, 1993, pp. 26–7.
5. Rachel Dwyer and Christopher Pinney (eds), *The History, Politics and Consumption of Public Culture in India*, Oxford University Press, New Delhi, 2001.
6. The work of Kathryn Hansen on Nautanki theatre of north India in trying to identify common features of classical performance traditions in India; she considers not the internal, textual features of the art but '. . . the sources of a tradition's authority, its

modes of reproduction, and its relation to dominant social groups'. Hansen is particularly concerned with the dynamic movement of performers as agents, who actively desire their work to be considered 'classical' in order to gain access to financial resources and audience support in contemporary India. She thus rejects any sort of static identification of art forms as folk or classical, including the folk/classical continuum suggested by Blackburn and Ramanujan, which acknowledged interplay and complexity between the two realms, but did not recognize agency on the part of performers. See Kathryn Hansen, *Grounds for Play: The Nautanki Theatre of North India*. University of California Press, Berkeley, 1992. Stuart H. Blackburn, and A.K. Ramanujan (eds.), *Another Harmony: New Essays on the Folklore of India*, University of California Press, Berkeley,1986.

7. Quoted in V. Geetha and S.V. Rajadrai, *Towards a Non-Brahmin Millennium*, pp. 6–7.

8. Ibid., p. 9.

9. As Besant exhorted the brahmins, 'Go back to your people and take your rightful place again as leaders still in India. Give to them your splendid intellect, give to them your wonderful eloquence, give to them the power of your past and the influence of your names crowned no longer with the crown of privilege but with the deathless crown of self-sacrifice', quoted in V. Geetha and S.V. Rajadorai, *Towards a Non-Brahmin Millennium*, pp. 6–7ff.

10. Ramaswami Sastri, *The Future of the Brahmin*, Madras, 1935.

11. Music was an important practice associated with the quotidian religious and social life of the community; in fact, even women even before they emerged in the public domain would appear to have had some access to it. See Sita Anantha Raman, *Getting Girls to School*, pp. 104–5ff. Anantha Raman quotes Savitri Rajan's reminiscences where she described the learning process for her family women: 'Girls there could not learn the Vedas but they were taught Sanskrit literature and music' Other brahmin women described similar experiences to Anantha Raman. Kamakshi Natarajan observed that some of her family women were unlettered but were orally conversant with Sanskrit and music. The case of Visalakshi (b.1875) was similarly revealing. Her musical talent and language skills in Tamil and Telugu were much appreciated by elders. On the other hand, there was the case of Nagalakshmi whose husband indulged her passion for music by arranging for her instruction by trained Kannadiga women of Madhava descent. Nagalakshmi herself even paid a devadasi woman to enter the family portals to instruct her daughters in singing and the veena.

12. K.V. Zvelebil, *The Story of My Life: An Autobiography of Dr U.V. Swaminatha Iyer* (English version), Institute of Asian Studies, Madras, 1994, pp. 14–20, 66–7, passim.

13. S.M. Natesa Sastri, *Hindu Feast, Fasts and Ceremonies*, Madras, 1903, pp. 53–5.

14. Ibid.

15. *JMAM*, 1944.

16. S. Ramamurthi, 'New Ferments in Karnatic Music: Talkies and Light Music', *The Indian Review*, vol. 39, February 1938, Madras, pp. 98–9.

17. Ibid.

18. In their critique of brahmin politics, V. Geetha and S.V. Rajadorai argue that the most complete expression of political Brahmanism was nationalism. To the brahmin, nationalism signified an atavistic desire to endow the Hindu past on a more durable

and contemporary basis. See V. Geetha and S.V. Rajadorai, *Towards a Non-Brahmin Millennium*, p. 320.

19. *Tevaram* refers to the corpus of Saivite temple hymns set to music, mainly ascribed to three revered poets and mystics, namely Tirunanacampandar, Tirunavakkaracar and Cundaramurti (approximately 6th–8th centuries) See Ludwig Pesch, *The Illustrated Companion to South Indian Classical Music*, p. 176.

20. Indira Viswanathan Peterson, *Poems to Siva: The Hymns of the Tamil Saints*, Princeton University Press, Princeton, 1989, pp. 15–21. The canonization of the Tevaram, we are told by Peterson, is mentioned in a fourteenth century work, namely *Tirumuraikantapuranam*, which was revealed to the poet Nambi Andar who with the help of his travelling partner was able to reconstruct the melodic aspect of the compositions.

21. T. Viswanathan and Mathew Allen, *Music in South India: Experiencing Music, Expressing Culture*, Oxford University Press, New Delhi, 2004, pp. 84–5.

22. Indira Viswanathan Peterson, *Poems to Siva*, pp. 64–9. Peterson points to a basic difference between Tevaram singing and Karnataka Sangeetam. Whereas in the latter, a metrical or non-metrical text is set to a raga tune and fit into a tala or rhythmic structure, the metrical pattern of the Tevaram acted as the rhythmic framework.

23. Congratulating the Academy for its efforts, the Secretary of the Krisna Gana Sabha of Trivandrum observed, 'Musical sabhas as ours in the presidency are by nature fit for only spade work. It may be argued that they do help to elevate the standard of taste to a degree but the work of pioneering ought to rest in such an executive body as the Music Academy with a wide field for experiment.', *JMAM*, vol. I, no. 1, 1930, p. 78.

24. Eugene Irschik, *Politics and Social Conflict in South India: The Non-Brahman Movement and Tamil Separatism, 1916–1929*, University of California Press, Berkeley, 1969.

25. Sumathi Ramaswamy, *Passions of the Tongue*, pp. 25–6.

26. Ibid.

27. M.S. Purnalingam Pillai, *Tamil India*, Tirunelveli, Madras, 1927. South Indian Saiva Siddhanata Works Publishing Society, Tinnevelly Ltd., p. 115.

28. The section on Tamil Isai is mainly based on the journals of the Tamil Isai Sangam (in Tamil) dating from 1943. All translations are mine.

29. *Ponnvizhakkollum Chennai Tamil Isai Sangattil Varalarru* (1943–93), Chennai. (A History of the Tamil Isai Sangam on the occasion of its golden jubilee celebrations, pp. 4–5.

30. Ibid. *Ponnvizhakkollum Chennai Tamil Isai Sangattil Varalarru* (1943–93).

31. Ibid., pp. 15–17.

32. Ibid. (hereafter *PCTISV*). Also see *The Hindu Speaks on Music*, edited by N. Ravi, Kasturi & Sons, Madras, 1999, p. 462.

33. *The Hindu Speaks on Music*, pp. 464–5.

34. Ibid., pp. 464–5.

35. *Ananda Vikatan* (Aadal-Paadal), November 3, 1940, pp. 38–9.

36. *JMAM*, vol. XII, nos 1–4, 1941. See presidential address, pp. 6ff.

37. Ibid., pp. 18–19ff. Ariyakudi Ramanuja Iyengar addressing the language issue on 29 December 1941.

38. Ibid.

39. *PCTISV*, p. 6.

40. *PCTISV*, pp. 6ff.

41. Ibid., pp. 6–10.

42. S. Theodore Baskaran, *The Message Bearers: The Nationalist Politics and the Entertainment Media in South India 1880–1945*, 1981, pp. 121–2. Baskaran mentions that the respectability which Tamil cinema acquired through its participation in the nationalist movement attracted a number of artists from classical music. Vidwan Kothamnaglam Srinivasan became a familiar figure in films, after 1935, Musiri Subramanian Iyer acted in *Tukaram*, (1938). M.S. Dandapani Desikar opened a career in cinema with *Nandanar* (1936) while T.S. Rajaratnam Pillai came into films with *Kavirathna Kalamegam*.

43. Thumilan *Nadaguru Chakravarti T.N. Rajaratnam Pillai* (in Tamil), Madras, 1988, pp. 114–25. The author describes how in 1925, when the drama *Dasaavatharam* was being staged by the Kanayya Company as the Troche Devar Hall, Govinda-swamy Pillai, Gopalakrishna Iyer, Dakshinamurthi Pillai and S.G. Kitappa were part of an enthusiastic audience and how Rajaratnam and Kitappa practiced together, spurring each other on.

44. Musicians like Tiger Varadachariar and Ariyakudi Ramnujam Iyengar took an active interest in popularizing Tamil compositions. The former, for instance, assisted by Tanjavur Sankara Iyer was responsible for preserving authentic versions of Go palakrishnan Bharati's compositions. See Ludwig Pesch, *The Illustrated Companion to South Indian Classical Music*, p. 193.

45. *PCTISV*, pp. 8–10.

46. Ibid., pp. 4–5.

47. Ibid., p. 8.

48. Ibid., pp. 13–18.

49. *The Hindu Speaks on Music,* pp. 468–9.

50. *JMAM*, 1941, pp. 19ff.

51. *Tamil Isai Sangam, Tamil Isai Araychi Kuzhu*, Proceedings of the Tevaram Research Committee 1960, Chennai (hereafter TIS Proceedings, 1960).

52. Ibid., p. 6ff. See presidential address delivered on 25 December 1960.

53. V. Geetha and S.V. Rajadorai, *Towards a Non-Brahmin Millennium.*

54. *Tamil Isai Natippu Kalaigal* by Periyar, Kudi Arasu, Erode, 1944, pp. 1–5, p. 12.

55. Sumathi Ramaswamy, *Passions of the Tongue*, pp. 235–6.

56. V. Geetha and S.V. Rajadorai, *Towards a Non-Brahmin Millennium*, pp. 295, 318, 320.

57. *Tamil Isai Sangam Proceedings*, 1960, pp. 19–41.

58. Ibid., pp. 11–12ff.

59. Here, it needs to be said that the Isai Sangam did commission musicians to write new musical compositions in Tamil. In 1941, Annamalai University commissioned T.N. Swaminatha Pillai to compose new musical settings for 60 kritis of Muttandavar, a seventeenth-century Tamil composer.

60. *Tamil Isai Sangam Proceedings,* 1960, pp. 11–13ff.

61. Ibid., pp. 24–6.

62. Ibid., pp. 25–9.

63. Ibid., pp. 28–9, 34.

64. Ibid., pp. 54–5.

65. On 13 October 2000, I had the privilege of interviewing Shanmugam Sundaram who came from a family, whose musical heritage had accrued over nine generations.

His grandfather and his brother had been nadaswaram players while his father Nataraja Sundaram Pillai began a school for nadaswaram in Swamimalai and Pazhani. He spoke of Raja Annamalai Chettiar's enthusiasm and single-minded commitment and of his own musical education with Musiri Subramania Iyer, Brinda and Chittor Subramanian. He referred to the depressed state of the community and to the fact that there were very few oduvars attached to the schools set up for tevaram singing.

66. Indira Viswanathan Peterson, *Poems to Siva*, pp. 56–7.
67. Indira Viswanathan Peterson, 'The Evolution of the Kuravanci Dance Drama in Tamilnadu: Negotiating the Folk and the 'Classical' in the Bharata Natyam Context'. *South Asia Research* 18 January 1998, pp. 39–72.

Epilogue

I n less than a hundred years, a modern classical music idiom had been constructed and placed at the service of the nation. The changes in the context of patronage had produced new modes of consumption that inevitably affected the art form, its practitioners, and its location in the cultural context of the nation state. The making of the modern classical was prefaced by a discourse that posited a basic separation of the world of music into classical and non-classical categories, which were seen as critical in the articulation of a nationalist cultural project. The discourse, itself was predicated on a set of meanings assigned to the consumption of culture by new patrons, for whom the appreciation of music was refracted by their engagement with modernity as a subjective experience. It is here that the role of imagination became important and suffused the auditory habit with overlays of meaning that helped the community of listeners experience a shared space of habit, practice, and aesthetic taste. At the same time, it was tied up with the larger agenda of social reform and modernization, which in the case of music and dance, was double-edged. Here, the point made by Partha Chatterjee[1] about the contra-modernity developed by the colonized western educated elite, and one that reinvented the categories of 'tradition' and 'modernity', is especially relevant. For the performing arts, the project spearheaded for the most part by the educated elite drawn primarily from high castes, involved at one level, the relocation of the performing arts within a new secular space of pedagogy and entertainment, which in turn resulted in a complex process of social engineering. On the other hand, the project celebrated the imaginative and affective space of solidarity constituted by a particular reading of religion and the sacral dimensions of performing culture, but one that was necessarily tied up with a Brahmanical reading of the same.

This was particularly true in southern India, associated with an influential branch of classical Indian music, which in its social organization had always been organized on the basis of caste and gender.

The assertion of linguistic nationalism combined with lower-caste social reform movements in southern India, touched briefly on the question of culture, on the definition of what was classical, and how the nationalist classical project was an exercise in exclusion, perpetuating the marginalization of lower castes and their histories. Inspired by the Madras Orientalists[2] who espoused the autonomy and importance of Tamil as a Dravidian language, which could legitimately command classical status at par with Sanskrit, the devotees of Tamil nationalism put forward their claims for an autochthonous music tradition that had its own reference terms and musical language, and a composition repertoire in the Tamil language. The tussle for custodianship of the classical went on for about two decades after independence; national institutions and state sponsored academies as well as those that represented the nationalist version of the classical like the Madras Music Academy held out against the challenges posed by the Tamil Isai Sangam, which had the specific endorsement of the state government that rested on the advocacy of a subaltern anti-caste platform. The reasons for the failure of the Tamil music movement, as I have argued, lay in the fact that for its advocates, the consumption of music and dance did not have the same expressive potential for solidarity. However, this is not to suggest that the nationalist version of the classical tradition went uncontested, or that the official version of *the tradition* remained in tact over time and space. In fact even as the Music Academy expanded and streamlined its agenda, there were important voices of criticism and self-reflection. Kalki Krishnamurthi (1899–1954) in particular, gave a special inflection to this reappraisal and represented the emergence of a music critic as the key participant in the reconstituted world of music. Kalki's writing skills quite apart from the advocacy of an ethico-moral standard became part of the overall social experience of listening and reflecting on music. Here was an instance when the entire project of music reform and revival, the organization of concerts and experts committee meetings for determining the attributes and features of songs texts and melodies, the conceptual and linguistic apparatus deployed to describe music, the antics of musicians and their patrons came under scathing attack. In the process, Kalki at one level endorsed the emerging consensus on performance aesthetics; at another he poked fun at the self-importance and righteousness of the Madras elite and thereby carved a space for a new expression of music criticism.

Kalki's Music and Dance (Aadal Paadal)

Kalki wrote on a variety of issues related to music—its patronage and consumption—and intervened quite decisively in his appreciation of both the technical aspects of the art form as well as the social dimensions of the altered context of its patronage[3]. For him, the debates that accompanied the concerts were not always very edifying; he described these *vidwat sabha*s as wrestling arenas, where expressions such as 'kick the *rishabha* a little higher', 'better take care of the *gandhara*', with a menacing stick to add emphasis, 'beat on the head of the *suddha dhaivata*' were too frequent for comfort. In his opinion, the debates were a waste of time and it was only the presence of Muthiah Bhagavatar, the leading light of the Music Academy of Madras, that made them tolerable. Kalki suggested that committees had to be reconstituted and experts were to be given the power and responsibility of deciding the various issues regarding *ragalakshanam* (features of ragas). This could have been an allusion to the Madras Academy's experts committee where musicians met every year to determine raga *lakshana*s. In fact Kalki was especially lavish in his praise of Sabesa Iyer, an other key figure in the Madras Academy debates—and here he drew attention to Sabesa Iyer's knowledge that enabled a profound and expanded interpretation of a composition in spite of his gruff voice.

The patrons of debates and concerts also came in for a fair measure of lampooning. The childish and naïve pleasure of being the key organizer so outweighed the aesthetic appreciation of music that some organizer when questioned about the quality of a particular concert, almost compulsively spoke of the seats that he had arranged for a high court judge, the rose garland that he had ordered for the chief guest, how there was a minor wrangle about who would garland the chief guest, and how stressful the entire business of organizing a first rate concert was. Some extracts of this dialogue are worth quoting. They offer us perhaps, the best insight into the social world of modern music as it was reconstituted around social celebrities, eager association members and enthusiastic volunteers for all of whom the experience was an extension of their self definition and identity.

'So how was the concert?' I asked.

'The concert was great. I had reserved a special sofa for a High Court Judge Alamelu Manga Sameda Thiruppathi Venkateswara Chettiar. But some body came and occupied the seat and along with a lady. I was really in a fix. When I requested him to get up, he refused to do so till I provided him with another. I myself dragged a couple of chairs. Yes Sir, if you are a secretary, you should be prepared to do anything and everything. But who realizes it?'

'You say the concert was good. What ragas did he sing?' I asked again.

'Not a single Raga was left out, heavy ones, light ones—sang everything... listen to one more gripe of mine! I had bought a rose garland for the judge costing me Rs.1 and a quarter. My god these flower men fleece you. But after all being a judge, he would be good for a hundred rupees at least. But how could I foresee he would bring his wife along. Kindly tell me what could I do. So I sent another boy to get a garland for a rupee and a quarter.'

'What important *kritis* did he (singer) sing', I persisted.

'He sang everything—*Thyagakeertanam, Nataraja keertanam, Diksitar keertanam, Ramayana padam*. He made mince meat of them all. Now the question was who should do the garlanding. You know my partner; he is there in name only but wants all the kudos. Just as were wondering what to do, the Judge showed signs of leaving. We panicked. The judge excused himself, saying that he had work to do but that his wife would stay back. I held my breath, sent a person to stop the second garland from being bought'.

'Did the musician's voice cooperate? You know sometime this is a problem,' I ventured again in an attempt to know about the concert.

'Oh yes. The voice was very good. But tell me should not a person have a sense of propriety? My partner is devoid of it. He insisted that since the Judge had left, he would like to garland the Judge's wife. I had to convince him that it would be very improper and that we would face boos and jeers from the audience.'

'You have gone into a lot of trouble. I hope you were pleased with the concert....'

'You say so, Sir. I know that I have worked hard but who realizes it? You know what one of them at the end of the concert said. Took two rupees and gave a rickety chair to sit on. For those two rupees, I could have bought a brand new chair. How do you like the comment? Who realizes how much I struggle to maintain the sabha without losses. Yesterday I requested the musician to reduce his rate by ten rupees. He refused. But what can I do? If I don't pay, he would have finished the concert an hour sooner. If this happens a couple of times, that would be the end of the sabha'[4].

The dialogue is telling. While Kalki was sympathetic with the sabha organizers, he was making an important point about the social dynamics that had accompanied the reception and consumption of music in the transformed public domain.

From the Local to the Global

The experience of the diaspora on the other hand has been somewhat different. In the case of the South Asian Diaspora in the United States, Indian music has been both part of an older inheritance as well as a resource to be deployed in new musical improvisations. The results have been interesting, especially in replicating existing tropes of tradition and modernity, spirituality and mysticism and in contributing to discourses on authenticity and global homogeneity.

It is in this context, that it may be pertinent to look at the south Indian Diaspora, and how contestations of language and content and interpretation are worked out in the diasporic imagination of South Asians for whom Indian music is both part of an older inheritance as well as a resource to be deployed in new musical improvisations, and how in the process, existing tropes of tradition and modern, sacral, and secular are replicated.

I will illustrate my position with some preliminary observations drawn from the experiences of Tamils in the United States, the nature of their engagement with Indian music and dance, and their efforts to negotiate diasporic identities from their vantage point. The question of academic courses and research on ethno-musicology and Asian music is also important and merits some investigation; how do these courses address the questions of tradition and modernity as categories in music, and in the process, reopen issues of authenticity in presentation and transmission?

To contextualize the consumption of classical music within the south Indian community in the United States, it may be instructive to look at modalities of repetition, a resource around which societies have been known to build regimes of periodicity and cultural practice. Another area would be to look at migrations and marriage networks that are expected to ensure circulation of practice and reinforce solidarity within a de-territorialized space. Finally, it would be pertinent to investigate the new imaginative spaces the second-generation immigrants occupy or would want to occupy.

The community of consumers and patrons of classical music in the United States remain for the most part upper-caste groups, mostly brahmins, for whom music has remained a social resource, a marker of status, and a key element in the imagining of the collective in much the same manner as organized modern religion and ritual worship operates.

The community makes strenuous efforts to maintain its marriage networks that stretch to the 'home'. With suitable brides equipped with a secular education—preferably of the scientific variety that can ensure employment and with at least a rudimentary knowledge of the arts—the community for the most part continues to consume and reflect upon classical music within the same frames of solidarity and identity. The engagement is part of the larger circuit of organized religion that is expressed through the building of temples consecrated by priests and practitioners imported from Madras, through the replication of the ritual ambience in the domestic space by recourse to audio-visual medium, and through a self-conscious attempt to infuse among the younger generation a nostalgia of the present. It is not, therefore, entirely coincidental that music festivals like the Tyagaraja Samaradhana[5] are replicated faithfully and that the Ohio chapter of this celebration should have become so important. Note the description that we have of this commemoration event, which records the instrumentality of imagination as a social practice.

On a cold gray morning in late April, a piercing wind whips in off Lake Erie. Several hundred people of South Indian descent who have come from across the United States and Canada hurry into a hall at Cleveland State University, wearing heavy winter coats over their light cotton dhotis and gold-bordered saris. They are drawn to this most un-South Indian climate for the aradhana, the annual festival honouring South India's most beloved composer, Tyagaraja (1767–1847). The celebration at Cleveland, just as those now taking place in many cities around the world with a sizeable South Indian population, brings elders thoughts of home while educating young South Indians growing up in the diaspora about their ancestral heritage.

At the festival, a range of performance stakes place, including evening music and dance concerts by vesting professional performers and many shorter presentations by young students or adult amateurs, all intent upon paying musical homage to the venerated composer. After Brahmin Hindu priests performed appropriate pujas, religious rituals, several groups of local musicians sang devotional songs called bhajans.[6]

On first appearances, as described so vividly by Viswanathan and Allen, the celebration in terms of the audience and the participants is not fundamentally different from the way it is observed in its local context, or in the way the state through its broadcasting and television channels showcases it as a 'national' cultural event. Further, given that the great majority of the advocates of classical music in the States maintain connections with the home, and share in a manner the terms of the mainstream discourse and sponsor artists who are recognized within official institutional spaces in the nation state (universities, teaching colleges, music academies), it would only be legitimate to expect a reinforcement of the official version of the classical and allow that to continue to inflect its reception.[7] So can we then look at the Cleveland event as an extension of the national project even if detached from its territorial locus or does it contain by the very logic of its spatial dynamics elements of 'cosmopolitanism'? The question is of some importance particularly if we take into consideration the trajectory of musical culture in the United States, the nature of official sponsoring of musicians from India, and the direction of academic interest and research in American universities.

One important vehicle for the transmission of music and dance has been the setting up of private schools and training workshops by Indian teachers, either hired on a temporary basis or by those who have combined their residence (following marriage usually) with some sort of pedagogical initiative. In most cases, this has amounted to an advocacy of certain styles associated with traditional music lineages in India and which are represented as the authentic version. By and large, this conforms to the official version of the classical that was put in place right through the last century, a version that the Madras Music Academy was chiefly instrumental in consolidating. The NRI investment in the Academy—in terms of both financial and social capital—has meant that the perpetuation of the mainstream version has been a significant concern, at least one segment in the diaspora. Not that this is not subject to contestation. But surprisingly this comes not from the advocates of Tamil music, but from second or even third generation students in US universities, American, Indian, and children of mixed marriages whose negotiation with world music, on the one hand, and with anthropology, on the other, critiques the universality of the modern nationalist representation. The emphasis is precisely on those communities of ritual performers whose repertoire was devalued as light classical, and on retrieving the silenced voices that suggest an alternative reading and representation of music. In part, this process has also to do with the somewhat special location of one family in the United States—associated with the legendary house of Veena Dhanammal—one that was marginalized in course of the nationalist imperative, and which migrated to the United States and subsequently earned a devoted following. This important intervention continues to contest the notion of the classical as set out by the state and its votaries within and without its borders, and deploys technology, ethnography to bolster its position. Finally, there is in this battle for imagination, a growing interest in fusion music—more pronounced in the field of rhythm and percussion—that articulates its own language of universality amidst diversity.

It is not my intention, here to draw any conclusions or even general propositions from these preliminary observations. The point that I would like to make is the fluidity that characterizes the reception and represent-ation of classical culture and the importance that continues to be assigned to its consumption and custodianship. Here, the fault lines that work within the boundaries of the nation state correspond somewhat even if not exactly to those in the diaspora, except that the terms of contestation are set not so much by the votaries of Tamil language devotion or indigenization as by the advocates of Indology and neo-Orientalism.

NOTES

1. Partha Chatterjee, 'Two Poets and Death: On Civil and Political Society in the Non-Christain World', in Timothy Mitchell (ed.), *Questions of Modernity*, University of Minnesota Press, Minneapolis, 2002, pp. 35–48. Also see Introduction.
2. Thomas R. Trautman, 'Inventing the History of South India', in Daud Ali (ed.), *Invoking the Past: The Uses of History in South Asia*, SOAS, Oxford University Press, New Delhi, 2000, pp. 36–54.
3. This section is based on the *Ananda Vikatan*, a Tamil weekly, where Kalki wrote regulalrly on the music performances of the day. The material used in this section is based on the Aadal Padal section of the years 1935–7.
4. 'Aadal Paadal', *Ananda Vikatan*, 18 October 1936.
5. *The Hindu Speaks on Music*, Chennai, 1999, pp. 449–50. Two reports on the Tyagaraja festival in Chicago and Cleveland are reported.
6. T. Viswanathan and Mathew Allen, *Music in South India: Experiencing Music, Expressing Culture*, Oxford University Press, New Delhi, pp. 1–2.
7. *The Hindu Speaks on Music*, pp. 448. The report on the Tyagaraja festival in Chicago in 1995 emphasized that for its participants, the festival was more than just a series of concerts. It attempted to reflect their culture as exemplified by the saint's life. In the words of the reporter, 'The traditional rituals at the altar of Tyagaraja, the music, the socialization (in many languages ranging from Sanskrit to Telugu), the fragrance of incense sticks, the aroma of typical South Indian home cooking, and the glittering clothes—all blend to create an ambience of the old country'.

Bibliography

I. Books and Articles

Allen, Mathew Harp, 'Rewriting the Script for South Indian Dance', *The Drama Review*, 41(3), 1997, pp. 63–100.

———, 'Tales Tunes Tell: Deepening the Dialogue between "Classical" and "Non-Classical" in the Music of India', *Yearbook for Traditional Music*, vol. xxx, 1998, pp. 22–52.

Anantha Raman, Sita, *Getting Girls to School: Social Reform in the Tamil Districts 1870–1930*, Stree, Calcutta, 1996.

Annamali, S.P., *The Life and Teachings of Saint Ramalingar*, Bharatiya Vidya Bhavan, Bombay, 1973.

Ayyangar, R. Ranga Ramanuja, *History of South Indian (Carnatic) Music From Vedic Times to the Present*, published by the author, Bombay, 1972.

———, *Musings of a Musician: Recent Trends in Carnatic Music*, Wilco, Bombay, 1977.

Ayyar, C.S., *Sri Tyagaraja Kritis for Beginners*, published by the author, Madras, 1898.

———, *The Grammar of South Indian (Karnatic) Music*, printed by R. Narayanaswami Iyer at the Madras Law Journal and published by the author, Madras, 1930.

———, *An Artists Miscellany on Society, Religion and Music*, Madras, R. Venkateshwar & Co., 1946.

———, *108 Kritis of Sri Tyagaraja*, published by the author, Madras, 1955.

Ballhatchet, Kenneth, *Race, Class and Sex under the British Raj: Imperial Attitudes and their Critics*, Weidenfeld and Nicolson, London, 1980.

Baskaran, S. Theodore, *The Message Bearers: The Nationalist Politics*

And The Entertainment Media In South India 1880–1945. Cre-A Publishers, Madras, 1981.

Basu, Susan Neild, 'Colonial Urbanism: The Development of Madras City in the Eighteenth and Nineteenth Centuries', *Modern Asian Studies*, 13(2) 1979, pp. 217–46.

——, 'The Dubashes of Madras', *Modern Asian Studies*, 18(1) 1984, pp. 1–31.

——, 'Madras in 1800: Perceiving the City', in Howard Spodek and Doris Srinivasan (eds), *Urban Form and Meaning in South Asia*, Hanover and London, 1993.

Bayly, C.A., *Rulers, Townsmen and Bazaars: North Indian Society in the Age of Expansion 1770–1870*, Cambridge University Press, Cambridge, 1983.

Bhatkhande, V.N., *A Short History of the Music of Upper India: A reproduction of a speech addressed by Pandit V.N. Bhatkhande at the first all India Music Conference, Baroda, 1916*, published by B.S. Suthankar, Bombay, 1934.

——, *A Comparative Study of Some of the Leading Music Systems of the 15th, 16th, 17th and 18th Centuries* (n.d.).

Blackburn, Stuart, *Print, Folklore and Nationalism in Colonial South India*, Permanent Black, Delhi, 2003.

Blackburn, Stuart, and A.K. Ramanujan (eds), *Another Harmony: New Essays on the Folklore of India,* University of California Press, Berkeley, 1986.

Booth, Gregory D., *Brass Baja Stories from the World of Indian Wedding Bands*, Oxford University Press, New Delhi, 2005.

Brihaspati, Acharya, *Musalman Aur Bharatiya Sangeet,* Raj Kamal Publishers, Delhi, 1934.

Buchanan, Francis, *A Journey from Madras through the Countries of Mysore, Canara and Malabar in three volumes*, John Murray, London, 1807.

Chatterjee, Partha, *The Nation and its Fragments: Colonial and Postcolonial Histories*, Oxford University Press, New Delhi, 1993.

——, 'Two Poets and Death: On Civil and Political Society in the Non-Christian World', in Timothy Mitchell (ed.), *Questions of Modernity*, University of Minnesota Press, Minneapolis, 2002, pp. 35–48.

Cousins, Margaret, *Music of Orient and Occident: Essays Towards Mutual Understanding*, B.G. Paul & Co., Madras, 1935.

Cousins, Margaret, *Indian Womanhood Today*, Kitabistan, Allahabad, 1941.

Cutler, Norman, 'Three Moments in the Geneology of Tamil Literary Culture', in Sheldon Pollock (ed.), *Literary Culture in History: Reconstructions from South Asia*, Oxford University Press, New Delhi, 2004, pp. 271–312.

Day, C.R., *The Music and Musical Instruments of Southern India and the Deccan* with an Introduction by A.J. Hipkins, FSA The Plates Drawn by William Gibb, original publication by Novells Ewer & Co., 1891. Low Price Publications, Delhi (Reprint) 1990, 1996.

Deva, B.C., *Indian Music*, Indian Council of Cultural Relations, Delhi, 1974.

Dubois, J.A., *Hindu Manners, Customs and Ceremonies*, translated from the author's later French manuscript and edited with introduction and notes by Henry K. Beauchamps, Clarendon Press, Oxford, 1897. Reprint, New Delhi, 1978.

———, *Pragmatism and Sociology*, Oxford University Press, Cambridge, 1983.

Durkheim, Emile, *The Rules of Sociological Method*, Collier Macmillan, London, 1969.

Dwyer Rachel, and Christopher Pinney (eds), *The History, Politics and Consumption of Public Culture in India*, Oxford University Press, New Delhi, 2001.

Erdman, Joan L. (ed.), *Arts Patronage in India: Methods, Motives and Markets*, Manohar, New Delhi, 1992.

Farrell, Gerry, *Indian Music and the West*, Clarendon Press, Oxford, 1997.

Fawcett, Fred, 'On Basavis: Women Who Through Dedication to a Deity Assume Masculine Privileges', *Journal of the Anthropological Society of Bombay*, vol. II, 1892, pp. 322–53.

Geetha V. and S.V. Rajadorai, *Towards a Non-Brahmin Millennium. From Iyothee Thass to Periyar*, Samya, Calcutta, 1998.

George T.J.S., *MS A Life in Music*. Harper Collins; India, a joint venture with India Today group, New Delhi, 2004.

Ghosh, Lokenath, *Music's Appeal to India: An Original, Instructive and Interesting Story (Complete) Agreeable to the Taste of both Young and Old*, M.C. Gangooly & Co., Calcutta, 1873.

Goetz, Herman, 'The Fall of Vijaynagar and the Nationalization of Muslim Art in the Dakhan', *Journal of Indian History*, 19, 1940, pp. 249–55.

Guha Thakurta, Tapati, 'Instituting the Nation in Art', in Partha Chatterjee (ed.), *Wages of Freedom: Fifty Years of the Indian Nation State*, Oxford University Press, New Delhi, 1998, pp. 89–122.

Guha Thakurta, Tapati, *Monuments, Objects, Histories, Institutions of Art in Colonial and Post Colonial India*, Columbia University Press, New York, 2004.

Hansen, Kathryn, *Grounds for Play: The Nautanki Theatre of North India*, University of California Press, Berkeley, 1992.

Heber, Bishop Reginald, *Narrative of a Journey through the Upper Provinces of India from Calcutta to Bombay 1824–25 with Notes upon Ceylon. An Account of a Journey to Madras and the Southern provinces*, 1826, and letters written in India by the Late Right Rev. Reginald Heber in two volumes. London, John Murray, MDCCCXXVIII.

Higgins, Jon. B., 'From Prince to Populace: Patronage as a Determinant of Change in South Indian (Karnatik) Music', *Asian Music*, no. 7, 1976, pp. 20–6.

Hopkins, Stephen Paul, *Singing the Body of God: The Hymns of Vedantadesika in their South Indian Tradition*, Oxford University Press, New Delhi, 2002.

Irschik, Eugene, *Politics and Social Conflict in South India: The Non-Brahmin Movement and Tamil Separatism, 1916–1920*, University of California Press, Berkeley, 1969.

Iyer, E. Krishna, *Personalities in Present Day Music*, Madras, 1933.

Iyer, P.S., *Articles on Carnatic Music*, printed at the Kamala Press, Tirupapuliyar, Madras, 1937.

Jackson, William J., *Tyagaraja, Life and Lyrics*, Oxford University Press, Madras, 1991.

———, *Tyagaraja and the Renewal of Tradition: Translations and Reflections*, Motilal Banarasidass, Delhi, 1994.

Jordan, Kay, *From Sacred Servant to Profane Prostitute: A History of the Changing Legal Status of the Devadasis in India 1857–1947*, Manohar, New Delhi, 2003.

Kannabiran, Kalpana, 'Judiciary, Social Reform and Debate on "Religious Prostitution" in Colonial India', *Economic and Political Weekly*, 30(43), pp. 59–69, 1945.

Kaul, H.K., *Travellers' India: An Anthology*: Chosen and edited by H.K. Kaul, Oxford University Press, New Delhi, 1979.

Kaufman, Walter, *The Ragas of South India: A Catalogue of Scalar Material*, Indian University Press, Bloomington, London, 1976.

Kinnear, Michael, *The Gramophone Company's First Recordings, 1889–1908*, Popular Prakashan, Bombay, 1994.

Lakshmi, C.S., *The Singer and the Song: Conversations with Women Musicians*, Kali for Women, New Delhi, 2000.

Lelyveld, David, 'Upon the Subdominant Administering Music on All India Radio', in Carol A. Breckenridge (ed.), *Consuming Modernity: Public Culture in Contemporary India*, Oxford University Press, New Delhi, 1996, pp. 49–65.

Love, Henry Davidson, *Vestiges of Old Madras*, vols 1–4, John Murray for Government of India, London, 1913.

Manuel, Peter, *Thumri in Historical and Stylistic Perspective*, Motilal Banarasidass, Delhi, 1989.

McNeil, Adrian, *Inventing the Sarod: A Cultural History*, Seagull Books, Calcutta, 2004.

Menon, Indira, *The Madras Quartet*, Roli Books, New Delhi, 1999.

Miller Barbara Stoler (ed.), *The Powers of Art Patronage in Indian Culture*, Oxford University Press, New Delhi, 1992.

Mines, Mattison, 'Individualism and Achievement in South Indian History', *Modern Asian Studies,* 26(1) 1992, pp. 129–56.

———, 'Courts of Law and Styles of Self-Representation in Eighteenth Century Madras: From Hybrid to the Colonial Self', *Modern Asian Studies*, 35(1), February 2001, pp. 33–74.

Miner, Allyn, *Sitar and Sarod in the Eighteenth and Nineteenth Century*, Reprint Motilal Banarasidass, Delhi, 1997.

Moro, Pamela, 'Constructions of Nation and the Classicisation of Music Comparative: Perspectives from Southeast and South Asia', *Journal of Southeast Asian Studies,* 35(2) 2004, pp. 187–212.

Mudaliar, A.M. Chinnaswami, *Oriental Music In European Notation*. Edited by Gowri Kuppuswami and M. Hariharan. Reprint, Delhi, 1982.

Nettl Bruno and Philip Bohlman, *The Life of Music in North India: The Organization of an Artistic Tradition*, Detroit Michigan Wayne State University Press, published in India by Manohar, New Delhi, 1980.

———, *Comparative Musicology and Anthology of Music*, University of Chicago Press, Chicago, 1991.

Neuman, Daniel, 'The Social Ecology of Indian Music' in O.P. Joshi (ed.), *Sociology of Oriental Music*, ABD Publishers, 2004, pp. 100–10.

Parker, Kunal M., ' "A Corporation of Superior Prostitutes", Anglo-Indian Legal Conceptions of Temple Dancing Girls 1800–1914', *Modern Asian Studies*, 32(3), July 1998, pp. 559–63.

Parthasarathy, T.S., 'Composers of Indian Music', in Gowri Kuppuswamy and M. Hariharan (eds), *Indian Music: A Perspective,* Sundeep Prakashan, Delhi, 1980, pp. 97–102.

Pathak,V.S., *Smarta Religious Tradition of Northern India c. 600 AD to c. 1200 AD,* Kusumanjali, Prakashan, Meerut, 1987.

Pesch, Ludwig, *The Illustrated Companion to South Indian Classical Music*, Oxford University Press, New Delhi, 1999.

Peterson, Indira Viswanathan, 'The Kriti, as an Integrative Cultural Form: Aesthetic Experience in the Religious Songs of the two South Indian Classical Composers', *Journal of South Asian Literature,* vol. 19, no. 2, 1984, pp. 165–79.

———, 'The Kriti: Sanskrit in Carnatic Music', *Indo-Iranian Journal,* no. 29, 1986.

———, *Poems to Siva: The Hymns of the Tamil Saints,* Princeton University Press, Princeton, 1989.

———, 'The Evolution of the Kuravanci Dance Drama in Tamil Nadu: Negotiating the Folk and the "Classical" in the Bharata Natyam Context', *South Asia Research* 18(1) 1998, pp. 39–72.

———, 'The Cabinet of King Serfoji of Tanjore: A European Collection in Nineteenth Century India', *Journal of the History of Collections,* 11(1), 1999, pp. 71–9.

Popley, H.A., *The Music of India,* Calcutta, 1921. Reprint Low Price Publications, Delhi, 1990, 1993, 1996.

Powers, Harold, 'Classical Music, Cultural Roots and Colonial Rule: An Indic Musicologist Looks at the Muslim World', *Asian Music* 12(1) 1980, pp. 5–39.

Prajnanananda, Swami, *Sangitasara Samgraha of Sri Ghanasyamadasa,* edited with an introduction by Swami Prajnananda, Ramakrishna Vedanta Math, Calcutta, 1956.

———, *Historical Development of Indian Music,* Firma K.L. Mukhopadhyay, Calcutta, 1973.

Price, Pamela, *Kingship and Political Practice in Colonial India,* Cambridge University Press, Cambridge, 1996.

Pukhraj, Malka, *Song Sung True: A Memoir,* Kali for Women, Delhi, 2003.

Raghavan, V., 'Notices of Madras in Two Sanskrit Works', in The *Madras Tercentenary Commemoration Volume,* (Humphrey Milford Oxford University Press London, Bombay, Calcutta, Madras, 1939, pp.108–10.

Rao, B. Dayananda (ed.), *Carnatic Music Composers: A Collection of Biographical Essays,* Triveni Foundation, Hyderabad, 1994.

Rao, T.V., *Studies in Indian Music,* Asia Publishing House, Bombay, 1962.

Rao V.N., David Shulman and Sanjay Subrahmanyam, *Symbols of Substance Court and State in Nayaka Period Tamil Nadu,* Oxford University Press, New Delhi, 1992.

Rao V.N., *Textures of Time: Writing History in South India*, Permanent Black, Delhi, 2001.

Ratanjhankar, S.N., *Pandit Bhatkhande*, National Book Trust, New Delhi, 1967.

Ramakrishnan, E.M., *Fundamentals of South Indian or Karnatic Music in a Nutshell*, Sakaraa, Madras, 1967.

Ramaswamy, Sumathi, *Passions of the Tongue*, University of California Press, Berkeley, 1997.

Ranade, D. Ashok, *Hindustani Music: India, the Land and the People*, National Book Trust, New Delhi, 1997.

Reddy, S. Muthulakshmi, *My Experience as a Legislator*, Current Thought Press, Triplicane, 1930.

———, *Autobiography of Dr (Mrs) S. Muthulakshmi Reddy*, MJK Press, Mylapore, 1964.

Reiss, Raymond, 'The Cultural Setting of South Indian Music', *Asian Music*, nos 1–2, 1969, pp. 22–31.

Rowell Lewis, *Music and Musical Thought in Ancient India*, University of Chicago Press, Chicago, 1992.

Sambamoorthy, P., *Great Composers*, The Indian Music Publishing House, Madras, 2nd edn., 1962.

———, *The Teaching of Music*, The Indian Music Publishing House, Madras, 1966.

———, *A Dictionary of South Indian Music and Musicians*, 3 vols, The Indian Music Publishing House, Madras, 1971.

Sastri, Natesa, *Hindu feasts, fasts and ceremonies with an introduction by Henry K. Beauchamp*, ME Publishing House, Madras, 1903.

Sathyanarayana, R., *Music of Madhava Monks of Karnataka*, Gnana Jyothi Kala Mandir, Bangalore, 1988.

———, *Karnataka Music as Aesthetic Form*, PHISPC, Centre for Studies in Civilization, New Delhi, 2004.

Seal, Anil, *The Emergence of Indian Nationalism*: *Competition and Collaboration in the Later Nineteenth Century*, Cambridge University Press, Cambridge, 1968.

Seetha S., *Tanjore as a Seat of Music*, University of Madras, Madras, 1981.

Sewell Robert, *A Forgotten Empire (Vijayanagar)*, London, 1900. Reprint, India Book House, New Delhi,1962, 1970.

Singer, Milton (ed.), *Krishna: Myths, Rites and Attitudes*, The University of Chicago Press, Chicago and London, 1971.

Srilatha, K., *The Other Half of the Coconut: Women Writing Self-Respect History: An Anthology of Self-Respect Literature (1928–1936)*, edited and translated by K. Srilatha, Kali for Women, Delhi, 2003.

Srinivasan, Amrit, 'Reform and Revival: The Devadasi and her Dance', *Economic and Political Weekly*, 20(4) 1985, pp. 1869–76.

Stein, Burton, *Vijayanagara: The New Cambridge History of India*, Cambridge University Press, Cambridge, 1994.

Story, Saskia Kersenboom, *Nityasumangali: Devadasi Tradition in South India*, Motilal Banarsidass, Delhi, 1st edn, 1987. Reprint Delhi, 1998, 2002.

Strangways, A.H. Fox, *The Music of Hindostan*, Clarendon Press, Oxford, first published 1914. Reprint, Delhi, 1965.

Subramanian, Lakshmi, 'The Reinvention of a Tradition: Nationalism, Carnatic Music and the Madras Music Academy', *Indian Economic and Social History Review*, XXXVI, (2) 1999, pp. 131–63.

——, 'Gender and the Performing Arts in Nationalist Discourse: An Agenda for the Madras Music Academy, 1930–47', *The Book Review*, 23(1–2), 1999, pp. 81–4.

——, 'Contesting the Classical: The Tamil Isai Iyakkam and the Politics of Custodianship', *Asian Journal of Social Science*, 32(1), 2004, pp. 66–90.

Subramanian, P., *Social History of the Tamils, 1707–1947*, Sundeep Prakashan, New Delhi, 1999.

Sundar, Pushpa, *Patrons and Philistines: Arts and the State in British India*, Oxford University Press, New Delhi, 1995.

Suntharalingam, R., *Politics and Nationalist Awakening in South India, 1852–1891*, University of Arizona Press, Arizona, 1974, Indian edition, Delhi, 1980.

Tagore, S.M., *Hindu Music,* first published 1882, 2nd reprint, Low Price Publications, Delhi, 1994.

——, *Universal History of Music: Compiled from Divers Sources Together with Various Original Notes on Hindu music by Raja Sourindro Mohun Tagore*, first published 1896. Reprinted in Low Price Publication, Delhi, 1990, 1999.

Thapar, Romila, *Early India: From the Origins to AD 1300*, Allen Lane, The Penguin Press, London, 2002.

Trautman, Thomas R., 'Inventing the History of South India', in Daud Ali (ed.), *Invoking the Past: The Uses of History in South Asia*, SOAS, Oxford University Press, New Delhi, 2002, pp. 36–54.

Vatsyayana, Kapila, *Traditional Indian Theatre: Multiple Streams*, National Book Trust, New Delhi, 1979.

Veer, Ram Avatar, *History of Indian Music and Musicians*, Pankaj, Imprint, New Delhi, 1987.

Viswanathan T. and Mathew Allen, *Music in South India: Experiencing Music, Expressing Culture*, Oxford University Press, New Delhi, 2004.

Wade, Bonnie C., *Khyal: Creativity within North India's Classical Music Tradition*, Cambridge University Press, Cambridge, 1984, Motilal Banarsidass, New Delhi, 1997.

Wagoner, Phillip B., 'Sultan Among Hindu Kings: Dress, Titles and the Islamization of Hindu Culture', *The Journal of Asian Studies*, 55(4), 1996, pp. 851–80.

Washbrook, David, *The Emergence of Provincial Politics: The Madras Presidency 1870–1920*, Cambridge University Press, Cambridge, 1976. Indian edition by Vikas Publications, New Delhi, 1976.

Weidman, Amanda, 'Gender and the Politics of Voice: Colonial Modernity and Classical Music in South India', *Cultural Anthropology*, 18(2), 2003.

———, *In the Kingdom of the Voice: Music and its Subjects in Modern South India*, Duke University Press, forthcoming.

Wheeler, J. Talboys, *Madras in the Olden Times*, 3 vols, Higginsbotham and Co., Madras, 1882.

———, *Annals of the Madras Presidency*, vols 1–3, Low Price Publications, Delhi, 1990.

White, Reverend E. Emmons, *Appreciating India's Music: An introduction to the music of India with suggestions for its use in the churches of India*, (Madras) Published for the Senate of Serampore by the Christian Literature Society, 1957.

Williamson, Thomas, *The Costumes and Customs of Modern India: from a collection of drawings by Charles D'Oyly*, engraved by J.M. Clark and C. Dubourg; with a preface and copious descriptions by Captain Thomas Williamson, printed and sold by E. Orme, London, 1983.

Wilson Anne C., *A Short Account of the Hindu system of Music*, Gulab Singh & Sons, Lahore. India, Simpkin, Marshall, Hamilton, Kent & Co. Ltd., London, 1904.

Zvelebil, K.V., *The Story of My Life: An Autobiography of Dr. U.V. Swaminatha Iyer* (translated), Institute of Asian Studies, Madras, 1994.

II. Contemporary Journals, Tracts and Publications (English)

Journal of the Music Academy Madras, Madras, 1930–73.

Sangeet Natak, 1977–9.

Hindu Music and the Gayan Samaj, Published in Aid of the Funds of the Madras Jubilee Gayan Samaj, Bombay, 1887.

Speeches and Writings on Indian Music and Art by Vijayadevi Maharana of Dharampur, 1938.

Sangit of India: Classical, Instrumental Music and Nautch by Atiya Begum, Bombay,1942.

Report of the Third All India Music Conference, Benaras, 1920.

Report on the Second All India Music Conference, 1919.

The Madras Congress and Conferences, Madras, 1908.

The Indian Review, G.A. Natesan & Co., Madras, 1932–40.

The Indian Social Reformer, Madras, 1899–1912.

Karunamirtha Sagaram on Srutis: A Treatise on Music or Isai Tamil which is one of the main divisions of Muttamil or Language, Music and Drama by Rao Saheb M. Abraham Pandithar, Original 1917. Reprint, New Delhi, 1984.

Sri Ariyakudi Ramanuja Iyengar Commemoration Volume, Published by Sri Ariyakudi Ramanuja Iyengar Commemoration Society, Madras, 1990.

III. Government/Official Publications

Aspects of Indian Music: A Series of articles and papers read at the music symposia arranged by All India Radio, New Delhi, Ministry of Information and Broadcasting, Publications Division, Government of India (first edition, 1957).

Census of India, 1891, vol. XIII, Madras, 1891. Report on the Census.

Census of the Town of Madras (1871) Printed by H. Morgan at the Fort St George Gazette Press, Madras, 1873.

Census of the Town of Madras 1871, printed by H. Morgan at the Fort St George Gazettee Press, Madras, 1873.

Collection of the Decisions of the High Courts and the Privy Council on the Law of Succession, Maintenance, &c. Applicable to Dancing Girls and their issues, Prostitutes not belonging to Dancing Girls' community, *Illegitimate sons and Bastards and Illatom affiliation upto December 1891*, C. Ramachandrier, Madras, and Illatom affiliation V. Kalyanaram Iyer, 1892.

Edgar, Thurston assisted by K. Rangachariar, *Castes and Tribes of Southern India*, vol. II, Government Press, Madras, 1909.

Fortieth Indian National Social Conference, Madras, 1927.

Government of Karnataka Selections from the Records of the Mysore Palace, vol. I, *Musicians, Actors and Artists*, Divisional Archive Office, Mysore, 1993.

Government of Madras, *Proceedings of the Madras Legislative Council*, Madras, 1928, 1929, and 1930.

Pillai, M.S., Purnalingam, *Tamil India*, South Indian Saiva Siddhanata Works Publishing Society, Tinnevelly Ltd., Tirunelveli, Madras 1927.

Proceedings of the Madras Legislative Council, vol. LI (nos 1–10), Madras, 1930.

Proceedings of the Madras Legislative Council, vol. XXXVIII, Madras.

Ramachandran, M., The Devadasi Secretary, Aryan Mission, Conjeevaram, June 1900.

Reddy, Muthulakshmi, 'Why Should the Devadasi Institution in the Hindu Temples be Abolished?' Chintadripet: Central Cooperative Printing Works Ltd., n.d.

Report of the Census of the Madras Presidency by Lewis McIver, 3 vols. Printed at the Madras Government Gazette Press, Madras, 1874.

Report of the Second All India Music Conference Held at Delhi, 14–17 December, 1918. Published in 1919.

Report of the Third All India Music Conference, Benares, held from 19–12 December 1919. Benares (Publication Mudrak, Chabinath Pandey, Sri Gyanmandal Yantralaya, Kashi, 1920).

Report on the Census of the Madras Presidency, 1871, Madras 1874.

Sastri K.S. Ramaswami, *The Future of the Brahmin*, 26 June 1935, Madras, 1935. This was the Presidential Address at the Tanjore District Brahmin Conference on 30 December 1934. Printed at CCP Works.

Sastri, Pandit S.M. Natesa, *Hindu Feasts, Fasts and Ceremonies*, Madras, 1903.

Smt. C. Saraswati Bai. Commemoration Volume issued on the occasion of the unveiling of her portrait at the Jagannath Bhakta Sabha Egmore, Saturday, 16 December 1939.

Journals/ Periodicals/ Publications in Vernacular (Tamil)

Ponnvizhak Kollum Chennai Tamil Isai Sangattin Varalaru, Tamil Isai Sangam, Chennai 1943–93.

Tamil Isai Sangam, Chennai Tamil Isai Araychi Kuzhu, 1960.

Tamil Isai Sangam, Ponn Vizha Chirppu Malar 1943–93.

Ananda Vikatan, 1929–36.

Tamil Isai Natippu Kalaigal by Periyar, Erode, 1944.

Tamil Isai Mutikkam, Madras, 1996.

Tamil Isai Makanadu, Madras, 1944.

Archival Sources

L/P and J/8/117 Collection 104/A—Government of India's Reports on Development of Broadcasting in India, 1940 (P&JB 406, P&J 4348) (India Office Library, London).

L/P and J104B No.119, Broadcasting Policy in India (IOL, London).

F/2/2/40, 'Communication from Delhi' dated 15 April 1940, (IOL, London).

L/I/1/445 File No.223/1 for Correspondence on Broadcasting in India Government of Madras, Public Works and Labour Department, 1932.

Huzur Political Office Education Department File No.77, Music Classes in the Baroda High School (Baroda State Archives).

Huzur English Office (Political) Miscellaneous Department No. 18, File 55/8A. Correspondence regarding 'The First All India Music Conference'.

Index